THE RUSSIAN HOFFMANNISTS

SLAVISTIC PRINTINGS AND REPRINTINGS

edited by

C. H. VAN SCHOONEVELD

Stanford University

XXXV

MOUTON & CO. · 1963 · THE HAGUE

THE RUSSIAN HOFFMANNISTS

by

CHARLES E. PASSAGE

Associate Professor of
Comparative Literature, Brooklyn College

MOUTON & CO. · 1963 · THE HAGUE

Publication of this volume was assisted by a grant from the American Council of Learned Societies as a result of a contribution from the United States Steel Foundation.

PRINTED IN THE NETHERLANDS

Dedicated

to the Memory of

HARVEY W. HEWETT-THAYER

OF PRINCETON UNIVERSITY

1873–1960

ASTUTE HOFFMANNIST
REVERED FRIEND

PREFACE

The significance of the Tales of Hoffmann for Russian literature forms the continuous thread upon which all parts of the present book are strung, but the author wishes to explain at the outset why the several parts, the beads upon the strand, are so diverse. Various points of fact needed to be made in this study and one major point of fancy needed, so to speak, to be unmade. Both processes required patient examination of details.

The point of fancy to be unmade was the irresponsible identification of Hoffmann's influence where no such influence, or very little, exists. Critics, both amateur and professional, made such claims from 1825 onwards and both kinds of critics have repeated the errors down to the present moment. The Countess Rostopčina provided the best example of such unwarranted claims when she dubbed Prince Odoevskij, in his own lifetime, "Hoffmann II". The resemblance between the two writers was generic but superficial; Odoevskij himself, an utterly honest man, disavowed the resemblance emphatically. Our examination of the facts of the matter has brought us to the conclusion that there was slightly more influence than Odoevskij *remembered* and vastly less than Countess Rostopčina *imagined*. Clarification of such points was time-consuming but necessary if a true judgment was to be arrived at. It is, however, incidental to the establishment of points of fact in this study, which is concerned with significant influences of Hoffmann upon Russian creative writers.

The sifting of evidence was a slow process. The seventy-odd prose Tales were available to Russian intellectuals, many of them in Russian translation, almost all of them in French translation; in most instances considered here the writers themselves knew enough German to read them in their original language, either easily or with difficulty as the case might be. There is no question whatever as to the availability of the Tales. Brilliant Russian authors, mediocre Russian authors, and poor Russian hacks all made tries at "Hoffmann's manner", each individual understanding a little something different by "Hoffmann's manner". It is the very number and variety of such attempts which made Hoffmann conspicuously important as a touchstone for the Russian mentality and which make the present study of clarification worthwhile.

The process of clarification confronted us with a sequence of author-personalities which in themselves were worth knowing. The graceful, minor talent of "Pogorel'skij" proved to have intrinsic value; his contribution to the formation of Russian literary patterns deserved to be distinguished amid its sad oblivion; the extent of his specifically Hoffmannian inspiration needed, of course, to be evaluated; but the man himself also seemed well worth telling about. Much the same could be said for the impetuous, well-intentioned, and irritating Polevoj, whose Hoffmann-enthusiasm and Hoffmann-propaganda were effective even if his Hoffmannizing stories deserve neglect, and for Prince Odoevskij, who was by no means minor, either as man or as artist. Our book accordingly assumed the form of a gallery of author-portraits, valuable, we believe, for their own sakes. Hence the over-all title: *The Russian Hoffmannists,* rather than an impersonal title like, for instance, *Russian Hoffmannism.*

The works of all three of these writers, as well as the story called *The Lonely Cottage on Vasil'evskij Island* and certain items discussed in Chapter VII, are to be found only in the Russian language and even there only in out-of-print editions difficult of access. Our study, on the other hand, is addressed to persons interested in Comparative Literature everywhere. Inevitably, therefore, fairly lengthy synopses of such works had to be included. Even with the well-known works of Gogol' and Puškin summaries of tales seemed inevitable when the subject under consideration involved so long an array of minute details. It is our hope that these synopses will abridge much time for readers concerned with surveying Russian Romantic fiction in general as well as for readers concerned with Hoffmann and his influences. If precisely such detailed information is lacking in the most important chapter, that dealing with Dostoevskij, it is because, as stated at the opening of that chapter, the detailed demonstrations are provided in the present author's separate monograph *Dostoevskij the Adapter,* with only the end-products of that study included here in order to put them in their true perspective amid the surrounding matter.

The entire subject has been presented in chronological order relative to the Russian authors. For readers taking Hoffmann's works themselves as a point of departure and working from the German productions outward, the total contents of the present study have been cross-indexed in Appendix III (pp. 253-261) with thematic ramifications to Russian authors listed in phrase form under each Hoffmannian title. Generalizations and deductions from the several detailed studies are set forth in Chapter IX, "Russian Hoffmannism in Retrospect".

Dansville, New York,   CHARLES E. PASSAGE
August, 1961

TABLE OF CONTENTS

INTRODUCTION

1. RUSSIAN HOFFMANNISM

At the beginning of the eighteenth century Peter the Great, the Tsar of immense vision and boundless energy, had snatched up Russian society like an oafish youth and held it, by sheer force and in spite of all its furious protests, beneath the well-pump of modernity, washed it vehemently, and sent it off to school. Bewildered and angry the oafish youth went as bidden, sullen in powdered hair and knee-breeches, resentful of being forbidden to grow a beard. But at school the disgruntlement quickly passed, the youth throve, both academically and socially, and before long was metamorphosed into a cultivated gentleman.

For there was genius in this Petrine society created by fiat. It had a personality and a will of its own, along with aspirations and noble thoughts and high sentiments. These it craved to express in durable artistic form. At school through the eighteenth century, it moved through stages of literary evolution, imitating primarily the French models which passed for Absolute on the continent, but also finding guidance in the literature of England. Awkwardly and diffidently it obtruded, rather than introduced, into its own compositions elements of the uniquely Russian feelings that so urgently demanded expression. By the reign of Catherine (1761—1796) it had mastered the external forms and for a time contemplated its achievement with a premature satisfaction. Yet genuine originality was only about to begin at the time when the Great Empress died, and its full realization lay forty years into the future.

By 1800 this French-speaking Petrine society had become so generally Gallicized that, without realizing the fact, it was dissipating its best energies in an effort to become a society of Frenchmen-away-from-home. Even its enthusiasm for things English was a form of Parisian *anglomanie*. Literarily speaking, the emancipation of the native genius was to be won, not by direct revolt from foreign models, but by the introduction of a new foreign model as counter-force to the old one. The new inspiration came from Germany. Conservatives found it bizarre and looked for its duration to be brief. It persisted, however, and through its medium were made most remarkable advances toward a literature that was to be genuinely national. Within this Germanizing movement, the influence of one author in particular — Hoffmann — had such a marked and extraordinary effect that it is possible to speak of "Russian Hoffmannism" as a significant phenomenon. It is with this phenomenon that the present study deals.

2. THE MUSCOVITE WERTHERIANS

It was in Moscow, rather than in Petersburg, that enthusiasm for Hoffmann was initiated and fostered. It was in Moscow, rather than in Petersburg, that German literature in general made its influence felt, and the Hoffmann vogue may be discerned as one of the phases in which that influence was manifested. A historical explanation underlies these facts. Since at least the sixteenth century the old capital had had its "German Suburb" (Nemeckaja Sloboda), populated largely by merchants and artisans. Peter the Great's connection with these foreign citizens is well known. Their role in Russian life was usually, but not always, utilitarian in nature. In the reign of Peter's father, Aleksej Mixajlovič (1645—1676), for instance, a Lutheran pastor from the colony assumed directorship of the first theatre in the country. Through the eighteenth century the city had known the operations of Peter's German-type bureaucracy as well as the effects of the court favorites of the Germanophile Empress Anne (1730—1740).

From an intellectual point of view, a significant German influence was to emanate from the University of Moscow, founded in 1755 as the first in Russia by Anne's successor Elizabeth, who was herself, ironically enough, a Francophile. In addition to its imposingly extensive curriculum, the institution had from its inception the extraordinary supplement of a theatre, and here, under faculty guidance and with student actors, were produced the early dramas of Schiller very soon after their German premières. The prime mover behind these theatrical ventures was a German of Russian citizenship and a professor, Johann Georg Schwarz, who was keenly interested in the literary achievements of the country of his origin. Besides delivering conventional lectures, he required his students to translate long sections from Lessing and Schiller, himself made detailed study of the new poetic medium of blank verse, and personally supervised dramatic performances. A whole generation derived a new literary taste from him. Directly prompted by Schwarz were the translations of Schiller's *Kabale und Liebe,* 1788, (under the title of *Luiza* and with a happy ending), and *Die Räuber,* 1792 (again with an altered final act), as well as of the unpublished version of Lessing's *Nathan der Weise.* By the end of the century or very shortly thereafter, other translators, some of them antedating Schwarz's era, had produced a total of works that included five plays of Lessing, at least three of Schiller's *Jugenddramen,* Goethe's *Clavigo,* and a miscellaney of lyric poems from various authors.[1] Many more books and authors were, of course, known in the original.

Housed within the university buildings was the preparatory school known as the Noble Pension (Blagorodnyj Pansion). Faculty members doubled as teachers for the younger boys, of whom there were from three to four hundred, aged from eight to the middle teens. The cultural orientation was much the same as that presented in the higher school, though preparation was directed toward the civil service and the army. The German language was taught along with Latin, French, and English, and some of the pensionnaires, for example the four Turgenev brothers, spoke it better than French, a most unusual accomplishment among Russians in 1800.

As a personal friend of Professor Schwarz, Ivan Petrovič Turgenev

---

[1]   a) Lessing: *Der junge Gelehrte* (1748), translated 1765 by A. Nartov. *Minna von Barnhelm* (1776), translated 1779 anonymously. *Miss Sara Sampson* (1755), translated 1784 (translator unknown). *Emilia Galotti* (1772), translated 1784 (translator unknown). *Nathan der Weise* (1779), translated by the students of the University of Moscow under the direction of Professor Schwarz, but not published.
b) Goethe: *Clavigo* (1774), translated 1780 by O. P. Kozdavlëv.
c) Schiller: *Kabale und Liebe* (1784), translated 1788 by Ivan Sokolov of the University of Moscow under the title of *Luiza* and with a happy ending; performed by the students of the University. A second translation was made by Nikolaj Sandunov in 1800, and a third by Smirnov in 1802. *Die Räuber* (1781), translated 1792 by Nikolaj Sandunov with the ending altered to have Karl Moor stabbed by his own highwaymen; performed by students of the University. The public première took place in 1829. *Fiesco* (1783), translated 1802 by Richter and again anonymously in 1803. *Don Carlos* (prose version, 1787): Act I alone was performed by amateurs of the court on the occasion of the thirty-third birthday of Grand Duke Paul (subsequently Tsar Paul I) in October 1787. The title was given as *Le fils royal,* names of the characters were changed (e.g. King Philip II became "Don Pedro") in order to avoid offense to royalty, and incidental music and lavish spectacle were added to make a quasi-operatic extravaganza.

entered his four sons in the Noble Pension as a matter of course. He was himself a Germanophile, personally acquainted with the Storm and Stress writer Lenz, a correspondent of Lavater, and had, even when the boys were small, engaged for them a Swiss tutor who made the lads learn by heart large numbers of poems by Gellert and Gessner. The fates of the four brothers were to be oddly varied. Sergej died insane in 1827; Nikolaj was ruined by the Decembrist conspiracy of 1825; Aleksandr lived a long life as an enthusiastic and talented littérateur; Andrej, who made the important translation of *Werther* in 1799, died prematurely in 1803. Yet Andrej is probably the best remembered of the four, not for his translation but for his friendship with Vasilij Andreevič Žukovskij, the future founder of Russian Romanticism.

Born in 1783, the fourth child and only son of a Russian nobleman named Bunin and his Turkish concubine, young Žukovskij's fate was entirely uncertain during his infancy. His name was assigned to him somewhat arbitrarily from the bailiff of Bunin's estate, who (at his master's suggestion) had brought the Turkish girl home captive from the wars. Bunin's legitimate wife gave birth to numerous progeny, but several, including all males, died young, a fact that perhaps accounts for the father's concern for his only surviving son. On his deathbed Bunin required his four remaining daughters to contribute 2,500 rubles each to the purpose of bringing up Vasen'ka as a gentleman. The boy's half-sisters dutifully complied, and in due time the talented youth was inscribed on the rolls of the Noble Pension.

The years of Žukovskij's attendance at the famous school, 1797–1801, correspond almost exactly to the reign of Tsar Paul I. It was a difficult era during which the mad ruler sought to seal Russia off from all Europe by prohibiting foreign travel, attendance at foreign universities, and importation of foreign books. In actuality it was an era of smuggled literature, ardent coteries, and equally ardent discussions of the rights of man. For Žukovskij personally it was a vivid time of youthful friendships and fascinating discovery of the province of German literature as revealed to him by his Germanophile friends, particularly Andrej Turgenev. Common interests with classmates led to the establishment in January, 1801 of the "Literary Society of Friends" (Družeskoe literaturnoe obščestvo), with a membership of ten. Here the members avidly discussed books in general and German books in particular. *Werther* in young Turgenev's translation was their Bible.[2]

---

[2]   The first translation of *Werther* (1774) was published anonymously in 1781, but the translator has been identified as F. Galčenkov. It was marred by

Wieland's *Agathon* was recommended by Turgenev as second in importance only to *Werther*. Spiess, he said, was also a noble writer, and in the area of the drama as well as in the novel, there was the admirable Kotzebue. From the year of the society's founding dates Žukovskij's four-volume translation of Kotzebue's *Die jüngsten Kinder meiner Laune* under the title of *The Boy by the Brook, or Constant Love* (Mal'čik u ručja, ili postojannaja ljubov').

Having left the Noble Pension in 1801, Žukovskij retired to his family estate of Mišensk, in Tula province not far from Moscow, and there closeted himself with a mass of books recommended by his friend. *Agathon,* he found, disturbed him profoundly, almost to the point of shaking his religious faith. Schiller's youthful dramas made him uneasy, but from them he passed to the momentous discovery of Schiller the lyric poet. He also discovered the lyric Goethe, as opposed to "the author of *Werther*", and presently, to his immense delight, Bürger. In the midst of his readings and solitude came the news of Andrej Turgenev's death on July 8, 1803. With a sentimental awe Žukovskij henceforward consecrated the dead youth to a sainthood of friendship, reverencing every remembered word and suggestion that had ever come from him. In this oddly circumstantial way the pursuit of German literature, which perhaps up to this time had been only a section of youthful exploration of the world, became a sacred obligation, from which Russian Romanticism received a German quality at the outset of its career.

Exploratory and tentative are terms which characterize the activities of these guileless youths in their "Literary Society of Friends". German literature was young. No social prestige attached to a knowledge of it

---

egregious errors explainable only from very imperfect knowledge of German. Uncorrected, it went through a second printing in 1794, and in 1796 was evidently used by Ivan Vinogradov as the basis for a "new" translation, again published anonymously as *The Sorrows of Young Werther, a Work of Mr. Goethe* (Strasti molodogo Vertera, soč. g. Gete). To the latter Vinogradov appended a popular Wertherianum: *The Letters of Charlotte to Karoline written at the time of her acquaintance with Werther* (Pis'ma Šarlotty k Karoline napisannye vo vremja eë znakomstva s Verterom), best known in Europe as *Lettres de Charlotte pendant sa liaison avec Werther* (1787), which in turn was "traduit de l'anglais par M.D.D.S.G. (Monsieur David de Saint-George)" and depended on the original *Letters of Charlotte during her connexion with Werther* (London, 1786), 2 vols. The third translation, a much improved one, was that of Andrej Turgenev, 1799, in the making of which some assistance was lent by A. F. Merzljakov, poet-professor at the University of Moscow. The fourth and definitive translation, that by Nikolaj Matveevič Rožalin in 1829, was a product of the Romantic generation.

in Russia. Under the earnest guidance of a professor these young men were exploring it in the spirit of sheer love of discovery. Their taste was faulty, their methods were cautious. In these respects, as in the loftiness of their intentions, they strikingly resemble that group of students at the University of Leipzig who, during the years 1745–1748, strove earnestly to create a new German literature by the publication of *Die Bremer Beiträge*.[3] Amid their hit-and-miss efforts, Andrej Turgenev's translation of *Werther* stands as the appropriate symbol for the accomplishments of the whole circle of Muscovite friends and of their generation. The death of young Turgenev marked the end of the first phase of German literary influence in Russia.

3. ŽUKOVSKIJ

The second phase was wholly Žukovskij's. It began imperceptibly as the continuation of the first and its progress traversed the stages and episodes of Žukovskij's personal life.

In 1805 Žukovskij's half-sister, Ekaterina Afanas'evna Protasova, was left a widow and in very straitened circumstances as a result of her late husband's unwise speculations and gambling. Pursuing a course of strict economy, she established herself with her two daughters, aged twelve and ten, in the town of Belëv, some two miles away from Mišensk. As a measure of further economy Žukovskij was to act as the girls' tutor. It was almost a German University program that he administered to his charges, and to perform his duty adequately he himself set about a vast plan of study. Literature of all ages and epochs was the basis of his curriculum, but he laid stress on Goethe, Schiller, and Bürger, or at least on selected lyric poems of those authors. For three years the study continued, with great profit for both teacher and students, and with the further result that Žukovskij gradually came to

---

[3] In the years 1745–1748 a group of some eight to ten students at the University of Leipzig, including Gaertner (1712–1791), A. Schlegel (1721–1773), A. Cramer (1723–1788), Ebert (1723–1795), Giseke (1724–1765), and Zachariae (1726–1777), had been admirers of Professor Gottsched, the dean of German letters in the early eighteenth century, and had contributed to his publications. After 1744 they came to disagree with his principles and founded their own magazine, *Die Bremer Beiträge,* with the declared intention of improving German taste. Without creative talent themselves, and making no claim to creative talent, their journalistic program of native German subject matter and matter appealing to bourgeois tastes was symptomatic of the new literature that developed spectacularly in Germany following 1748.

realize that he was in love with his elder pupil, his half-niece Mar'ja Protasova.

By 1808 he had acquired a reputation among his acquaintance as a man of extraordinary breadth of learning, especially in literature and aesthetics,[4] and some measure of fame with the general public on the basis of his poems and translations. It was in this year that he made his first adaptations of poems by Goethe and Schiller, an endeavor which was later to bring him signal renown. Meanwhile he had developed a close connection with Karamzin, former founder and editor of *The Messenger of Europe* (Vestnik Evropy), but currently too busy with the composition of his famous *History* to take more than a casual part in the magazine's affairs. For two years, 1808–1810, Žukovskij, at Karamzin's invitation, moved to Moscow to assume the editorship. Another period of retirement among books followed his newspaper career. Then came the abrupt change to military duty during the Napoleonic invasion. His patriotic war poems gained him nation-wide respect and the particular interest of the imperial family. Again a period of withdrawal, and then the vivid summer of 1815 in Dorpat.

Mme Protasova was fond of her half-brother but her strict religious scruples led her to forbid categorically any possibility of marriage between him and her daughter. Perhaps she anticipated with relief the forthcoming move to Dorpat, whither she and Mar'ja were to go as part of the household of her younger daughter's husband, Voejkov. She was certainly most displeased to find that Žukovskij had followed them there, taken a house, and declared his intention of residing near Mar'ja. By autumn she had persuaded him to renounce finally his hopes of marriage and to move to Petersburg.

But the summer had been a revelation to the poet. In Dorpat, particularly in the University circles, he was accepted as a famous writer. The intellectual climate delighted him. With Professor Bock he could sit and listen to intimate details of Berlin intellectual life and to reminiscences of Goethe. The lectures of Professor Gustav Ewers dwelt on a very Romantic Middle Ages with an ardor hardly matched by August Wilhelm Schlegel. And the curator of the university district was that very Friedrich Maximilian Klinger (1752–1831) who had

---

[4] A letter of January 8, 1806 to A. I. Turgenev requests the sending of such books as: J. J. Engel, *Der Philosoph für die Welt*, 1801. Garve, *Versuche über verschiedene Gegenstände aus der Moral, der Literatur, und dem geselligen Leben*, 1792–1800. Eschenburg, *Entwurf einer Theorie und Literatur der schönen Wissenschaften*, 1783. Sulzer, *Allgemeine Theorie der schönen Künste*, 1772.

been a Storm and Stress dramatist and had known Goethe in the
Werther years. Klinger was a very different man now. He refused to
have his published works introduced into Russia, preferred the rôle of
the high functionary, and paraded his sentimental dedication in friendship with the aged Professor Ewers, lecturer in theology and father of
the history professor. The whole faculty had a German air about it.
Their talk was of German literature. Žukovskij expected to hear — as
he did — of Goethe, but he also expected to hear of Schiller and
Lessing, of Bürger and Ramler and Kotzebue and Hebel. To his surprise he discovered that these writers were now considered passé.
Enthusiasm was all for the new Romantic generation. Two years later,
in 1817, Žukovskij was to propose in a letter to his friend Daškov a
program of translations from Tieck, Fouqué, Novalis, the Schlegels,
and Uhland, as well as from older writers like Goethe, Schiller, Herder,
and Jacobi. It is problematic whether he had actually read, or was ever
to read, many of these new authors.[5] Of the younger generation in
Germany, only Uhland really appealed to him, and only Uhland, of all
German authors since the beginning of the new century, was to inspire
any significant compositions of his own. Inevitably he heard in Dorpat
of the Tales of Hoffmann, which were then in the midst of their decade
of composition in Berlin. But of Hoffmann's name he made no
mention.

Saddened but not broken by his renunciation of Mar'ja, Žukovskij
arrived in Petersburg in the autumn of 1815 for what was to be the
most momentous period of his life. Attending the theatre with friends
on the evening of September 23rd, he found himself witness of a
satirical farce directed against himself and his own poems. The piece
was Prince Šaxovskoj's *A Lesson for Coquettes, or the Leipzig Waters*
(Urok koketkam, ili Lipeckie vody).[6] It spoke for the literary and social

[5]   The letter to Daškov specifies clearly enough five items from Tieck: *Die
Elfen, Der Pokal, Liebeszauber, Der blonde Eckbert,* and extracts from *Sternbald.* In the case of Fouqué, Žukovskij refers merely to extracts from the *Erzählungen,* with a parenthetic remark that "there is a quantity of very fine things
there". The remaining items are so vaguely indicated as to be difficult or
impossible to identify, and the impression conveyed is that he is listing from
hear-say: *"Jean-Paul's Geist,* just extracts, the whole thing is impossible." (No
such book is known.) — "Novalis: *Der Poet. Erzählung* (very beautiful)."
(Chapter III of *Heinrich von Ofterdingen,* perhaps? or the lyric from that
chapter?) — "Schlegel: extracts from the Dramaturgy." (By "the Dramaturgy",
does he refer to *Über dramatische Kunst und Literatur?* Was he aware that
there were two Schlegels?). — For a discussion of this point, see Marcelle
Ehrhard: *V. A. Joukovski et le Préromantisme russe* (Paris, 1938), pp. 323—326.
[6]   Prince Aleksandr Aleksandrovič Šaxovskoj (1777—1846) — the Arzamas

conservatives who looked upon the new Romantic poets as preposterous and slightly dangerous. For a decade these reactionary individuals had held formal meetings at the home of the aged poet Deržavin, the laureate of Catherine's reign, for the purpose of keeping literary taste pure and literature archaic. Their "Society of the Russian Word" advocated the superiority of the antiquated Church Slavic language over the modern spoken idiom. The reaction of Žukovskij's friends was immediate. On October 14th they founded a society of their own, known as the "Arzamas". The name was taken from the town of Arzamas, famous for its geese. Roast goose figured in their banquets and members swore their oaths: "by the sublime goose of Arzamas". Special names were conferred upon the members: Žukovskij was called "Svetlana" from the heroine of one of his ballads; Aleksandr Turgenev was dubbed "the Æolian Harp" from his stomach rumblings; M. Orlov was named "the Rhine". The youngest member, aged sixteen, had the nickname of "the Cricket" (Sverčok), but to the public he was known as Aleksandr Sergeevič Puškin. Speeches were delivered, and some were recorded by Žukovskij-Svetlana, as secretary — to eulogize some "cadaver" of the "Society of the Russian Word", that is to say the very much alive conservatives. Above all, the group vowed to propagate Romanticism.

Beneath the hilarity and high-jinx of the Arzamas dinners lay a serious purpose which probably no member could have defined exactly. They were agreed in opposing the moss-backs and in favoring Romanticism. By "Romanticism" most of them understood a new type of literature from England, represented primarily by Sir Walter Scott and Lord Byron. Their general intellectual views were wholly determined by training in French classical and post-classical works. They respected Žukovskij's Germanic enthusiasms without sharing them except in a vague and general way. During the three years (1815—1818) that the organization lasted, Žukovskij was their most distinguished member and Russia's leading poet.[7] In those same years his translations and adap-

---

dubbed him "Šutovskoj" (Funster) — was a prolific dramatist, courtier, and wit, particularly gifted in the parody of living persons. By temperament and training he belonged to the late eighteenth century French tradition, though he later became an Anglophile and made dramatic adaptations of *Ivanhoe*, *The Tempest*, and a part of *Henry IV*. His quarrel with the sentimentalists goes back at least as far as 1807, when his one-act farce, *The New Sterne* (Novyj Stern), heaped elaborate ridicule upon those in Russia who sought to be real-life Yoricks.

[7] In 1818 Alexander I commissioned Žukovskij's friend Bludov to translate all diplomatic documents since 1814 into Russian. The new Russian translation of the Bible from Church Slavic was gaining widespread favor at this time.

tations of German lyric poetry appeared in thickest profusion and had their greatest fame.[8] But his Arzamas colleagues accepted his Russian products without seeking further contact with their sources of inspiration. After 1818 events took a new turn. The Arzamas disbanded, Žukovskij was called to other pursuits, and the rapid fame of Puškin eclipsed that of his predecessor and attracted a following with different ideals. Puškin himself could seldom muster more than tepid enthusiasm for the Germanic Muse. His guides were Scott, Byron, Shakespeare, and the late Rococo poets of France. Thus by 1820 it was a Franco-British type of Romanticism that established itself in Petersburg and which achieved predominance in Russian letters.

Displaced Žukovskij might be as leader of Russian literary life, but his career was far from ended. Yet after the dispersal of the Arzamas his story became the story of a single individual writer. The evolution of circumstances brought him ever closer to Germany until, in 1841, at the age of fifty-eight, he married a German girl and took up permanent residence in Düsseldorf.

Late in 1817 the imperial family selected him as Instructor in Russian to the bride of Grand Duke Nicholas, later Tsar Nicholas I. A kind of special favor attached to the young bride, who in Russia was known as Aleksandra Fëdrovna but in her native Berlin as Princess Charlotte, daughter of Frederick William III and Queen Luise. She was allowed to bring with her many of her childhood German friends and to maintain a German atmosphere in her household. It was she who introduced the custom of the Christmas tree into Russia and who made the Russian Christmas a family festival. She was an eager Romanticist in the current German sense of the word. In her album she had copied out sections of Tieck's *Sternbald*; at her request Žukovskij was later (1837) to make a hexameter version of Fouqué's *Undine*; she knew large quantities of German poetry by heart. With fine pedagogical sense, her tutor exploited this knowledge by making translations of poems by Schiller, Körner, Hebel, Goethe, and Uhland, and having his pupil learn Russian by comparing the two versions. A thin volume of these bi-lateral texts was printed under the title of *For the Few* (Dlja nemnogix).

An illness of the Grand Duchess in 1820 was compensated by a vacation journey to her native land. Žukovskij attended her as a

---

[8] A total of twenty-nine poems was translated from the German by Žukovskij in the years 1815—1818, representing 9 from Goethe, 5 from Schiller, 7 from Uhland, 6 from Hebel, 1 from Körner, and 1 from Ramler.

member of the imperial entourage, witnessing the festivities of greeting in Berlin upon arrival and also making his own private tour of Germany, Switzerland, and northern Italy before return. The tour was a literary man's pilgrimage to famous writers. In Berlin he met Fouqué, whom he did not much like, Chamisso, Brentano, and Bettina Brentano. The last he actively disliked. Since all these persons knew Hoffmann, who was then at the peak of his fame in Berlin, it is plausible that Žukovskij met him as well, though no record attests the fact. In Dresden he spent considerable time with Tieck, who told him at length about Wackenroder and who talked at great length about art. He also became good friends with Caspar David Friedrich, the Romantic painter par excellence. (Žukovskij was an enthusiastic painter of some skill.) In Bayreuth he called on Jean-Paul. In Weimar he was disappointed to miss Goethe, but at the insistence of Grand Duchess Mar'ja Pavlovna,[9] pressed on to Jena where Goethe was staying. The reception by the Olympian was curiously cool, though subsequent events created a more pleasant relationship.[10]

Once back in Russia, Žukovskij lived for a time amid his literary friends and literary work. Suddenly, in March of 1823, came the news of the death of Mar'ja Protasova in Dorpat. It was the Grand Duchess, no longer his pupil but always his friend, who urged him to find solace in new employment. Specifically she proposed his acting as tutor to the German bride of Grand Duke Michael and to prepare himself for undertaking the duties of tutor to her son, the future Tsar Alexander II. For six years, 1823—1829, Žukovskij acted in the latter capacity, and if ever Prince had a high-minded director of youth, the Tsarevich had

[9]   Grand Duchess Mar'ja Pavlovna (1786—1859), the sister of Tsars Alexander I and Nicholas I, married Karl Friedrich, son of Goethe's patron, Duke Karl August of Weimar, in 1804. Her residence in Goethe's city and her alliance with the Ducal family made her an important intermediary between Goethe and the Russian Goetheans. Her reports of him as a non-revolutionary also helped remove prejudice against him in the circle of the imperial family.

[10]   Goethe may possibly have been slightly put out by the persistent visitor. The conversation was begun in French, but when Žukovskij observed that Goethe's French was not particularly fluent, he changed over to German, thereby perhaps adding to his host's annoyance. At any rate, Žukovskij wrote the Grand Duchess Aleksandra Fëdrovna that this interview had been "like a boat trip on the Rhine swathed in mist, although he received me amicably". Before he left the country a letter of particular cordiality from Goethe overtook him, which Žukovskij answered — in French. A far more cordial visit of four or five days' duration took place in September 1827, on which occasion Goethe is said to have sent his pen by Žukovskij's hand as a gift to Puškin. Žukovskij also made a third visit to Weimar in 1833, the year after Goethe's death.

such in Žukovskij. Not the least of the poet's services to Russia was the bringing to the throne of a Tsar of benevolent intention.

When his service with the imperial family was concluded in 1829 almost a quarter of a century of Žukovskij's life was waiting yet to be used and lived, and he did use it conscientiously. His literary work, much of it distinguished and valuable, continued until his death in 1852, crowned near the end by his monumental translation of the *Odyssey*.[11] But the truth of the matter is that history had by-passed him. If the last dozen years of his life were passed in deserved happiness with his young wife and his children in the Rhineland, he was an anachronism in Germany as he was in Russia. Spiritually he was a man of 1800, and the nineteenth century disconcerted and dismayed him. History has steadily acknowledged his capital importance as "the father of Russian Romanticism". Modern criticism tends to rediscover in him a purity of style and language long obscured by shifting tastes. In some senses it is to be regretted that he preferred all his life long to translate the works of others, from the English, the French, the German, and the classical languages, rather than compose original works. Yet his translations enriched Russian literature enormously, and, somewhat in the spirit of the German Romantic translators, he brought world literature to his fellow-countrymen and made it their own.

Relative to his role as intermediary between Germany and Russia, the importance of which is hard to exaggerate, it may be said that upon the narrow basis of the Muscovite Wertherism which he inherited he constructed a literary edifice of size where many German writers were enshrined. Yet almost all of these writers belonged to the eighteenth century. Even after extensive travels in the West and after the passage of many years, the Romantic generation of Germany were, save Uhland alone, antipathetic to him. To the end he venerated Goethe, Schiller, and Bürger above the rest. He made their poems Russian poems. The second phase of German literary influence in Russia may be distilled into two terms: "sentimental lyric" and "Žukovskij".

[11]   Žukovskij knew only a smattering of Latin and no Greek, and all his classical translations were made through the medium of French or German or English. In the case of the *Odyssey* he worked with the direct personal assistance of Varnhagen von Ense in Berlin in 1843. (Varnhagen's comment about him was: "Es ist ein gutmütiger redseliger Alter, etwas zu demütig gegen den Hof.") It was Žukovskij's intention to begin a great new field of endeavor, translation from the classics, to correspond with the new era of his married life and also to bring the Greek and Roman writers directly to his countrymen in their own language. An editor in 1935 praises his *Odyssey*, saying that, with its errors, it is still superior to more scholarly translations.

4. THE MOSCOW SCHELLINGIANS

Students who entered the University of Moscow in the 1820's, either directly or after promotional examinations from the Noble Pension, had swords conferred upon them in formal ceremony, but they also wore government uniforms, took stern oaths of allegiance to the Tsar's government, and abjured secret societies. The political cabales of the German Burschenschaften and the memory of Kotzebue's murder in 1819 were fresh in everyone's mind. There was no equivalent of the picturesque frivolity of the German Burschen, but rather an atmosphere of urgent intellectual seriousness among the students. Early in Alexander I's reign Russia's second University had been founded in Petersburg, followed in 1811 by the establishment of the Lyceum at Tsarskoe Selo as a parallel to the Noble Pension, but the older schools continued to attract brilliant pupils and future celebrities — Lermontov, Gončarov, Turgenev the novelist, Herzen, Prince Odoevskij, Belinskij, Griboedov, Čaadaev. The four-fold curriculum offered a concentration in Literature as well as in the traditional branches of Politics and Morals, of Physcis and Mathematics, and of Medicine. The courses in literature tended decidedly toward conservatism. Perhaps the best the faculty could offer there was Professor Merzljakov, a school-mate of Žukovskij's, who had long since renounced whatever brashly pro-Romantic views he might ever have held. History was better taught by Kačenovskij, Žukovskij's one-time co-editor on *The Messenger of Europe,* and by Mixail Petrovič Pogodin, who in 1826 assumed direction of *The Moscow Messenger* (Moskovskij Vestnik). Both presented a skeptical point of view, both made use of the scientific method. Best taught of all and most stimulating to literary-minded students, were the scientific courses, both those given by native Russians and those given by Germans who lectured in Latin. Here the doctrines of Schelling's nature-philosophy were enthusiastically presented by Professors Davydov and M. G. Pavlov. The latter, who was also editor of the literary review *Athenaeum* as well as Professor of physics and agriculture from 1820 to 1840, carried on a lively debate with his colleague Fischer von Valdenheim, a student of Cuvier, about the relative merits of experimental science and Schellingian theory. Yet ideologies like Schelling's could be dangerous. Ubiquitous police spies darkened the intellectual atmosphere generally. In 1826 Davydov was officially silenced. The same year saw the poet Poljaev sent for a soldier for satirical verses, and famous student expulsions for alleged political reasons included

Belinskij (1832), Ogarëv and Herzen (1834), and possibly Lermontov (1831).

Whatever was omitted in lectures, however, was discussed in private gatherings. A whole series of "discussion groups" concentrated the eager intellectual life in semi-formal societies meeting in various homes. Around Professor S. E. Raič (1792–1855), himself a poet and translator, gathered a large and significant group of varying membership from both the student body and the faculty.[12] One development of their discussions is reported by Pogodin under the date of March 11, 1823:

Among us a group of friends has been organized. We meet a couple of times a week and read our own compositions and translations. We have proposed, among other things, to translate all the Greek and Roman classics . . . , and Plato, Demosthenes, and Livy have already been begun.

A journal entitled *Hermes* brought the classical translations of the group to the public, but Pogodin's publication *Urania* in 1826 reflected an even more significant aspect of their thinking. Eager philosophers of science that they were, they were still primarily literary men and they wished to see the thought of Schelling transmuted into artistic forms. It was precisely such transmutation that they found in Goethe. Goethe was their arbiter of aesthetics, the complement of Schelling — "Schelling applied to literature". This great artist must be brought to the Russian reading public. Therefore Pogodin set to work himself on a translation of *Götz von Berlichingen,* while his friend Ševyrëv was preparing Schiller's *Wallensteins Lager* — which Goethe had suggested to Schiller — and while Dmitrij Venevitinov was undertaking *Egmont. Urania* was to be pervaded with Goethe during its very brief existence. Even the "Science" section of the magazine was filled with translations from Goethe's scientific writings.

Among the student members of this circle the average age was less than twenty. It was a duplication of the days and doings of the "Literary Society of Friends" of 1801, but on a larger scale. The numbers were larger in 1823, the persons vastly more sophisticated, the enthusiasm more exuberant and more public. Most of these young men, upon completion of the three-year university course, entered government service in the Archive Department of the Ministry of

---

[12] Among the Raič circle were: Prince V. F. Odoevskij, V. I. Obolenskij, M. P. Pogodin, V. P. Titov, D. P. Oznobišin, V. L. Androsov, N. V. Putjata, S. P. Ševyrëv, A. N. Murav'ëv, P. I. Kološin, A. F. Tomaševskij.

Foreign Affairs in Moscow, and from this fact came to be known collectively as the "Archive Youth" (Arxivnaja junost'). Entrants there in 1824 included, among others: V. P. Titov, A. I. Košelëv, S. P. Ševyrëv, and D. V. Venevitinov, all of whom were intimately involved in the expansion of Russian Romanticism.[13] Their work among the dusty historical files was sometimes tedious but never arduous, free time was plentiful, and the association with one another yielded an exhilaration that found its direct expression in literature.

Whether they met among themselves or with their university friends or in the salons, the talk centered about two names, Schelling and Goethe, and about the creation of a synthesis of philosophy and aesthetics. It was a new aspect of Goethe that they admired. *Werther* they accepted with enthusiasm, as the previous generation had done. Their translations from Goethean lyric included areas previously worked by Žukovskij but went further to include the anthology verse and the philosophical poems. Wholly new in Russia was their admiration for *Faust* and for *Wilhelm Meister*. In other words, they were at the point corresponding roughly to the year 1798 in Germany, when the Romantic generation there, inspired by these very works, set out to surpass the master of Weimar. A difference in time and in milieu forced the "Archive Youth" in another direction from that taken by the Romantiker. Their preoccupation with philosophy led them, in spite of themselves, away from art and toward the dangerous fields of speculative thinking. The course followed may best be seen in the instance of the "discussion group" known as the "Lovers of Wisdom" (Ljubomudry).

There were five members in this group which met secretly in the private study of their host, Prince Vladimir Fëdrovič Odoevskij: Odoevskij himself, a future novelist and short-story writer; Aleksandr Ivanovič Košelëv, the most practical-minded of the quintet; Nikolaj Matveevič Rožalin, who was to make the definitive translation of *Werther* in 1829; Ivan Vasilevič Kireevskij, grand-nephew of Žukovskij, future critic of distinction and co-founder of the Slavophile movement; and, above all, the brilliant and versatile poet, the secretary of the group, Dmitrij Vladimirovič Venevitinov (1805—1827). Years later Košelëv recalled with nostalgia the secret meetings at Prince Odoevskij's, where the talk was all of

---

[13] Besides the four mentioned, the "Archive Youth" also included: A. V. Venevitinov (brother of Dmitrij), the brothers Ivan and Pëtr Kireevskij, F. S. Xomjakov, N. A. Mel'gunov, S. A. Sobolevskij, I. S. Mal'cov.

... German philosophy, i.e. Kant, Fichte, Schelling, Oken, Görres, etc. There [he continues] we used to read our philosophical compositions, but more often still and for the largest part we talked about the works of German lovers of wisdom whom we had read. The foundations on which all human knowledge must be built constituted the favorite subject of our conversations. Christian doctrine seemed to us fit only for the masses, but not for us Lovers of Wisdom. We valued Spinoza especially highly and reckoned his works far above the Gospel and other sacred writings.

Some public reflection of the ideas of this quintet was to be seen in the journal *Mnemosyne* (Mnemozina), founded in 1824 by Prince Odoevskij and Puškin's friend, V. K. Küchelbecker, with the avowed purpose of publishing serious literature and as much philosophy as they dared. But *Mnemosyne,* Russia's first philosophical magazine, ran for only four months, January to October 1824, and the ill-fated political revolt of December 1825 put to rout the philosophizing friends. Küchelbecker, who *was* involved in the conspiracy, was first condemned to death, then sent on reduced sentence to twenty years in Siberia. The Lovers of Wisdom, who were *not* involved in the conspiracy, were at least guilty of having friends who were, and of holding secret meetings. In his mémoires Košelëv says:

I vividly recall how immediately after that unfortunate date [December 14th] Prince Odoevskij summoned us together and with particular solemnity committed to the fire in his grate both the statutes and the protocols of our Lovers of Wisdom society.

5.   VENEVITINOV

It was a significant chapter of Russian intellectual life that was committed to the fire in Prince Odoevskij's grate that evening. If it could be resurrected, we should be able to see, among other things, a most interesting phase of German-Russian ideological relations about which only conjecture is now possible. The practical applications of the lost protocols to literature might, in turn, be more evident, had not death abruptly carried off Dmitrij Venevitinov shortly after his twenty-first birthday. He had been the most imaginative of the speakers in the secret conclave. As secretary of the group he had composed the lost documents. His human and his poetic personality, both remarkably attractive, brought him close to Puškin, who felt on the whole alien to the other members of the group. In fact, he alone could have united the

Moscow and Petersburg factions of Russian Romanticism and beyond his unfortunate death lies one of those wistful histories of speculation on the Might-have-been.

Into the last two hectic years of his life he poured an extraordinary amount of experiences — his desperate love for the Princess Zinaida Aleksandrovna Volkonskaja, imprisonment and release after charges of seditious associations, the founding of *The Moscow Messenger,* the composition of most of his small but striking body of lyric poems and a significant set of translations. The broad outlines of his aesthetic and ideological concepts are, to be sure, clear enough, and they may be taken as indicative of the whole Archive Youth and Lovers of Wisdom. His original verse has wit and charm, lucidity, and, above all, an impressively lofty sense of dedication to beauty and to truth. His ideal was Goethe, and the selections translated from Goethe are in themselves an index to Venevitinov and to his generation. Those from *Faust* [14] testify to a mind speculatively philosophical and religiously non-conformist. The cautiously chosen fragments from *Egmont* [15] hint at political criticism. Two early poems (1774) of Goethe about Art and the Artist, *Künstlers Erdewallen* and *Des Künstlers Vergötterung,* show a concern with a rationale of art to which is given a vivid expression in the fine original poem *To Puškin* (K Puškinu). Here Goethe, the aged Olympian of Weimar, is invoked as a Romantic demigod of Poetry and the hope is expressed that Puškin may be his successor. The irregularly rhymed fifty-two lines conclude:

> Our master, thy master,
> He is hidden in the land of dreams,
> In his native Germany.
> Until now his withering fingers
> Have fled at times over the strings,
> And intermittent tones,
> Like the sweet voice of old friendship
> After dreary separation,

---

[14] *Faust I: Vor dem Tor,* lines 1064—1141 (Faust i Vagner, za gorodom); the lyric, *Meine Ruh' ist hin* (Pesn' Margarity); and the opening monologue of Faust in *Wald und Höhle,* lines 3217—3250 (Monolog Fausta. Noč'. Peščera). The last appeared in *The Moscow Messenger,* 1827; the first two were printed posthumously in Venevitinov's collected works, 1829.

[15] *Egmont,* I. *Palast der Regentin* (Dvorec pravitel'nicy), the dialogue between Margaret of Parma and her secretary Machiavel on state policy in the Netherlands; *Egmont,* I. *Bürgerhaus* (Meščanskij dom), the scene between Klara, her mother, and Brackenburg, including the lyric *Die Trommel gerühret.* The lyric was printed in *Dennica* (Dawn) in 1830, the remainder — with cuts — in 1831; the complete text was not released by the censor until 1855.

Have turned us to well known thoughts.
Until now the heart has not chilled within him,
And believe me, with keen joy,
In his harbor of sad old age
He will yet hear thy voice,
And perhaps captivated with thee,
Inspired with a last warmth,
Answering, the swan will burst into song,
And with a music of farewell,
Directing his triumphant flight toward heaven,
In the rapture of divine dreaming
Will call, o Puškin, upon thee.

Posthumously published in 1827 in *The Moscow Messenger* was another piece of translation by Venevitinov, which for reasons unknown was left a fragment to be completed by his brother. It was one of the Tales of Hoffmann, known to modern readers as *Der Magnetiseur* (The Hypnotist) but originally entitled *Träume sind Schäume*. The Russian version, imitating the latter, was called *As Foam in Water, So (are) Dreams in the Head* (Čto pena v vode, to sny v golove). By virtue of the long "philosophical" first section of that story with its speculative analysis of dreams, the conclusion may be drawn that it had entered into the Schellingian evenings as an example of the unification of philosophy and literature. At any rate, the impression was to be persistent in Russia that Hoffmann was a purveyor of philosophical allegories, and that within his story-shells were kernels of original and profound ideological matter for those who were willing to crack the nut. In printing the story *The Moscow Messenger* was serving two ends. It was honoring its founder, to be sure, but it was also in a sense taking a stand relative to its competitor, Nikolaj Polevoj's *Moscow Telegraph* (Moskovskij Telegraf). Since its founding in 1825, the rival journal had made open avowal of its universality of interests. Tentatively, it had experimented with Hoffmann, thereby anticipating the new turn which Russian Romanticism was about to take. Almost as a corrective, to insist upon a philosophical Hoffmann and a Schellingian tradition, the *Messenger* presented *Der Magnetiseur*. In the three years of its existence (1827–1830), the *Messenger* was to offer further *Die Irrungen* — one of the rare instances of political concern in Hoffmann's writings —, the critical piece *Zacharias Werner,* and the artist-problem-tale *Die Jesuiterkirche in G.* It seems plausible that an editorial policy inherited from the Lovers of Wisdom and from Venevitinov governed these choices.

6. THE MOSCOW CIRCLES 1825–1840

After the catastrophe of 1825 intellectuals in Moscow, as elsewhere, understandably eschewed secret societies. The disciples of Schelling spoke in whispers, but they continued to speak. Two Moscow salons afforded them opportunities for gathering. The first, known as "the pleasurable republic of the Red Gates", was that of Avdot'ja Petrovna Elagina, a half-niece of Žukovskij and mother of Ivan Kireevskij by her first marriage. The second, known as "the enchanted castle of the realm of music", was that of Princess Zinaida Aleksandrovna Volkonskaja. At the latter, Venevitinov carried on his hopeless suit for the hostess, who was as beautiful as she was talented, herself a writer, shrewd literary critic, and liberal thinker. But the personalities of the mid-'20's were gradually disappearing from the scene. Venevitinov was now dead; Prince Odoevskij, V. P. Titov, and A. I. Košelëv migrated to Petersburg; Rožalin, Ševyrëv, and finally Princess Volkonskaja herself left Russia in 1829 for prolonged stays in Italy. *The Moscow Messenger* came to an end in 1830.

At the University likewise, the names and faces were all changed from the times of the Archive Youth. A cholera epidemic in 1830 had forced the closing of the institution for a whole year, and upon its reopening a close observer might have noted a revival of the para-University intellectual life of pre-Decembrist days. But with a difference. A new revolution in France had just raised depressed liberal spirits everywhere. A new set of ideas was beginning to displace Schelling's predominance. The "Stankevič clique" [16] at the beginning of the decade took cognizance of recent political trends, though its orientation was still Germanophile. By 1834, the "Herzen clique" [17] might still pay

[16] To the "Stankevič clique" belonged: V. G. Belinskij, the famous critic; Pëtr Kireevskij, co-founder of the Slavophile movement; Konstantin Aksakov, son of Sergej Aksakov, the author of *A Family Chronicle;* A. P. Efremov; two minor poets, V. I. Krasov and I. P. Ključnikov; Ja. M. Neverov; etc.
[17] To the "Herzen clique" belonged: Nikolaj Ogarev, Herzen's life-long friend; N. M. Satin, V. V. Passek, Baron Kelčer, and N. Sazanov, the latter two being passionate admirers of German thought. Members of this "clique" were arrested in 1834 and exiled to widely separated points in the Russian empire. Within a year the "Stankevič clique" came to include persons far more dangerous than the exiled "Herzens": M. A. Bakunin the revolutionist, V. P. Botkin, M. N. Katkov, and future Professor T. N. Granovskij. The striking thing about these groups is their inclusion of members who, a decade later, were to be vehement opponents, e.g. Belinskij the Westernizer and Kireevskij the fanatic Slavophile; the doctrinaire revolutionist Bakunin and the conservative Katkov. The real-life conflicts

allegiance to German thought, but the name of Saint-Simon was spoken among them more and more frequently. Through the decade as a whole the prestige of Schelling waned, until, by 1840, he could be mentioned as a mere fore-runner of Hegel. With the waning of Schelling, the primacy of Goethe waned. When the Romantic movement ended in 1841, the whole tally of Moscow Germanophiles had been transformed into political revolutionists, at least in theory, some of them moving through the Westernizer position to the extreme left, more of them moving to the mystical position of the Slavophiles.

As the temper changed from idealistic to political, literary objectives likewise changed. Venevitinov's view of Goethe as universal genius and sublime Poet had somehow proved inadequate to the spiritual needs of Russian thinkers and artists. The view had exalted Goethe, as it were, beyond reach. Closer to the mood of the times was Hoffmann, whose narrative art beguiled, whose aesthetic was certainly allied to Schelling's philosophy, but in whom there was an agitation of spirit more attractive than the remote and unattainable calm of Goethe, at least of the late Goethe who was contemporary with the rising generation. His recurrent theme of the juxtaposition of two worlds, Real and Ideal, implied strife, unending strife between irreconcilable opposites. Whatever the author's original intention might have been, the strife seemed perfectly calculated to express the irreconcilable opposition between Utopia and Russian actuality. Groping their way from a philosophy of aesthetics to a philosophy of politics, the young men of 1830 found in Hoffmann an author who wrote about Art and Anti-Art, but whose conflicting worlds could quite well stand parable-wise for other conflicts, political-social conflicts with which these young men were faced daily. In their own adaptations of Hoffmannian themes and situations, the Russian Hoffmannists will never make explicit this transposition of ideas. Their opposed worlds will be prudently invested with a Christian raiment. The Real will often appear as a Vale of Tears, the Ideal will often suggest a vision of Heaven. The logical hero for a story will be the Artist, be he poet or painter, or at least a youth of artistic temperament. Such a hero, by his very nature, will perceive the Ideal and be destroyed by the implacable Real. The heroes of Hoffmann may attain to happiness at last, may reach the realms of Art far from the madding Philistine throng, or they may become "mad", which is to say that their contact with higher reality makes them *seem*

in ideologies which will inform Dostoevskij's later novels are here in the making, at the University of Moscow in the 1830's.

mad to dull folk around them; the Russian heroes always perish and their not infrequent madness is literal and clinical.

Hoffmann, the successor to Goethe, was the last foreign import to exert strong influence on Russian literature. Enthusiasm for his works extended far more widely than among the coteries that had cultivated Goethe, except for the *Werther*-readers. The Russian reading public had multiplied notably since the beginning of the century. Their demands were making themselves felt, and their demands were, like those all over Europe, for more and more of the fascinating Tales. The public at large, not the critics, not the philosophers, created the Hoffmann craze. The Russian authors, attempting to make his unique manner their own, met with widely varying degrees of success, but in their search for his secret they discovered the secret of their own national genius.

7. HOFFMANN IN RUSSIA IN THE 1820's

Interpretations of his works so divergent as these from his own intentions would have sent Hoffmann back to his manuscripts in puzzlement to see what he could have written to give rise to such ideas. He was himself a tolerably learned man and holder of a law degree from the University of Königsberg, but he never laid the slightest claim to being a philosopher. In fact, in his student days he had never once attended the lectures of Königsberg's most illustrious professor, Immanuel Kant. Nor were his post-university readings systematic or extraordinarily broad. He read the recent German authors and read them with attention and perceptive sympathy, but avoided aesthetic polemics in the manner of Friedrich Schlegel. To political theory he was profoundly indifferent. The Napoleonic campaigns disrupted his personal life repeatedly, but he considered the disturbances part of the trials of existence and never became embroiled in arguments about international affairs. By profession he was a jurist in the employ of the Prussian government, with station at various points in Poland until the sudden collapse of his government under Napoleon's impetus left him jobless. By preference he was an artist, skilled in varying degrees with painter's tools and musican's instruments, until the same disaster to the Prussian government forced him to turn music instructor to keep body and soul together. Subsequent jolts of fate brought him to a four-year stay in the south-German city of Bamberg, where he served as theatrical director and producer, orchestra leader, composer, scene-painter, and impresario, eking out the wretched salary for this multifold position by giving singing lessons in spare time. Meanwhile he had published quantities of musical compositions in almost all the forms as well as extensive articles of musical criticism. Some time in the winter of 1808—1809, when he had passed his thirty-second birthday, and under circumstances which are unknown, he wrote his first piece of fiction, a short story entitled *Ritter Gluck*. The four Bamberg years, which were just then beginning, brought him vivid and poignant experiences and ultimately transformed him from a capable musician into a literary man of genius. Only toward the end of those years, when he was nearing the age of thirty-seven, did he finally take to writing in all seriousness. At some point in the same period he unofficially altered his third name from Wilhelm to Amadeus, in honor of Mozart, thus producing the signature Ernst Theodor Amadeus Hoffmann. Theodor was his preferred name. From 1813 until his death on June 25, 1822, during which years he was a steady and reliable employee of the restored Prussian government in Berlin, he composed two novels — one of them unfinished —, three long Märchen, and some sixty short stories. These shorter works were normally published individually, then gathered up into collections, usually with the addition of some new items to make the books attractive to purchasers. In this way three major omnibus sets of tales were created: *Fantasiestücke in Callots Manier,* 1814—1815 in four volumes; *Die Nachtstücke,* 1817 in two volumes; and *Die Serapionsbrüder,* 1819—1821 in four volumes. To these may be added the two-volume collection published posthumously in 1825 with the title of *Die Letzten Erzählungen.* The fame of these works was instantaneous and enormous. Public demand for them would not be satiated. Their popularity continued through the years immediately following his death, though at first nothing seemed to indicate that it would transcend the frontiers of the German-speaking world with anything like the intensity familiar at home. Slowly the devious operations of Fame brought the Tales to Paris, whence in the French translations of Loève-Veimars they reached all Europe, achieving everywhere a popularity greater than that of any German author in foreign lands.

Not the least striking aspect of Russian Hoffmannism is the fact that it anticipates the European vogue for the Tales. The first translation was made in 1822, the very year of the author's death, and the choice was *Das Fräulein von Scudery.* Somewhat oddly, the magazine which carried it was *The Son of the Fatherland* (Syn Otečestva), the re-actionary journal founded by N. I. Greč in 1812 as a war propaganda sheet and later converted into a literary paper. Possibly the story's setting in the classical Paris of Louis XIV made it palatable to the editors. An analogously remote and literarily familiar Venetian setting of long ago may further account for the same magazine's second choice for translation in 1823, *Doge und Dogaresse*. Thereafter the editors recognized the inappropriateness of a Romantic author in their columns and printed no more works of his until 1829, when the force of popular demand was making itself felt. Even then, with so harmless a piece as *Signor Formica,* they felt obliged to counter their manifestations of liberalism by publishing the same year a translation of Sir Walter Scott's article *On the Supernatural in Fictitious Composition,* which had originally been printed in England in 1827 under the title of *Novels of Ernest Theodore Hoffmann.* Sir Walter held that Hoffmann allowed his considerable gifts to sweep him away into depths of unwhole-someness.

Meanwhile in 1823 the story *Spielerglück* had appeared in *The Messenger of Europe,* the moderate-conservative magazine which had been founded in 1802 by Karamzin for the purpose of transmission of European culture and of which Žukovskij had been the editor for two years, 1808—1810.

Apparently *Das Fräulein von Scudery* had made an impression on the reading public, for its decidedly inferior companion-piece, *Die Marquise de la Pivardière,* was the first Hoffmann work to be selected by Nikolaj Polevoj's newly founded *Moscow Telegraph* in 1825. The story had originally been published in the autumn of 1820 but had been included in the posthumous collection of *Die Letzten Erzählungen,* and was therefore a current item in Germany itself when the Russian version was made. For his annual supplement issue — the bonus expected by subscribers in those days —, Polevoj published the genuinely terrifying little ghost story which occurs without title amid the frametale conversations at the end of Volume II of *Die Serapions-brüder* and which is known by alternate editor's titles as either *Eine Spukgeschichte* or *Der schwebende Teller.* Again from the recent *Letzten Erzählungen* he printed a version of *Datura fastuosa* in 1826 under the title of *The Botanist* (Botanik).

It was at this juncture that the Moscow Schellingians created their own journal *The Moscow Messenger* to offset the eclecticism of Polevoj's magazine and to give expression to their philosophical point of view. Here appeared in 1827, as has been mentioned, Venevitinov's translation of *Der Magnetiseur,* to be followed in 1829 by *Die Irrungen* with its implied criticism, so rare in Hoffmann, of current politics, in this case of the enthusiastic arm-chair fighters for Greece against the Turks.

In 1829 Paris made the discovery of the Tales and the general European vogue set in. The year 1830 saw six new Russian translations appear. *The Moscow Messenger,* now in its third and final year, carried the critical-historical piece *Zacharias Werner* and the art-problem-tale *Die Jesuiterkirche in G.* Polevoj's *Telegraph* printed two of the famous eerie tales, *Das Majorat* and *Der Sandmann,* while the middle-of-the-road *Messenger of Europe* gave its readers *Das Sanctus* and the beautiful miniature story *Rat Krespel.* Moscow magazines all. By 1831 the Petersburg *Son of the Fatherland* felt obliged to comply with public demand and to print — of all things — *Die Brautwahl,* one of the seven new Hoffmann items of that year. The *Literary Gazette* and *Northern Archive* also joined the general tide that year. The great preponderance of Hoffmann translations, however, stemmed from Moscow, the home territory of the Germanophile Romanticists.

Interest in Hoffmann began slowly with 1822, increased sharply at 1829 when he became the rage of Europe, held at full tide until about 1835, decreased slowly until 1840, and with the end of Romanticism fell into sudden disfavor. Meanwhile through the 1820's the first Russian imitator of Hoffmann was unobtrusively at work.

"POGOREL'SKIJ", THE GENTLEMAN-AMATEUR

In March of 1825 the magazine *News of Literature* (Novosti Literatury) carried the first Russian story written in imitation of Hoffmann. Its title, more cumbersome in English than in the original, was *The Poppy-seed-cake Woman of the Lafërtov Quarter* (Lafërtovskaja Makovnica). The work was signed "Antonij Pogorel'skij". Puškin, in a letter of March 27th, 1825 to his brother, declares he has read the little work through twice at a single sitting, so delighted was he with it, and then adds: "'Pogorel'skij' is surely Perovskij, isn't it?" The guess was quite correct, and probably many readers divined behind the pseudonym the authorship of the wealthy nobleman Aleksej Alekseevič Perovskij, proprietor of the vast estate of Pogorel'cy in the northern Ukraine.

Poetic justice begins the line of Russian Hoffmannists with this same Perovskij-"Pogorel'skij", a man of Hoffmann's own generation or very nearly so, and a representative of the more amiable traditions of Russian aristocracy before the nineteenth century cleavages first cracked, then shattered its serenity. Wealth, leisure, graciousness, and taste were his, together with all the qualities of a gentleman except for his name, which, properly speaking, was no more Perovskij than it was "Pogorel'skij". Yet Perovskij was the name adopted by him, by his sister Anna Alekseevna, and by his two brothers, all illegitimate offspring of Count Aleksej Kirillovič Razumovskij. The ancient family of the Razumovskijs, originally shepherds and Cossacks, had come into particular prominence in the eighteenth century. Count Kirill, the author's grandfather, became hetman of the Ukraine, the last, incidentally, to hold that office, while his brother Aleksej was long the favorite and finally the secret husband of the Empress Elizabeth (1741—1761). As commander of the famous Izmajlovskij Regiment, Count Kirill was also one of the chief supporters of Catherine II in the coup d'état of 1761. The author's father, though less distinguished, was not obscure. His liaison with Mar'ja Mixajlovna Sobolevskaja was quite open and he presided over his household of four illegitimate children with paternal solicitude, sparing no effort to advance their worldly welfare.

Little is known of Perovskij's childhood or early youth until the time of his entry into the University of Moscow August 16th, 1805. He was then eighteen years old. By October of 1807 he had acquired a doctor's degree, having presented the required triple dissertation in German, in French, and in Russian. The botanical subjects were not inexpertly treated, as may be judged from the printed versions of 1808.[1] Yet Perovskij did not become a botanist. For four years he worked in the civil service, where native intelligence and loyalty to duty, rather than family prestige, advanced him in rank. In the general mobilization of 1812 he served as a Cavalry Captain of the 3rd Cossack Regiment, seeing action in the battles of Dresden and of Kulm in 1813. Rather than follow the armies to Paris, he chose to remain through 1814–1815 in Dresden on the staff of his brother-in-law, Prince Volkonskij, governor-general of Saxony. Upon return to Russia it fell to his lot to act in the government office for the control of religious affairs in the provinces. The post was something less than congenial to him but he retained it for five years, 1816–1821, largely out of loyalty to his chief, the brilliant littérateur and friend of Žukovskij, A. I. Turgenev. Amid the clique of literary amateurs that surrounded Turgenev began undoubtedly Perovskij's preoccupation with belles-lettres. With the death of his father came a certain independence, and at age thirty-four he resigned from government service and retired to his Ukrainian estates.

Meanwhile he had acquired a kind of family of his own. In 1816 his sister, Anna Alekseevna Perovskaja, had married Count Konstantin Petrovič Tolstoj and a year later a son had been born to them. Scarcely six months after the child's birth the parents separated. The action seems to have been wholly amicable and, in fact, amicable relations between all parties concerned were maintained as long as they lived. But Anna Alekseevna never returned to her husband. She and her infant son took up residence with her brother and henceforth constituted a regular part of his household. The infant son was later to become the very distinguished poet, dramatist, and novelist, Count Aleksej Konstantinovič Tolstoj.[2]

---

[1] The three dissertations of 1807, published 1808, bear the following titles: 1. *Wie sind Thiere und Gewächse von einander unterschieden und welches ist ihr Verhältnis zu den Mineralien?* 2. *Sur le but et l'utilité du système des plantes de Linné.* 3. *O rastenijax kotorija by polezno bylo razmnožat' v Rossíi* (Concerning plants which it would be useful to propagate in Russia).

[2] A distant cousin of Leo Tolstoj. The principal works of Aleksej Konstantinovič Tolstoj (1817–1875) are: *Prince Serebrjannyj*, historical novel, 1862; a

With sister and nephew and with a great provision of books sent down from the capital, Perovskij came in 1821 to his estate of Pogorel'cy in the province of Černigov. The manor house surveyed a fine English park immediately surrounding it and thence wide prospects of pine forests which abounded in game of all sorts, even to foxes and wolves. Not long afterward the amiable bachelor moved for a time to an even finer house on his adjoining estate of Krasnyj Rog. A vast octagonal hall was one of the principal features of the mansion which the Italian architect Rastrelli had built for his grandfather, Count Kirill Razumovskij; ten horses abreast could turn on the main linden avenue; and, as at Pogorel'cy, the belvedere commanded panoramas of pine forests. In this setting the gentleman-amateur of letters, reading Hoffmann's Tales, was prompted to adapt one of them to make a story of his own.[3]

1. *THE POPPY-SEED-CAKE WOMAN OF THE LAFËRTOV QUARTER*

The old woman to whom the title refers was renowned in the Lafërtov Quarter of Moscow for her poppy-seed-cakes. Every day, rain or shine, she could be found seated by the tollgate, her cakes aligned on a neat cloth before her. Twilight invariably saw her home, and darkness often brought her visitors, chiefly persons eager to have her tell their fortunes with cards, in coffee-lees, or by other devices. Neighbors disliked her. Some had even denounced her to the police as a witch, but search of her premises had never revealed anything untoward. Following such denunciations, the informant's wife would often fall ill, some odd accident would befall a child of his, or a perfectly healthy cow would unexplainably sicken or die. Her Tom-cat had an almost human way of escorting her to the gate each morning and of meeting her there when she returned at twilight.

At length her nephew Onufrič, a God-fearing employee of the Moscow postal service, felt impelled to exert himself, against his wife's warnings, to alter his old aunt's ways. For his pains he received her curses and the withdrawal of her promised dowry for his baby daughter Maša.

---

trilogy of dramas: *The Death of Ivan the Terrible,* 1866; *Tsar Fëdor Ivanovič,* 1868; and *Tsar Boris Godunov,* 1870; two long narrative poems and some three hundred lyrics published throughout his lifetime.
[3] Biographical information has been drawn chiefly from the article on "Pogorel'skij" in the *Russian Biographical Dictionary* (Russkij Biografičeskij Slovar') and from André Lirondelle, *Le Poète Alexis Tolstoi,* thèse pour le doctorat ès lettres (Université de Paris, 1912).

Years pass. Onufrič's poverty never varies. Maša's beauty attracts suitors a-plenty, but her lack of dowry brings no offers of marriage. Her mother, Ivanovna, concludes that the old woman must be reconciled and, without Onufrič's knowledge, sends the girl to effect it. The reception is at first hostile, then relenting, and Maša with misgivings agrees to return for a second visit at the uncomfortable hour of eleven at night.

This time her aunt is cordial. Only the Tom-cat is with her. A crimson candle is lighted, the lamp is extinguished. A glow fills the room. Blood-red filaments stretch from floor to ceiling. The old woman cries an incantation. The Tom-cat howls. Then, to Maša's horror, the cat assumes human face and form, appearing in the uniform of a civil service officer. She faints at the sight. When she revives, the old woman tells her she has won her favor, that a suitor will presently come to claim her hand, and that at her marriage he will disclose a treasure. By that time the witch will be dead. She gives the girl a key as pledge of her promise, and, with the key in her hands, Maša makes her frightened way homeward beneath the late pale moonlight.

The very next night the poppy-seed-cake woman dies. At her funeral Ivanovna is sure the corpse tried to bite her as she made her bow to it, yet she rejoices to be able now to move into the house in the Lafërtov Quarter, for Maša's sake, as she says. Maša, for her part, is dismayed to leave the vicinity where the young man Ulian lives and still more dismayed to learn of the arrival of a suitor, Titular Councillor Aristarx Faleleič Murlykin. [Murlyka means "Tom-cat".] When her father summons her to meet the gentleman she recognizes with horror the half-human cat of the incantation, implores her bewildered father to bid the visitor remove his gloves and show his claws, and when her words have no effect, flees from the room. From her upstairs window she has the satisfaction of seeing the Titular Councillor speed in decidedly feline fashion before the onslaughts of the neighbors' dog.

At the glum supper table Onufrič is called away by a letter. An old comrade-in-arms from the Turkish campaign is asking for Maša's hand for his son. The girl agrees to any suitor so long as it not Murlykin. To her delight, the new suitor proves to be none other than Ulian. A joyous marriage is held in the old house. Amid the merriment word comes that the witch's house collapsed at the very moment when the bride pronounced her vows.

Readers of Hoffmann will readily recognize in the witch and her cat the counterparts of old Liese Rauerin and her Tom-cat henchman, the sworn enemies of Archivarius Lindhorst in *Der goldene Topf* (1814).

Midway through the "Fifth Vigil" — the chapters, somewhat preciously, are thus designated — of the German story, the pretty bourgeoise Veronika Paulmann is serving afternoon coffee to her friends the Oster sisters. Angelika Oster is telling at length how an old fortune-

teller named Rauerin interprets figures in a magic mirror and has given
her detailed information about her absent fiancé. Veronika is immediately interested, for she is dubious about being able to win the love of the
student Anselmus. Angelika Oster is able to inform her further that
the old woman receives clients, preferably alone, on Tuesdays, Wednes-
days, and Fridays, from seven in the evening until sunrise, in a house
situated in a remote street before the Lake Gate.

Veronika arrives at a suitable hour at this house. The sole living
creature in view is a large black Tom-cat who, with back high-arched
and tail waving, gravely escorts her to a closed door. Two meows elicit
a human voice from within bidding Veronika enter. A witch mon-
strously ugly sits inside surrounded by squeaking animals, human-faced
bats, and conventional witch's gear. A whisk dipped in a kettle and
sprinkled over the hearth transforms this paraphanalia into conventional
cottage furnishings. To Veronika's sharp annoyance she is told that
Anselmus will never in this world be hers. She turns with a curt "Good
Night!", but the witch detains her to disclose that she is Veronika's
former nurse, old Liese, and that she looks upon the girl as a daugther.
Moreover, the cause may not be hopeless after all, if Veronika has the
courage to attend certain rites at the crossroads on the equinox.
Veronika asserts that she has the requisite courage.

Two "vigils" later, just as the clocks are striking eleven, Veronika
arrives amid wind and rain at the crossroads. The witch is likewise
prompt. The Tom-cat, whose eyes dart blue lightnings, guides her steps.
In terms of a ghastly materialization of a painting by Rembrandt or
Breughel the incantation is elaborately detailed. Through all the horrors
Veronika keeps her promised courage until, at the climax, a great
eagle swoops down and the voice of Lindhorst disperses the spirit
rabble. At this, Veronika faints.

The story pursues other matters with only occasional mentions of the
witch and her cat up to the "Tenth Vigil", where, in a passage of rather
stronger physical violence than is common in Hoffmann's writing, the
evil spirits are destroyed by the good spirits under Archivarius Lindhorst. The Tom-cat, seized by Lindhorst's parrot, spurts fiery blood
from its jaws, while the witch burns to death under the folds of Lindhorst's robe of flame. The lifted robe afterwards reveals merely an
ugly beet-root, the true essence of the witch.

As for the relationship of witch and cat, it may be noted that in the
"Ninth Vigil" Veronika counters a disparaging remark about the pair
by saying:

That is a vile slander! Old Liese is a wise woman and the black Tom-cat is not a hostile creature at all, but an educated young man with fine manners, and her "cousin germain".

At a glance it may be seen that fairly commonplace invention has supplanted the vivid and unique Hoffmannian imagination. Maša is a demure maiden quite out of the class of the headstrong and plucky Veronika Paulmann. She is wholly blameless and passive, and the point should not be missed that "Pogorel'skij" brings her home from her nocturnal ordeal beneath a misty Žukovskian moonlight, as if she were one of those sweet but troubled angels, like the Svetlana of Žukovskij's ballad, who sadly tread the earth's dark paths. Action is initiated and guilt incurred by her mother, who, by being called merely Ivanovna, is identified as the shrewd, but still unwise, wife of traditional folk-tales. Veronika Paulmann's mother has died long before the story began. Onufrič too is a type borrowed directly from the simple but honest fathers of folk stories and owes nothing to the incarnate Philistine, Konrektor Paulmann, who serves as the butt of Hoffmann's humor. All of Liese Rauerin's complex relationships with human and spirit characters and all her significance within the framework of the elaborate Nature myth of *Der goldene Topf* have likewise given place before a purely conventional witch whose motivation is merely the search for wealth. She meets no grandiose annihilation and her obscure death "off stage" is mentioned only in passing, though presumably her destiny does not lie with the angels.

In short, "Pogorel'skij" drew no more than a few threads out of the gorgeous tapestry of Hoffmann's tale, and these he refashioned into a modest pattern of his own. This will be the procedure of almost every Russian Hoffmannist until Dostoevskij, who will reverse the method to superimpose whole stories of Hoffmann one on top of the other. Some writers will, to be sure, borrow more than a few threads, but always they will borrow less than the whole scheme of any given work. Their technique will rely on the recasting of one or more excerpted episodes.

Lost, then, to "Pogorel'skij's" fairy-tale, or rather disregarded, are all the intricacies of plot of Hoffmann's *Märchen*. Gone is the grandiose Nature myth which lent *Der goldene Topf* an extra and significant dimension of meaning. Gone are the magic, the colors, gone are the agile irony and the sprightly humor. Happiness in the Russian tale comes to a cozy wedding in a soberly rationalistic world, the very antithesis of the close of the German work, with its glimpse of "Atlantis", the land of Art's desire, where Anselmus may withdraw from the prosaic world in which Maša and Ulian find their joy. "Pogorel'skij" chooses to ignore the opposed worlds of Real and Ideal, indispensible to his source-work, to concentrate all his attention on the world of everyday. His supernatural elements are adjuncts to human agents, and good and bad human beings are the only creators of conflict which he recognizes. His view was, in this story as elsewhere, that literature's purpose is moral, and other Russian Hoffmannists will differ from him only in the degree of subtlety or directness with which they convey the moral sense. In the present instance he minces no words but puts the lesson of his fable clearly when he makes Maša's peasant-woman neighbor say explicitly: "Money does not make happiness".

The Poppy-seed-cake Woman of the Lafërtov Quarter is a moral fable designed to entertain *and* edify. Its author's mentality was founded on sturdy eighteenth century enlightenment, yet its rationalism was of the modified sort not uncommon in the age of Mesmer, for "Pogorel'skij's" concern with the occult was genuine if not particularly profound. The romanticism of the story is rudimentary, its Hoffmannism is purely external. Yet Puškin's delight as he read the tale in March of 1825 was not without justification. The story is well told, the style is pure, the humor is gentle and pleasing, remote as it may be from Hoffmannian wit, and the Žukovskian heroine has an unpretentious charm that persuades us to believe in her adventure.

2. THE DOUBLE

In the same year as the publication of his first story Perovskij - "Pogorel'skij" emerged from the seclusion of his Ukrainian estates in compliance with a request from the Minister of Education to administer the school system of the Xar'kov district. This and other government assignments occupied him extensively until his final retirement from official service on March 20th, 1830, with the notable interruption for the European journey of 1827. Accompanied by his sister and nephew, he made the trip both a learning experience and a pilgrimage. The major event was the visit to Goethe in Weimar. The aging Olympian, who was then preparing the second part of *Faust,* took the ten-year-old Aleksej Tolstoj on his lap and talked to him with pleasure and with a paternal kindness. Within less than a year the memorable excursion was ended. Its memories were treasured by all three travelers, but they kindled extraordinary excitement in the ten-year-old, who, to his uncle's disapproval, began now to have notions of becoming a poet.

To Perovskij-"Pogorel'skij", literature was an adornment of life, noble and ennobling. To create it was a gentleman's privilege. But a gentleman did not seek to make money that way, and it was quite out of keeping with his proper function in society if he allowed it to intrude too much upon his time and consciousness even as an avocation. A gentleman had prior obligations to his Tsar's government and to his own social caste. The paradox is that, in the five years 1825 to 1830, when "Pogorel'skij" was conscientiously busy in government posts at Xar'kov, Taganrog, and elsewhere, he also produced almost all of his moderately extensive literary works. His nephew was away at school now in Petersburg, his sister had moved to the capital to be near her son, and perhaps the absence of his "family" gave him freer time for books and writing.

The new bachelorhood at "Pogorel'cy", from which excursions were made to his official rounds, forms the setting of his next and most ambitious production, a set of tales within a frame-story bearing the over-all title of *The Double, or My Evenings in Little Russia* (Dvojnik, ili moi večera v Malorossii), published in book form in 1828.

The book opens with a description of a manor house and village named "P***", located in the northern Ukraine, and an amicable address to the "benevolent reader" formally presents to him the narrator, Mr. Antonij Pogorel'skij, the inhabitant of the place. Mr. Pogorel'skij goes on to say that he has dwelt here for several years. The time has been neither wholly gay nor wholly dull amid the solitude, a point on which he expatiates with gentle melancholy.

One evening as he is seated at the window meditating on the past and dreaming of the future, the door noiselessly opens and a strange gentleman appears in the room before him. The newcomer announces that he has come to keep him company. Startled but not frightened, the narrator inquires his name and is told that the visitor can have no name since he is "your form which has appeared to you" (obraz vaš, javivšijsja vam). With a tremor the narrator recalls that such an encounter is considered to be an omen of approaching death. The visitor laughs at his crass superstition, assures him that no harm impends, and proposes a pact of friendship. But what name shall he use? Friends need to call each other by name. To which the stranger replies:

I have already told you that I have no particular name. Beings of my sort scarcely have a designation in the Russian language, and for this reason I am actually at a loss to answer your question. In Germany, where such apparitions occur more frequently, our brotherhood are termed "Doppelgänger". It would, of course, have been possible to take over this word into our language and it would have been no less à propos than others; but since they say that we already have too many foreign words, I venture to propose calling myself a "Double" (Dvojnik). What do you say to that, my esteemed friend?

"Antonij Pogorel'skij" agrees that "Mr. Double" will do excellently, thus countenancing the minting of a new Russian word which will have its own fate and history in the course of Russian literature.

Host and guest now enter into an animated discussion of doubles and other aspects of the occult. The visitor, it appears, is much traveled and comes crammed with anecdotes. For instance, there is the case of a ghostly personage from the age of Louis XIV who paid a call on the poet Pope. In Prague fifteen years ago he himself spoke with an aged librarian who had inadvertently summoned evil spirits simply by reading from an ancient manuscript of spirit-lore. The author is engrossed in his guest's tales, but at the stroke of midnight the latter announces that it is time for bed. Are doubles compelled to depart at the stroke of midnight?, asks his host, only to be laughed at again for his crass superstition. All hours are equal to spirits, but it is good that mortals should go to bed by midnight. The double, as he retires, adds further that the crowing of cocks is of no concern to him either.

So ends the section marked "First Evening". The "Second Evening" opens with the reappearance of the double at ten o'clock the following night. Both gentlemen are in a jovial mood, and the visitor most gracefully inquires whether his "dear Antonij" would be so kind as to read him one of his works, for he is aware that Antonij is an author. After some faltering apologies for his slight productions, Antonij is coaxed to read aloud his manuscript of a tale entitled *Izidor and Anjuta*. The organization of a frame-tale with story insets is now apparent.

The device of the frame-tale, popular in the Middle Ages and thereafter fallen into desuetude, had been revived by German authors at the end of the eighteenth century. Credit is often assigned to Goethe, whose *Unterhaltungen deutscher Ausgewanderten* (1795) is imitated from Boccaccio, and whose *Die guten Weiber* (1801) is modelled on the collection of Margurite de Navarre. The aged Wieland also composed such a work entitled *Hexameron von Rosenhain*. More successful was Tieck's large miscellaney of prose and verse called *Phantasus,* put together between 1812 and 1816 from works of various dates. But the frame-tale par excellence of modern literature is generally conceded to be Hoffmann's four-volume collection of 1819—1821, *Die Serapionsbrüder.*

Unlike his two earlier collections, which were merely series of un-related tales, *Die Serapionsbrüder* presented its contents as stories composed by a group of friends who called themselves the "Serapion Brethren" and who met regularly in a club to read aloud their productions to one another. The device closely parallels that of Tieck's *Phantasus,* except that, where Tieck's seven authors were, by his own avowal, seven aspects of his own personality, the Serapion Brethren represented in part real persons who did actually meet with Hoffmann in a club called the "Serapion Brethren", where stories were read aloud and commented upon. Thus the Ottmar of the frame-tale discussions and conversations is the equivalent of Eduard Hitzig, the loyal real-life friend of the author; Sylvester represents the minor Romantic writer Contessa; the moody Vinzenz reflects Dr. Koreff, who later was instrumental in bringing the Tales of Hoffmann into fashion in Paris. Three others, Theodor, Lothar, and Cyprian — who frankly seize the lion's share of importance — embody various aspects of Hoffmann himself. All stories are, of course, products of Hoffmann's pen, but the vividness of the frame-tale conversations is doubtless due in some degree to the fact that they transcribe parts of actual discussions of the same stories by living people.

"Pogorel'skij's" frame-tale in *The Double* is conceived on a much more modest scale, with only two characters, who, after all, involved but a single model. There are further significant differences from the German works, as the Russian scholar Ignatov has pointed out: [4] the two Antonij's meet by chance, whereas the Serapion Brethren were an organized club; their discussions range widely but prefer "philo-sophical" topics and very little space is allotted to discussion of the stories themselves, whereas the German figures give first attention to critical comment; finally, the Russian tales are entirely heterogeneous, making no effort to conform to a "Serapiontic principle". It is possible to question whether there is any case for an imitation of Hoffmann in this instance. No final demonstration is possible but, given the range of alternate possibilities and considering the nature of the story insets as well as the presence of the Double-concept even to the title, the statement may be ventured with reasonable certainty that "Pogo-

[4] Sergej Ignatov, "Gofman i Pogorel'skij", *Russkij Filologičeskij Vestnik,* LXXII (1914), pp. 249—278; p. 261.

rel'skij's" frame-tale is a graceful, modest, original, and successful adaptation of the more elaborate frame-tale in *Die Serapionsbrüder*. A derivation from Tieck's *Phantasus* is also plausible, but the Hoffmannian source for two, perhaps three, of the separate tales makes the connection with *Die Serapionsbrüder* the more likely.

3. THE DOUBLE: SECOND EVENING
IZIDOR AND ANJUTA

Through approximately half of the "Second Evening" Antonij reads aloud to the Double his tale called *Izidor and Anjuta* (Isidore and Annie):

Izidor, an officer of the Cuirassiers, comes home to Moscow just as Napoleon's troops are about to enter the city and discovers that his mother is dying. Unwilling to leave her and unwilling to transport her out of the doomed city, he determines to remain with her. He wishes also to protect his fiancée Anjuta, an orphan girl who has grown up in his family. The dying woman, however, is shocked that her son should desert his army post at this critical moment and that he has even buried his uniform beneath the old maple tree of the garden in order to pass as a civilian before the invaders. Begging him to defend his Tsar and Fatherland at all costs, she persuades him to dig up the uniform and return to duty. Anjuta bravely shows him a dagger: this shall protect her honor during his absence. With heavy heart he rides away.

Six weeks later he reenters Moscow, his arm wounded, but with a decoration for valor on his breast. Only a heap of rubble marks the site of his home. The old maple tree alone remains amid the devastation; Izidor faints.

That evening, after recovering consciousness, he goes out to the maple tree. A comrade hears him address it as though it were a person. Four successive nights the ghostly conversations continue. On the fourth morning the comrade finds him dead upon the ground. His withered hand clutches a dagger. A half rotted human skull lies at his side.

The Double is not especially pleased with this tale because he finds the events "impossible". The modern reader is not especially pleased either, for it is a poor tale told with excessive sentimentality. Ignatov is puzzled to know the source but feels sure it is not to be found in Hoffmann. Quite possibly the story consists of nothing more than a patriotic war anecdote upon which has been superimposed a lugubrious ghost element from the repertory of popular Romanticism. A certain kinship may be observed with Žukovskij's ballad of 1808, *Ljudmila,* which in turn is a close imitation of Bürger's internationally famous ghost-ballad *Lenore* of 1774. The Russian poem opens with a scene in which the heroine searches in vain among victorious returning soldiers for her lover and its principal sequence portrays the lover's coming by night as a ghost to carry her off to his tomb forever.

Some suggestion of the story may have been found in the very passage from *Der goldene Topf* whence came the material for *The Poppy-seed-cake Woman of the Lafërtov Quarter*. As Veronika Paulmann was serving coffee to the Oster sisters in the "Fifth Vigil" of that work, Angelika Oster related how old Liese Rauerin had given her specific information about her absent fiancé Viktor:

... my Viktor is well and I shall see him again in a short time as a Cavalry Captain, adorned with a Decoration for Valor which he has earned by his unlimited bravery. A serious but not at all dangerous wound in his right arm, received from a sabre thrust of an enemy Hussar, prevents him from writing, and the rapid change of position still makes it impossible for him to send me word, since he absolutely does not wish to leave his regiment. But this evening he will receive definite instructions to go and have himself cured. He will set out tomorrow morning on his way here, and as he is about to mount the carriage he will learn of his promotion to Cavalry Captain.

That this passage furnished anything more than incidental details cannot be maintained, yet it relates to the occult and is curiously juxtaposed with material known to have been used by "Pogorel'skij". Moreover, it is interesting to observe Angelika's refutation of Veronika's skepticism in terms which would well serve the narrator Antonij in the face of the dogged rationalism of the Double:

Suffice it to say that I cannot give up this belief in certain mysterious things, because often enough they have entered my life, I might say, in a wholly visible and tangible manner.

In life and in the frame-tale, "Pogorel'skij" was obviously eager to believe in the supernatural, yet prevented from so doing by his eighteenth century indoctrination. The pair of Doubles in the present instance show his awareness of the conflicting aspects of his own character, pure rationalist and amateur romanticist. Something like Hoffmannian irony has invested the real narrator with the romantic aspect, while the hallucinatory Double embodies the aspect of doctrinaire rationalism.

Comment on *Izidor and Anjuta* leads directly into a lively debate on ghosts in general. The narrator cites the case of a learned Leipzig

doctor who attested in detail to the apparitions of his deceased wife
and wrote a treatise on the subject. The Double points out that fifteen
years after the event that very Leipzig doctor confessed his treatise was
a hoax. As the midnight departure is at hand, the Double promises
Antonij a story of his own for the following evening, an actual
experience this time, which he will relate in the very words of his
friend, Colonel F., from whom he heard it.

4. THE DOUBLE: THIRD EVENING
THE BALEFUL CONSEQUENCES OF AN UNBRIDLED IMAGINATION

Needless to say, "Colonel F." is a fiction, for his "actual experience"
proves to be a point-by-point reworking of the Olimpia episode from
Hoffmann's *Der Sandmann.* Ignoring the symbolism of the magic
glasses and of the mechanical doll, "Pogorel'skij" has made the detached episode a case of fantastic and willful self-delusion of the hero,
upon which he pronounces his moral condemnation at the outset by
the ponderous title, *The Baleful Consequences of an Unbridled Imagination* (Pagubnye posledstvija neobuzdannogo voobraženija).

Intrinsically, *Der Sandmann,* despite several brilliant passages, deserves probably only second-class rating among Hoffmann's tales, but
the nineteenth century consistently accorded it the attention due to a
masterpiece. Some of its more striking sections occur at the beginning
and deal with the childhood of the hero, there named Nathanael. Cast
in the form of letters, those early pages portray, from within the hero's
personality, the mental anguish of a hyper-sensitive child and deftly
convey the impression of a mind predisposed to madness. By omitting
these episodes "Pogorel'skij" deprived himself of the necessary psychological preparation for the sequel, and by making "Colonel F." see
exactly the same things as the protagonist, he removed entirely the
theme of evolving madness which was central to the original concept.
By omitting the terminal episodes and forcing a conclusion directly
after the experience with the mechanical doll, he eliminated some
rather strained melodrama which one misses less. He further discarded
the mixed narration so dear to the German Romanticists, in this case,
epistolary form followed by third-person narrative, and rejected all
attempts at impressionistic technique by means of selected and care-
fully lighted episodes. He chose a unified sequence developed from an
isolated section of the original and told it in consistent third-person

narrative. Probably his basic grounding in French literature accounts for this procedure. Both French and classical is the name "Al'cest" (Alceste) which he assigns to his hero, as opposed to Hoffmann's folkish "Nathanael", and there is a significant substitution of the Francophile and "smart" University of Leipzig for the Romantic Heidelberg — though Hoffmann's failure to identify his university town except through subtle details could easily have led to a misunderstanding. Nevertheless, such minor alterations add wrong accents to the already wrong procedure. They show the more plainly how the author was out of his element when he ventured into this kaleidoscope of lights and shadows and muted inferences, wrenched out a section, lighted it uniformly with cold white reason, and left his product an absurdity.

Hoffmann's symbols were shrewdly chosen and effective: the magic lenses that distort reality; Nathanael's obsessed and compulsive dancing all night long with the doll until the candles are burned away and the orchestra has all gone home; the needle-fine double irony of the mechanical doll as a parody of the heartless society belle *and* of the soulless salon coloratura; his Professor Spalanzani (called Andronij in the Russian) who is a caricature of the eighteenth century in art and philosophy by virtue of his counterfeiting Nature so expertly as to produce a mechanical woman. Moreover, the whole story may be construed as a parble of the human heart deceived by consummate artifice, and a note of philosophical horror is sounded when the consummate artifice is seen to be manipulated by a malignant Power. Failing to perceive these things, "Pogorel'skij" presents all actions as sober facts with two witnesses, thereby plunging his story into a slough of preposterousness. In the process of simplification characteristic of the Russian Hoffmannists, he rejected the multiple symbols of illusion: telescopes, lenses of all kinds, retaining only the human eyes. These are mentioned so late in the narrative that the mention of them, far from having a cumulative effect, seems irrelevant or merely part of a repulsive physiological inventory along with nose and pearly teeth. Why Al'cest should rush away with the automaton's eyes is left quite unexplained. Worst of all was the substituting of the conjugal couch for the scene of the hero's disillusionment, in place of Hoffmann's making the hero witness the two scoundrels fight for possession of the doll until her eyes fall out. With a poor economy of means, "Pogorel'skij" shifted the scoundrels' quarrel to his exposition section. But is was the portrayal of the bridegroom pawing the heartless bosom of his bride to tatters that dropped the story down beyond recovery into the depths of the ghastly and the hilarious. Waters of oblivion should mercifully close over this scene.

"Pogorel'skij's" second villain, Venturino, should by rights be the exact equivalent of Dr. Coppelius, alias Giuseppe Coppola, of *Der Sandmann,* even as Andronij corresponds to Spalanzani, but actually he bears very little resemblance to that memorable figure of violence and irrational horror. The disparity is not due to "Pogorel'skij's" ineptitude, nor is it to be explained as the result of the usual softening of violence to be observed with the Russian Hoffmannists, with "Pogorel'skij" even more than with his successors. Rather, Venturino is not Coppelius at all but a substituted character. By his red cloak, his guffaws of sarcastic laughter, his "poisonous glance", his interest in pandaring, he reveals himself as a variant of the devilish Spanish Jesuit, Fermino Valies, of *Datura fastuosa.*[5] Herewith is explained the odd circumstance that the two apparently Italian villains should have been heard quarrelling in Spanish. Parenthetically it may be remarked that Hoffmann's Spaniard was quite undifferentiated from his Italians. Like Venturino, Fermino Valies practised his machinations without convincing motivation, except in so far as he was intimated to be an extra-terrestrial devil in human form. At best, however, both are stage devils quite devoid of the gruesome, elemental quality and of the savagely consuming evil of Coppelius. The substitution is a subtle commentary on "Pogorel'skij's" sensitivities. Moreover, it is, in itself, a neat bit of literary mortise-work.[6]

Antonij, with some justice, rebukes the Double for doubting the apparitions of Anjuta to Izidor only to ask in return that *he* should believe in a life-like doll. The debate waxes lively. The Double bids Antonij reflect on the moral of the tale, as if "Pogorel'skij" had not driven that point home. Consider, he says, all the people, of both sexes, who stroll the streets, dance at parties, curtsy and smile, even as the automaton in the story, yet have no hearts. He goes on to relate other instances of automaton construction, just to prove that it is not so preposterous after all: a Latin-orating raven owned by a Roman emperor, the "Android of Albertus Magnus" which took over thirty years

[5] *Datura fastuosa,* published posthumously in 1822, then republished in *Die Letzten Erzählungen,* 1825; translated as *The Botanist* (Botanik) in *The Moscow Telegraph,* VIII (1826).
[6] Ignatov, "Gofman i Pogorel'skij", *op. cit.,* p. 268, mentions that Venturino's role is unclear and that he is a poor imitation of Coppelius, but offers no explanation of the fact.

to construct, and finally an automaton which he himself had observed in Paris, created by the physicist Robertson and operated by a keyboard. Popular mechanics and the poetic imagination were close neighbors in "Pogorel'skij's" mind. By this token he shows more affinities to Poe than to Hoffmann. But bed time has arrived and the colloquy rather abruptly breaks off.

5. THE DOUBLE: FOURTH EVENING

The "Fourth Evening", which also begins Part II of *The Double,* is devoted to "philosophical" debate. The subject is nothing less than the analysis of the compound parts of an intelligent human mind. First on the list, the Double explains, is "sound judgment". Then follow: sagacity, comprehension, profundity, prudence, clarity, ingenuity (which the author glosses as "le tacte"), acuteness (glossed as "Scharfsinn") not to be confused with sharpness (glossed as "der Witz"); the latter, like cleverness, falls into a subsidiary category. All these components are analysed, defined, hierarchized, and finally hung on the branches of diagrams. The diagrams may in turn be manipulated to demonstrate the evolution of the vices.

For a long evening both Antonij and the Double show themselves to be eager, and ingenious, psychologists. Their armchairs survey limitless vistas.

6. THE DOUBLE: FIFTH EVENING

It is now Antonij's turn to tell a story and the Double arrives eager to hear. Antonij first inquires whether he ever reads *News of Literature,* and when the Double says he does not, Antonij explains that he is about to read him a story of his own creation "published a few years ago in the aforementioned *News*", and therewith plunges directly into the text of *The Poppy-seed-cake Woman of the Lafërtov Quarter.*

When the reading is concluded, the Double pronounces the story much superior to *Izidor and Anjuta,* a judgment in which the modern reader readily concurs. The reading unleashes a whole pack of memories from the Double's mind. There was a famous clairvoyante, Madame Le Normand in Paris, whom the Double himself consulted. But she proved a fake. Her sole interest was in her exorbitant fees. Yet all ages have entertained such beliefs. He cites examples from Greece and Rome, from the France of Henri IV and from Reformation Germany, from the Spain of the Inquisition, and from modern nations. Finally he quotes at length a curious passage from *The Golden Ass* of Apuleius which he had read in the antiquated Russian translation of 1780. (Clearly "Pogorel'skij" was an omnivorous reader!) Again the colloquy abruptly breaks off.

7. *THE DOUBLE: SIXTH (AND LAST) EVENING*
THE JOURNEY BY STAGECOACH

The Double once again claims that his contribution shall be an actual experience related in the very words of the Muscovite friend who was his informant. The title, *The Journey by Stagecoach,* really applies only to the setting within which the real narrative was first heard. In other words, "Pogorel'skij" here creates a miniature frame-tale within the greater one. The unnamed Muscovite friend has boarded a stagecoach for Petersburg with only one fellow-passenger. The latter is silent all during the first day's drive except for indispensible courtesies. When the driver is about to light the lamps, however, he suddenly turns to the Muscovite and begs him to persuade the driver to leave them in darkness. Some fear obsesses him. A conversation is thus engaged, which, through the two remaining days of the journey, develops into the story of his life.

His name is Colonel Van der K . . . , formerly in French service. His father, after years in the service of the United States, had settled in Borneo. There, as a child of four, Van der K . . . had been carried off to the jungles by the dreaded ape-packs that occasionally raid human settlements. While his family believed him dead he was actually claimed and cared for by a great female ape named Tutu. From Tutu he learned to climb for coconuts and bananas, from the rest of the pack he learned to travel through the tree-tops for long stretches of jungle distance. And always he was happy.

One day he espied a human settlement, descended to investigate, and found himself amid his astonished and delighted family. At first he was glad to be with them, but their fear and hatred of the animals distressed him. Asleep one night, he was awakened by a sound outside his window. It was Tutu, come to see him despite all the sentries. Night after night she came until one dreadful occasion when his father pursued her with a sabre, cutting off a paw as she fled. The boy fainted.

Years passed. His brothers entered government service, his sisters married, and he was left alone and disconsolate. He made long treks to the jungle, alleging them to be hunting trips. On one of these he met Tutu and in her embrace realized that here was the sole creature he loved. At the annual island festival he met a girl named Amalia, for a time fancied he loved her, and even became engaged to be married. Her jealous curiosity about his jungle excursions brought him to tell her the whole story. Amalia was horrified and gave him an ultimatum forthwith: either herself or Tutu. Utterly wretched, he shouldered his gun next day to go and kill Tutu. Meeting her, he found himself unable to perform the act of murder. Then the old ape's clumsy caress accidentally broke the locketchain on which Amalia's picture hung about his neck. He ordered her away. When she attempted to follow him, he leveled his rifle and shot her dead.

Since that day he has had no peace. He never saw Amalia again. He left Borneo, entered the service of the French (first) Republic (!), saw battle. Now he is traveling from Moscow to Petersburg. Waking and sleeping, he is haunted by the image of Tutu.

The Muscovite heard much later that Colonel Van der K... migrated to New Holland, where he was eaten by cannibals.

With this variant of the "noble savage" theme "Pogorel'skij" moves in spirit from Hoffmann well backwards into the eighteenth century, though the immediate source was probably as recent as 1825. In that year *The Moscow Telegraph* carried a translation of a story called *Jocko* with which its author, Charles Pougens, had created a sensation in Paris and which related how a female ape died for love of a human. A footnote to the translation cited the Parisian fad of the tale, of its stage version, and of numerous imitations that had followed it.[7] In composing still another of these "Pogorel'skij" is showing himself an up-to-the-minute writer. In juxtaposing it with the other tales in *The Double* he demonstrates the odd category to which Hoffmann was assigned by the Russian public of the 1820's, a category of the exotic and the bizarre. The uniqueness of Hoffmann had not yet been perceived.

[7] The original story of 1824 by Charles Pougens, entitled *Jocko, épisode détaché des Lettres inédites sur l'instinct des animaux*, was dramatized with enormous success in 1825 by Rochefort and Gabriel as the two-act *Jocko, ou le Singe de Brésil.* "Jocko" hair-styles, "Jocko" color, and the like, became the rage. The translation in *The Moscow Telegraph*, II–III, No. 8, 9, and 10, was called *Jocko (An Indian Tale)* — Žoko (Indijskaja Povest'). See P. N. Sakulin, *Iz Istorii russkago idealizma. Knjaz' V. F. Odoevskij* (Moscow, 1913), Vol. I, Part II, p. 370, footnote 2. Ignatov, "Gofman i Pogorel'skij", *op. cit.,* p. 267, believes that *The Journey by Stagecoach* was derived, not directly from the story by Pougens, but from one of the numerous (lost) imitations mentioned in the *Moscow Telegraph's* editorial footnote.

Once again Antonij feels that his rationalistic Double has strained credibility by his story and once again the Double stresses the moral significance: A man who repays life-long devotion with murder deserves to be haunted by his own ingratitude. Even if Tutu was only an ape, the moral is no less applicable. Antonij wonders aloud whether such apes may still be found in Borneo. The Double promises further information on the morrow. But even as he promises, his voice and figure fade away. Apparently he never returned, for the concluding paragraph of the entire work says:

The Double disappeared, and his last words were so little audible that to this day I do not know whether he actually pronounced them or whether it only seemed so to me.

While *The Double* sometimes seems cluttered with miscellanies and while passages in it sometimes seem to wander without a goal, a closer examination will reveal an almost pedantic order of its components. Perfect symmetry governs its divisions:

Part I: First Evening — Introduction: the time, the place, the characters. General discussion of the nature of the occult.

Second Evening — *Izidor and Anjuta.*

Third Evening — *The Baleful Consequences of an Unbridled Imagination.*

Part II: Fourth Evening — Debate on the component parts of the human mentality.

Fifth Evening — *The Poppy-seed-cake Woman of the Lafërtov Quarter.*

Sixth Evening — *The Journey by Stagecoach.*

The whole collection is divided into two equal parts. Each part begins with an "evening" devoted to "philosophical discussion", one treating the irrational, the other treating the rational aspect of human experience. Each is followed by two stories, the first fairly short and told by Antonij, the second somewhat longer and told by the Double. It would seem that the author intended the Double's stories to be wholesome correctives to Antonij's "mysticism" as shown in the other stories, though the modern reader perceives the antitheses rather dimly. Subject matter aside, all the tales are told with the same sober clarity and forthrightness. At the end of the sequence the author undoubtedly felt that he had, through an entertaining medium, inculcated the following precepts:

1. Faithfulness into death is noble. (*Izidor and Anjuta.*)
2. He who allows excessive imagination to overwhelm sound Reason, loses life itself. (*The Baleful Consequences of an Unbridled Imagination.*)
3. Money does not make happiness. (*The Poppy-seed-cake Woman of the Lafërtov Quarter.*)
4. He who rewards kindness with unkindness, even though he kills only an ape, will be conscience-haunted forever. (*The Journey by Stagecoach.*)

In the last analysis, this didacticism does not irritate but conveys a quaint and touching earnestness. There is no attempt to force a philosophical system on the reader. Only home truths are unpretentiously reaffirmed. Apart from the hapless bathos of Al'cest's bridal night, the infelicities of the stories themselves may be easily forgiven. For the most part they fly low but gracefully.

The memorable part of the whole work is the frame-tale, where the author has spoken from his heart rather than in contrived fictions. The lonely man moved to invent a Double to bear him company in the long evenings moves us. Almost twenty years later Dostoevskij, in a story likewise entitled *The Double,* will distil that scene into a single chapter, electrifying it with torment and anguished loneliness. But in 1828 "Pogorel'skij" could write it with gentle wistfulness. The conversations with the Double float like blue successive smoke-rings from a good cigar, and where the smoke-rings dissolve, we catch glimpses of a quiet study and earnest books and windows full of stars. Outside, rural vastnesses enclose the scene, and it seems incredible that anything could disturb the settled order which has disposed things thus for centuries.

8. THE BLACK CHICKEN

Unperturbed by the attacks from *The Northern Bee*,[8] which found *The Double* in deplorable taste because of its pandaring to faddish

---

[8] *The Northern Bee* (Severnaja Pčëla), a thoroughly reactionary journal, was founded in 1825 by F. V. Bulgarin (1789—1859). A man of many political faces, Bulgarin was a Pole by nationality and fought in Napoleon's Polish Legion against Russia. After the Napoleonic débacle, he assumed a position of loyalty to Russia but with liberal tendencies. By 1825 he had further shifted ground to take a strongly reactionary stand and later served as an agent of the "Third Section" (the Secret Police). The critical orientation of *The Northern Bee* may be seen repeatedly in its reviews of major works. Of Chapter VII of *Eugene Onegin* it said "the complete collapse of Puškin's talent"; of Gogol', that he was "the Russian Paul de Kock"; of *The Inspector General,* that it was a libel on Russia; etc. Bulgarin's associate on the magazine was N. I. Greč, who had been the editor of the reactionary *Son of the Fatherland* since 1812.

Romanticism, "Pogorel'skij" in the very next year (1829) published another Romantic work. Its title was *The Black Chicken, or The Subterranean Dwellers* (Čërnaja Kurica, ili Podzemnye Žiteli), expressly designated as a "Fairy-tale for Children" (Volšebnaja povest' dlja detej). Here was a genre where the author felt at liberty to indulge his imagination without apology.

The hero of the tale is a boy named Alëša who attends a boarding school in Petersburg far from his parents. His real-life model was patently Aleksej (diminuitive: "Alëša") Tolstoj, the author's nephew, now aged twelve and in attendance at a boarding school in the capital, though his parents, or at least his mother, were not so very far away. The distance lay between him and the lonely uncle writing the story in remote Pogorel'cy. The lad was also undoubtedly the intended recipient of the moral exhortation of the tale, which, we may assume, had many an oral predecessor.

The Alëša of the narrative is a good student, popular with teachers and companions, and happy at school except for the lonely vacations. He has a great fondness for the headmaster's flock of chickens, particularly for Čërnuška (Blackie), and one day in the lonely week between New Year's and Epiphany rescues him from the cook's ax.

That night Čërnuška emerges from the shadows of his moonlit room, perches on his bed, and bids him follow him. Hundreds of tiny candles rise in silver holders from beneath the floor to light their way. Despite explicit directions, Alëša breaks silence to address the cat of the old ladies next door. As a consequence their path is barred by two knights in armor and the journey must be postponed. The following night the boy follows instructions, the armored knights are sunk in sleep, and the travelers reach the tiny race of dwellers underground.

Čërnuška, dressed all in black velvet as Prime Minister of this nation, presents Alëša to the king, who gravely thanks the boy for rescuing his Minister from the cook's ax and bids him ask any boon. After some pondering, Alëša asks to know his lessons without studying them. The king is displeased but gives him a hemp-seed which, as long as it is on his person, will confer such knowledge. Visitors and courtiers then go on horseback for a great rat-hunt, for rat and mouse fur are prized as precious pelts by the subterranean folk, and also see fabulous jewel-trees and menageries of strange animals. Alëša promises never to mention his visit. The underground folk must avoid contact with mankind, since mankind has become so wicked, and if their dwelling place is known they will be forced to migrate.

With the hemp-seed in his pocket Alëša becomes the envy of his classmates, until, inevitably, the hemp-seed is lost. Shame and disaster follow. That night Čërnuška brings him the lost talisman to his room where he is confined supperless. But his refound glibness at recitation rouses his teacher's suspicions, and a whipping elicits the whole story.

That night Čërnuška in full Prime Minister's regalia comes to Alëša's bed. Golden chains bind his hands. He must wear them forever for being the cause of his nation's disaster. The subterranean dwellers, weeping and lamenting their lost homes, are passing into exile. Overcome with remorse, Alëša vows to mend his ways. Henceforth he is a model boy.

Despite the too long postponement of the crucial motif of the hemp-seed, the story is well and charmingly told. The departure of Čërnuška in chains, even golden chains, is a striking scene bordering on the tragic and almost too solemn for the surrounding matter. The reader feels the sacrifice all out of proportion to the betterment of a single schoolboy. Perhaps some particular instance made "Pogorel'skij" feel he should speak in strong terms to his nephew.

Of the two disparate elements in *The Black Chicken,* a journey to fairyland and a schoolboy's escapade, only the first suggests a literary prototype. The second is patently *ad hoc* reality. Immediately after the story's publication, *The Moscow Messenger* defined it as an adaptation of Tieck's fairy-tale of 1811, *Die Elfen.*[9] This was a story about the little girl Marie who wandered off while playing to enter the forbidden hovels of some "gypsies". To her wonderment the "gypsies" proved to be fairy folk living in realms of indescribable beauty. For seven years the child remained among them, unaware that she had tarried more than a night. Ultimately the king decides that she must not stay with them and sends her home. As a parting token she receives a jewelled ring and willingly gives her promise never to reveal where she has been, for disclosure of their presence will force the fairies to depart forever. Marie goes home, resumes her former life, grows up, marries, and has a daughter of her own. Suddenly she is alarmed to learn that one of the fairy folk comes to play with her child. When her peasant husband makes the same discovery he vows to drive away these miserable "gypsies" once and for all. Impulsively Marie cries out that these are not gypsies but fairies, thereby breaking her promise of secrecy. That night frightful storms rage, and down by the river the ferryman sees a whole nation of departing people cross the stream and disappear. Thereafter the countryside withers and becomes wholly desolate.

---

[9] *Die Elfen,* 1811, was subsequently included in Volume I of the collection *Phantasus,* 1812—1816. It was one of the works of Tieck specifically proposed by Žukovskij for translation in his letter to Daškov, 1817. (See note 5 of Chapter I.)

Tieck's fairies are nature spirits who tend the roots of plants, channel underground waters, work mines, and control terrestrial warmth and cold. They are also spirits of everlasting childhood faith and innocence. "Pogorel'skij's" subterranean dwellers, on the other hand, are merely decorative figures with no symbolical significance. All differences apart, however, it was from *Die Elfen* that he got the elements of his plot: an unglamorous earthly inhabitant befriended by a mortal and proving to be a member of a fairy race; the visit to the fairy realm; the token pledge of the visit; the promise of secrecy; betrayal of the secret; the disconsolate migration of a whole nation of fairy folk.

Without explaining his reasons, Ignatov denies all connection between *The Black Chicken* and *Die Elfen,* proposing instead a source in Brentano's *Gockel, Hinkel, und Gackeleia.*[10] Except for the fact that Brentano's fairy-tale deals with chickens, there is no resemblance at all between these two works. The wishing-ring possessed by Gockel is a precious family heirloom, the theft and regaining of which provide the matter for a whimsical episodic variant of the picaresque tradition, and is no parallel to the fairy boon of the hemp-seed. Ignatov's suggestion is wholly incorrect.

Scarcely more helpful is the author of the "Pogorel'skij" article in the *Russian Biographical Dictionary,* who states that *The Black Chicken* derives from Fouqué and Hoffmann, as well as from German folk tales, but omits to name any specific titles. Aspects of the Russian work may have been drawn from Hoffmann's Christmas fairy-tale, *Nussknacker und Mausekönig,* in which the real-life children of his friend Eduard Hitzig appeared as the chief characters. As with Aleksej Tolstoj, the story was written for and about them. Moreover, as will be recalled by persons familiar with Čajkovskij's ballet version, the story includes a battle between the gallant Nutcracker and the seven-headed, seven-crowned Mouse King, a battle which Hoffmann depicted in strict conformity with the manual of military tactics, and which suggests the rat-hunt witnessed by Alëša underground. The Nutcracker and the little heroine Marie also journey to the dazzling wonders of the Doll Kingdom by way of the Christmas Forest, encountering en route the most wondrous candy trees, lemonade brooks, macaroon gates, and the like, before they arrive at *Marzipan*-Castle. But marvellous sights are also encountered in Tieck's *Die Elfen,* and in other fairy-tales. In the final count, *Nussknacker und Mausekönig* can have

---

[10] Ignatov, "Gofman i Pogorel'skij", *op. cit.,* pp. 276—277.

suggested only secondary details at best. The primary source was Tieck's *Die Elfen,* as *The Moscow Messenger* declared in 1829.

9. *THE HYPNOTIST*

For reasons unknown, "Pogorel'skij" left as the merest fragment a novel which he had begun with the title of *The Hypnotist* (Magnetizër). One chapter and three pages of a second chapter exist as they were printed in the first two issues of the *Literary Gazette* (Literaturnaja Gazeta) in 1830, and if any more of the work was composed, the continuation has been lost.[11]

The title duplicates the well known early story of Hoffmann, *Der Magnetiseur,* which had appeared in Venevitinov's Russian translation in *The Moscow Messenger* of 1827, and the brief text insures that the theme will concern an evil mesmerist in his desire for an innocent girl. The setting is the remote Ural mountains town of Ekaterinburg (modern Sverdlovsk), and the characters are well-to-do bourgeois. Provincial settings are the exception in Russian literature, especially specific provincial town settings, and non-aristocratic characters, other than peasants, are rarer still. That "Pogorel'skij's" purpose was to exploit local color seems unlikely, since the Ural mountains region was unfamiliar to him, and if he sought remoteness to facilitate mysterious action, the specificity is puzzling. That he, the aristocrat, should depict bourgeois circles is more puzzling still, for the source work suggested nothing of the sort. His choice is at least a generation ahead of his time.

Chapter I presents a family at tea-time. Anasim Anikeevič Fejsjurin is intrigued by a newspaper account of hypnosis (magnetism) and asks his daughter Pašen'ka, who has just returned from Petersburg, whether she has heard of the matter in the capital. It happens that she has had direct experience with it.

A Petersburg friend, Countess N., was deeply concerned about a serving girl named Katerina who was subject to alarming fits of hysteria. Tears and laughter alternated until violent convulsions set in. Doctors were baffled. One evening, just as such a seizure was taking place, a certain Neapolitan Marquis offered to help the girl. He took her hand, cast one glance into her eyes, and the attack ceased. Pašen'ka

---

[11] All diaries and private papers of "Pogorel'skij" have been lost. Ignatov explains (p. 257) that: "The former manager of the estate (Pogorel'cy) was a lover of fine foods, particularly of cutlets in paper wrappings, and in his long stay at Pogorel'cy he used up all of the writer's papers for his favorite food"

had gasped at the sight, whereupon the Italian turned his terrifying gaze upon her. In the ensuing weeks she was oppressed with melancholy. She felt certain that only the Italian could cure her depression, yet dreaded meeting him again. Gradually her good spirits returned and she had come home to Ekaterinburg. Recently, however, she has noted something of her former melancholy.

The three pages of Chapter II begin an account of Fejsjurin's life when he worked in his father's store. Acquaintance with a second-hand book-dealer had given him a passion for reading and he wished he might own a book-shop himself just to have many books around him.
(Here the text breaks off.)

The opening scene of drawing room talk suggests less the opening of *Der Magnetiseur* than of Hoffmann's own variant story, *Der unheimliche Gast*,[12] in which the evil hypnotist is a Sicilian count. The latter's earlier embodiment was named Alban, with no nationality specified. In line with either story, however, Fejsjurin's life would almost certainly have brought him into some relationship of enmity with the Neapolitan, and his daughter would inevitably serve as an instrument of belated revenge. Further guesswork would be hazardous, unless the author intended another extensive plagiarism as in the case of *Der Sandmann* and *The Baleful Consequences of an Unbridled Imagination*.[13]

10.   THE GIRL FROM THE CONVENT SCHOOL

In lieu of continuation of *The Hypnotist*, the *Literary Gazette* of 1830 promised its readers a different novel by "Pogorel'skij", a colorful

---

[12] All told, Hoffmann wrote three variants of his story about the sinister hypnotist, each time with less satisfactory results: 1. *Der Magnetiseur,* written 1813, published 1814 in Volume II of *Fantasiestücke in Callots Manier.* 2. *Der unheimliche Gast,* written 1818, published 1819 separately and in 1820 in Volume III of *Die Serapionsbrüder.* 3. *Der Elementargeist,* written 1820, published 1821 separately and in 1825 in *Die Letzten Erzählungen.*

[13] The motif of an evil man's long postponed revenge by destroying the child of his enemy had already been used at the close of *The Baleful Consequences of an Unbridled Imagination,* where Al'cest's father writes frantically and too late to his son's friend, saying that in his son's description of Andronij he has recognized a fiendishly clever mechanic and ventriloquist who many years ago in Madrid vowed to destroy him and his family. Quite probably, *Der Magnetiseur* or *Der unheimliche Gast,* or both, should be added to *Datura fastuosa* and *Der Sandmann* as sources for *The Baleful Consequences of an Unbridled Imagination.* Quite possibly, too, the awareness of having used the motif before, even though inconspicuously, was among the causes for "Pogorel'skij's" abandonment of his novel.

portrayal, it claimed, of Ukrainian life and manners, entitled *The Girl from the Convent School* (Monastyrka). This time a long Part I promptly appeared in two installments, only to be followed by a two-year hiatus, with the second half delayed for publication until 1832. (The author's second European journey intervened.) In view of "Pogorel'skij's" career the book is astonishing. Instead of the expected Romanticism, it offers a self-possessed realism not unlike that of Jane Austen or a Russian equivalent or George Eliot's *Middlemarch!* Conservative magazines like Raič's *Galatea* voiced relief and hearty approval; Polevoj's *Moscow Telegraph* was glum with disapproval. To the twentieth-century reader the book is worthy though not great, but it uncannily anticipates the evolution of Russian literature as a whole from various stages of Romanticism (Hoffmannism being one) into unequivocal realism. And this at the very beginning of Romanticism's heyday in Russia!

With sympathy and gentle humor the novel traces the unsmooth course of a young love. The heroine, Anna (Anjuta) Trofimovna Orlenkova, has just finished her studies at the famous Smolny convent school in Petersburg and has come to stay with her aunt in the Ukrainian countryside. Here she finds kindly relatives, her parents being dead, as well as an eligible young Army officer whose love she wholeheartedly reciprocates. Their marriage is all arranged, when suddenly her aunt somewhat belatedly recalls that the girl's legal guardian has not been consulted. The impatient bridegroom undertakes to travel to a distant village and procure the permission of the guardian, Klim Sidorovič Djundik. But Klim Sidorovič proves to be a scoundrel, and his wife, Marfa Petrovna, still worse. The poor hero offends both. He demonstrates that their daughters' French is hopelessly bad, he sees no charm in their attempts at urban manners, and he totally overlooks the fact that one of them is in love with him. Their mother determines that he shall pay bitterly for his slights, and thus he returns with no permission to marry Anjuta.

Part II begins with the aunt's attempt to persuade Klim Sidorovič by letter. Her efforts only bring that sly gentleman on a visit to fetch his "dear ward" to his own home for a time. Everyone mistrusts his purpose, but Anjuta feels obliged to go with him. At first she is entertained as a guest by her guardian and Marfa Petrovna, but before long her entertainment passes into detainment by force and finally into outright captivity. Picturesque flight and rescue bring the story ultimately to a happy end. Like Rip Van Winkle's wife, Marfa Petrovna dies of a fit of anger.

11.   "POGOREL'SKIJ'S" LATTER YEARS

These literarily fruitful years,[14] which included a brief membership on the staff of the magazine, *The Butterfly* (Babočka), in 1829, had reduced "Pogorel'skij's" government service to a nominal occupation. Upon final retirement in March of 1830 he chose to establish himself in Moscow, though not until he had taken his sister and nephew on another extensive European tour. His novel might wait in abeyance until his return. Italy claimed the greater part of the travelers' attention. Museums and historical sites were visited, studios of artists were inspected, and quantities of paintings, statues, and jewels were purchased to adorn the Moscow mansion. In Rome, Ševyrëv introduced them into artistic circles difficult of access and on one occasion took them to call on Thorwaldsen. Once settled in his Moscow quarters, "Pogorel'skij" adopted the attitude of a Maecenas, entertaining men of letters and even keeping the painter Brjullov for some time as his house guest. He worked meanwhile at the completion of the novel, but no new literary projects were undertaken.

The career of his nephew occupied him considerably. By 1834 that seventeen-year-old was eager to devote his life to writing. Since the age of six he had composed verse and since the Italian journey he had been feverishly dreaming of prose tales of romance and terror. His uncle had no wish to stop him from writing, but he was determined to subordinate writing to some suitable career. Accordingly, he took a quantity of the youth's effusions to literary friends and saw to it that they appeared in print. With satisfaction he watched the adverse reviews and their cooling of the young man's ardor. With further satisfaction he saw his nephew enrolled that year in at least a sub-office of the government, in the archive section of the Ministry of Foreign Affairs. As a belated "Archive Youth", Tolstoj made good use of his time amid those dusty files and documents. Years later they were to be metamorphosed into his historical novels and dramas. His was to be a long servitude in government bureaus, however, before the latent artist in him disclosed its varied and splendid achievements.

[14] All of "Pogorel'skij's" works have been discussed in this chapter except for his amusing *Letter to Baron Humboldt* (Pis'mo k Baronu Gumboldtu), composed in 1829 both in Russian and in French translation. The letter purports to be a defense of the use in Russian orthography of the alphabet letter known as the "hard sign", written by the alphabet letter itself. The able little essay presents all the arguments in favor of retention of the sign, which was eliminated, almost entirely, from Russian spelling after 1917.

Meanwhile, Perovskij-"Pogorel'skij", aged only a little beyond forty-five, began to fail in health. In the summer preceding Puškin's fatal duel with D'Anthès he felt so seriously unwell that he determined to travel to Nice to take the cure. Before he could even reach Warsaw he was stricken. He died in that city, in his nephew's arms, July 9th, 1836.

Graceful talent, rather than genius, characterizes "Pogorel'skij" and it is an unmerited oblivion into which his works have slipped. As a stylist he is admirable. He brought to Russian prose that same limpid clarity and ease that marked the verse of Žukovskij. Historically he may be identified as a kind of prose corollary to Žukovskij's poetic innovations, an identification of no mean significance in the evolution of Russian literature. As for Russian Hoffmannism, it is true that it might have been initiated by another, by Polevoj, for example, or by Venevitinov, had he lived, but the fact remains that "Pogorel'skij" was the first to exploit this lode of useful ore. His productions within the genre were important and popular in their own day. They are readable more than a century later. The sole collected edition of "Pogorel'skij's" works, that edited by Aleksandr Smirdin in 1853,[15] deserves revival at least in excerpt.

[15] *Works of Antonij Pogorel'skij* (Sočinenija Antonija Pogorel'skago), edited by Aleksandr Smirdin (St. Petersburg), Imperial Academy of Sciences Press, (1853), two volumes in one.

POLEVOJ, THE JOURNALIST

Completely antithetical in personality to "Pogorel'skij" was his slightly younger contemporary, Nikolaj Alekseevič Polevoj, whose Hoffmannism was only one of the many facets of his versatile mind. Before all else, Polevoj was a journalist, one of those persons who breathe easily only in an editorial office amid the good strong smell of printer's ink. He loved both the managing of publications and the producing of copy. His pen was rarely idle. Tirelessly he composed poems, plays, stories, novels, learned articles on an astonishing variety of subjects, history, and criticism, but, as he himself acknowledged with bitter dismay, practically all of his writing was outmoded before his death in 1846. His real masterpiece was *The Moscow Telegraph,* the magazine which he founded and edited with loving zeal from 1825 to 1834.

Such an editorship had been his dream from boyhood, but is cost him many a hard struggle to achieve it. Born June 22, 1796 in the town of Irkutsk in remote Siberia, of an old merchant family long associated with trade in the Far East, it was assumed that he would become a merchant in the tradition of his forebears. His father, in fact, would hear of no alternative and made no provision for his son's education. Yet the boy had learned to read by the age of six and later recalled how, in that "far-off homeland rich in gold and dreaming forests", he had devoured quantities of books before the age of ten. Literary works pleased him, but history pleased him far more. His favorite book was Captain Cook's accounts of his travels. The happy, schoolless boyhood presently found expression in quantities of original verse, in the historical drama called *The Marriage of Tsar Aleksej Mixailovič,* before he had ever seen a theatre, and, above all, in a home newspaper written out entirely in long-hand. On a trip to Moscow at the age of fifteen (1811) with his father, he discovered the marvels of the dramatic stage, the book shops, the University lecture halls,[1] and the great city itself. To his rugged-tempered father all this was indifferent

---

[1] At the University Polevoj heard lectures by Merzljakov on literature and by the "skeptical" M. T. Kačenovski on history.

so long as it interfered in no way with the serious business of business. His wife might read the novels of Richardson and Mme de Genlis if such stuff pleased her, but his son's hankering after books and art was another matter. It had often stung him to fury, and now, as a result of this Moscow visit, he discovered among the lad's papers a tragedy, a short story, a continuation of Elagin's history, and other rubbish. He burned the lot of them. He sent the youth on travels to various parts of the country to acquaint him with commercial conditions, but invariably the youth fell in with persons interested in letters. With visitors at home he never talked merchants' talk but picked up piece-meal knowledge of foreign languages, which led to more books. Whenever business took the young man to Moscow or to Petersburg [2] he seized the opportunity to seek out editors and professors and writers. After his father's death in 1822, Polevoj settled in Moscow, nominally in order to take charge of the family business. It was not long before he was writing copy for the *Northern Archive* (Severnyj Arxiv). He met Prince Odoevskij, heard him expound Schelling, and soon began to write for the ill-starred *Mnemosyne*. Finally, in 1825, he impatiently cast off all pretense of being a business man and put all his energies into his great project, *The Moscow Telegraph*.

1. *THE MOSCOW TELEGRAPH* (1825–1834)

The learned journal as a form of publication distinct from the newspaper was a British-Scotch creation of the latter eighteenth century, and politics, rather than literature, had given rise to it. The Whigs in 1773 had devised *The Edinburgh Magazine and Review,* after 1802 called simply *The Edinburgh Review,* and the Tories in London had countered with *The Quarterly Review* in 1812. Polevoj was aware of their primacy and pre-excellence, but to his chagrin realized that his lack of English kept him from direct knowledge of them. It was their continental imitations with which he was familiar, particularly the *Revue encyclopédique,* edited from 1819 to 1833 by the famous Jullien de Paris. To a Europe-wide audience this publication regularly offered analysis of new works of literature, science, and art from all the languages of Europe and America.

Precisely such scope and purpose Polevoj hoped to offer in *The*

[2] In 1820 he met Kačenovskij personally in Moscow. In 1821 in Petersburg he met Žukovskij, Griboedov, Greč, and Bulgarin.

Moscow Telegraph. He felt, however, that the Russian reading public would never support an exclusively learned journal and planned accordingly to give over sizeable portions of each issue to new literary works of all kinds, both native and foreign. The initial number in 1825 announced an editorial policy of being a review of reviews, drawing on the *Revue encyclopédique* itself as well as on the *Bulletin universel,* the *Journal des Débats,* the *Allgemeines Repertorium,* and the learned *Anzeigen* of Halle, Jena, Leipzig, and Göttingen, in addition to which the paper would "transmit to its readers not merely Russian works but everything excellent, pleasant, and useful that was to be found in the national and in all the ancient and modern literatures".

Underlying this dual policy was a splendid and unlimited pedagogical ideal. By that paradox which should give educators pause, Polevoj, who had never had any formal education, was interested in everything. Moreover, he was interested in teaching everything and fancied that everyone shared his own insatiable thirst for knowledge. The goal of his journal was nothing less than the education of the whole Russian nation. The translations of foreign authors should serve not merely to entertain passively; they were to be spurs to native authors. The scholarly reviews should stimulate every branch of learning, and if some subjects remained untreated, he would himself write articles to fill up the deficiency.

The general public accepted the publication and its policy very well. It was with the literati that a little sense of ironic detachment or of humor might have saved Polevoj many difficulties, for he not only proclaimed his purpose with loud solemnity but was equally solemn in proclaiming his fitness for the task. In expressing such self-confidence he was at no pains to mask his contempt for existing journals and their editors. His contempt was understandably resented, and herewith began the enmities that were to plague him for a lifetime. Some persons were merely jealous. Some differentiated between the admirable work and the exasperating man. Yet there was some foundation for the recurrent charge against his presumptuous half-knowledge. Still short of his thirtieth year and without formal training, he could not be other than superficial when he wrote now on linguistics, now on Oriental art and religion, now on economics, now on Byzantine history. The fact remains, however, that he did educate a whole generation of Russians — precisely as he had intended to do.

In the early stages of planning the *Moscow Telegraph* Polevoj had an able supporter in Prince Vjazemskij, whose prominence in the

Puškin circle attracted the entire Petersburg group to contribute to the magazine. By 1830 Polevoj had managed to antagonize all of them. Their alienation was accomplished *en bloc* and for ideological reasons. In 1829 he had embarked on his ambitious three-volume *History of the Russian People*, a highly controversial work that directly controverted the somewhat hagiographic but nevertheless standard work of Karamzin, the late imperial historiographer. Karamzin was dear to the Puškin circle both as personal friend and as venerated writer. Their chief place of meeting was at the salon of Karamzin's widow. Thus Polevoj's attack came as a personal affront. The "skepticism" of the same three-volume history also gave it an unpatriotic, dangerous, quasi-revolutionary quality by conservative standards. *The Northern Bee* and *The Son of the Fatherland* missed no chance to attack Polevoj. It was pressure from their quarter that finally ruined him. As a historian and a writer of dramas, Polevoj felt quite competent in 1834 to review Kukol'nik's jingoistic play, *The Hand of the Almighty Saved the Fatherland* (Ruka Vsevyšnjago otečestvo spasla). He fancied that he had written with gentle caution, but S. S. Uvarov, Minister of Education, used the tempered condemnation as a pretext to terminate the license of *The Moscow Telegraph*.

The blow was rude. For a time Polevoj was all at sea. Within the year, while still under censorial disapproval, he became the anonymous editor of an art review.[3] An article on a monument to Peter the Great elicited favorable mention from Nicholas I himself, and Count Benkendorff, the Chief of the Secret Police, showed his personal sympathy. With odd logic, Polevoj determined to move to Petersburg and work with Greč and Bulgarin, editors of *The Northern Bee* and *The Son of the Fatherland* respectively. Apparently he nourished the hope of modifying their rigid conservatism and aesthetic wrong-headedness. In this hope, as anyone could have told him, he was quickly disappointed. He resigned from *The Northern Bee* in 1838 and from *The Son of the Fatherland* in 1840. Whereat his financial condition, already bad, became worse. Without editorial work he was wretched. The censor continued to plague him. His personal quarrels multiplied. In 1841 his previously popular Romantic fiction came under attack in the beginning of the anti-Romantic phase of Russian literature and criticism, while his new plays were shown to have little merit. His health was declining. Gloomi-

---

[3] Semeon's *Živopisnoe Obozrenie*, Russia's first illustrated review. Here appeared Polevoj's article, "The Monument to Peter the Great" (Pamjatnik Petra Velikago).

ly he remarked in a letter to his brother Ksenofont (Xenophon): "To stop talking in time — that is the great thing; I should have stopped talking in 1834." In 1842 he attempted to take over the editorship of *The Russian Messenger* (Russkij Vestnik), but the attempt came to nothing. There seemed nothing to do but swallow his pride and return to Greč and Bulgarin. Seizing at a straw, he accepted a post on A. A. Kraevskij's *Literary Gazette* in January of 1846, but before he was scarcely started, death claimed him, February 22, 1846.

If any one phase of Polevoj's creative career may be said to predominate, it was the phase of the historian. His *History of the Russian People* (1829—1834), intrinsically and in the evolution of Russian historiography, has significance. His semi-fictionalized history of tenth century Constantinople in *Byzantine Legends* (1841) is a worthy successor to Thierry's *Récits des temps mérovingiens*. He was less felicitous in his historical novel, *The Oath at the Holy Sepulchre* (Kljatva pri grobe gospodnem) (1832), the immediate model for which was Vigny's *Cinq-Mars*.

Given the predominance of this aspect of his literary work, it is easy to see how the historical novel was emphasized by *The Moscow Telegraph*. Selections from Walter Scott frequently appeared in its pages, along with imitations of Scott by wholly forgotten Germans. Victor Hugo in general and his *Notre Dame de Paris* in particular were accorded very special attention. Space was disproportionately allowed to native tyros at this genre, Bestužev-"Marlinskij", Lažečnikov, Zagoskin. In fact, the touchstone of Polevoj's ardently championed Romanticism was the historical romance. Primarily, as the Moscow Schellingians complained, he was a Russian proponent of *Walter-Scottisme*.

The Moscow Schellingians complained further at the predominance of French works in the *Telegraph*. In an article of the initial issue Polevoj had written: [4]

How much is still unknown or curious to us that is essential for a European to know! [Polevoj never doubted that Russia rightly was part of Europe.] English, Spanish, Italian, Oriental literatures are about as well known to us as the language of the Iroquois — and is not German literature wholly unknown to us?

---

[4] The article was entitled "Letter to N. N." (i.e. to "anyone") and appeared in *The Moscow Telegraph*, 1825, No. 1; cited by N. K. Kozmin, "Očerki iz istorii Russkago Romantizma, N. A. Polevoj", in *Zapiski istoriko-filologičeskago fakul'teta imperatorskago S.-Peterburgskago Universiteta*, LXX (1903), p. 23.

Lament as he would, Polevoj was constrained by linguistic limitations and by popular taste — especially by popular taste — to recur more frequently to France than to any other country. In the nine years of the *Telegraph's* existence the Orientals were all but by-passed. Italian and Spanish literatures were represented by only a few critical articles. From English literature, Scott and Byron predominated; Shakespeare was represented by extracts from *Hamlet, Lear,* and *Othello,* while opinion about him was derived from Hugo's Preface to *Cromwell*; otherwise, only minor bits appeared from pre-Romantic or minor Romantic authors: Milton, Young (*Night Thoughts*), Tom Moore, Southey. From French, however, the list was long: Hugo, Vigny, Benjamin Constant, Charles Nodier, Mérimée, Eugène Sue, Balzac, Mme de Genlis, Chateaubriand, Jules Janin, Victor Ducange, as well as nonfiction writers like Barante, Quinet, Michelet. Native Russian works of all genres were given generous representation.

As for the Germans, their number fell about midway between greatest and least. From Herder and Novalis only tiny fragments were given; nor did Schelling fare any better. Wackenroder's *Joseph Berglinger,* with attribution to Tieck,[5] and an essay of August Wilhelm Schlegel[6] appeared in 1826. The forgotten fictionalists Fan der Felde and Blümenhagen provided one item each. There were short fragments from Schiller's plays and from Goethe's plays and poems, while four tales by Zschokke were offered from 1825 to 1829.

The oddity on this list was Hoffmann, with eight titles.[7] Alert journalist that he was, Polevoj selected items which were still novelties

---

[5] *Das merkwürdige musikalische Leben des Tonkünstlers Joseph Berglinger,* one of the important essays by Wilhelm Heinrich Wackenroder in the *Herzensergiessungen eines kunstliebenden Klosterbruders,* published anonymously 1797 with a preface by Tieck. The Russian translation was made by Švyrëv and appeared in *The Moscow Telegraph,* 1826, No. 9, under the title: "Primečatel'naja i muzikal'naja žizn' xudožnika Iosifa Berlingera" (sic).

[6] A. W. Schlegel's *Über dramatische Kunst und Literatur,* in *The Moscow Telegraph,* 1826, No. 3—4, under the title: "O dramatičeskoj poèzii i teorii izjaščnago". This was the first Russian translation from the work of the Schlegels. *The Moscow Telegraph,* 1831, No. 12, carried an article by Friedrich Schlegel entitled *Fragments of a course of theory and history of the fine arts* (Otryvki iz kursa teorii i istorii izjaščnyx xudožestv), representing the opening section of *Gespräch über die Poesie,* 1799—1800.

[7] Kozmin, *op. cit.* (See footnote 4 above), lists a ninth translation, that of *Die Irrungen,* as appearing in *The Moscow Telegraph* in 1829 under the title of "The Enchanted Portfolio" (Očarovannyj Bumažnik), but other authorities list this item as appearing in *The Moscow Messenger.* See: *Universitetskija Izvestija* (Kiev, 1908), No. 10 (October), pp. 127—184, under *Priloženie 2*; and also: P. N. Sakulin, *V. F. Odoevskij, op. cit.* (Footnote 7 of Chapter II.)

in their native Germany when he chose for publication in 1825 and 1826 respectively *Die Marquise de la Pivardière* and *Datura fastuosa,* the former reprinted from 1820, the latter first printed in the posthumous collection of *Die Letzten Erzählungen* of 1825. *Eine Spukgeschichte* (alias *Der schwebende Teller*) figured in the *Telegraph's* "supplement" for 1825.

Thereafter a four-year hiatus occurred before Polevoj returned to Hoffmann. The five translations of 1830–1831 drew attention from the periphery to the core of Hoffmann's work: *Der Sandmann, Das Majorat, Der goldene Topf,* selections from *Kater Murr,* and *Fragment aus dem Leben dreier Freunde.* Coming as they did in the prime of the international enthusiasm for the Tales, these translations established among the Russian reading public a new vision of Romanticism as a genre of vivid color and breathless mystery. Beside the new star, the star of Byron, already waning, waned the more. Indeed, most of the literary firmament seemed a little less bright than formerly. Creative writers of the vanguard were in particular attracted by its brilliance, and by 1833 they began to vie with one another in the creation of works in the Hoffmann manner. Polevoj was himself caught up in the fashion which he had helped to create and in 1833 published, in lieu of more translations, two stories of his own for which Hoffmann was the point of departure. In retrospect, however, the translations he published are seen to have been more important than his efforts to imitate them, just as the totality of *The Moscow Telegraph,* greater than the sum of its parts, outranks all of Polevoj's creative works. The journalist in him surpassed the poet.

2. *THE FELICITY OF MADNESS*

The first of Polevoj's Hoffmannizing stories appeared in two installments in the January issues[8] of *The Moscow Telegraph* for 1833, bearing the title: *The Felicity of Madness* (Blaženstvo Bezumija).[9] The story proper is told as a recollection of Leonid, who is patently Polevoj himself, within a frame-tale setting that presents a literary soirée. It begins:

[8] *The Moscow Telegraph* was published semi-monthly, and every four issues comprised a "čast".
[9] *The Felicity of Madness* (Blaženstvo Bezumija), a novelette published in two parts in *The Moscow Telegraph,* January, 1833, No. I, pp. 52–96 and No. II, pp. 228–272.

We had read Hoffmann's story *Meister Floh.* Various impressions had
flashed quickly through each of our minds as Hoffmann, that wild
child of fantasy, that poet-madman, himself afraid of the spectres he
created, led us out of the realm of the marvelous into the most commonplace world, from the world of magic into the German beer-cellar,
as he joked, laughed at our expectations, deceived us continually, and
finally vanished like a dream passing into deep slumber.

The discussions get under way. The women preferred the prosaic parts,
"while the men were in raptures over the most fantastic scenes", but
Leonid is silent. He is challenged on his silence by "a young girl who
could not get her fill of the bookbinder's daughter described by Hoffmann". A coy quibble ensues on the appropriateness of the word "like"
as applied to the author of *Meister Floh,* until Leonid fervently ex-
claims:

I simply *do not like* Hoffmann, just as I do not like a storm with
rolling thunder and blinding lightning. I am astonished, astounded, the
silence of my soul expresses my whole being at the very moment of the
storm, and afterwards I cannot give an explanation to myself: at that
time I did not exist for the world. And how would you have me repeat
to you my feelings in the cold language of reason and word? Kindle my
words with fire and then I will light my feelings in the soul of another
with letters such as he will comprehend. . .

How Hoffmann would have received such praise one can only specu-
late. We know what he would have thought of the literary soirée here
in progress: abomination. And we can divine with no effort what he
would have felt about the badinage in the manner of a Fontenelle-
turned-bourgeois which follows Leonid's outburst:

"Doesn't he write poetry?" the interrogating girl asked her silent friend.
"Really, now, that is some sort of poetic metaphor or some expression,
and I don't understand it at all . . ."
   "Ah! how well *I* understand him!" — murmured the other softly,
clasping her hands and raising her blue eyes upwards.

The events of *Meister Floh,* Leonid maintains, are not far-fetched at
all. They remind him of how "in Petersburg a few years ago when (he)
was serving in the Ministry of . . . (he) knew a certain činovnik [holder
of a government bureaucratic rank]". Perhaps these words should be
paraphrased: "a decade ago (1823) in Moscow I knew a member
of the 'Archive Youth' who worked in the Ministry of Foreign Affairs."
Leonid now engages the story proper with a description of his činovnik
friend, Antiox.
   Antiox, somewhat older than Leonid, passed for cold and morose.

He invited guests only once a year, on his name-day, much as Peregrinus Tyss, the recluse hero of *Meister Floh* held solitary commemorative feasts four times a year with imaginary guests. Like Peregrinus, too, he was handsome, though ladies unflatteringly called him "erudite", and widely traveled, though he would never discuss his travels any more than Peregrinus would talk about *his* trip to "India". He performed his duties effortlessly, a Russian touch, this. He knew Latin, French, Italian, and German, especially German. He was passionately devoted to music, though he disliked dancing and did not play an instrument. He adored Beethoven. He was "a strange person". When his father died of cholera, Antiox was received by his harsh, proud, old maternal grandfather who was rich and who brought the lad up as a gentleman. Antiox attended the University of Göttingen and made a tour of Italy and the Swiss Alps, dutifully returning to Russia for his grandfather's funeral. He longed for the past days of the Napoleonic wars when there was opportunity for heroic action; failing that, he longed to indulge in the arts of peace. "O Raphael, o Mozart, o Schiller!" he cried, "Who gave you your colors, tones, and words? Why were they given to you and not to me?"

In short, Polevoj has, in creating his supremely poetic hero, stitched together almost every cliché of the era: Byronic beauty and Byronic pose, Schillerian *Freiheitsmelancholie,* Žukovskian piety, Rousseauistic sensibility, the frustration of the Russian intellectuals of Nicholas I's reign, and artistic ideals which the author fancied were Romantic but which were really more characteristic of the 1790's.

The heroine is no less a preposterous medley. Her name is Adelheid. "She resembled a wild symphony of Beethoven, or the Valkyrie maidens of whom the scalds of Scandinavia used to sing." She is pensive, charming like a Dürer Madonna, auburn-haired, dressed in white like Schiller's Muse that inspired Thekla, or Goethe's Muse when he created Mignon. She is an *artiste* who performs at the genteel private showings staged by her father. Appearing after a few pieces by the chamber orchestra and after light refreshments for the guests, she normally began her part of the program with a selection rendered either on the piano or on the harp. The selections were wholly improvisations, during which her eyes flashed ecstatic fire. These were followed by readings from Goethe, Schiller, Bürger, or Klopstock. At the end of the program she retired with dignity, never acknowledging applause.

Her father, Ludovik von Schreckenfeld, is not an artist, not a savant, but a peregrinating charlatan. His "mnemo-physico-magic evenings" attract hordes of visitors despite high prices of admission. He exhibits astonishing machines, automata, fireworks, – and the accomplishments of his daughter Adelheid. Only by invitation may people attend these evenings, and only the wealthy are invited. Gambling tables are provided for those who are restless, and large sums of money change hands at these tables. For his part, Schreckenfeld never touches a card, merely stands and watches everyone with his green frog's eyes, chattering in five or six languages with his guests. To these evenings comes first Leonid, then, at his insistence, Antiox.

Patently, the situation, the characters, and the simple linear story which now follows, are all developed from four or five pages in the "Second Adventure" (chapter) of *Meister Floh,* where the author is briefly summarizing *antecedent action* of "several years ago". At that time, young George Pepusch had come to Berlin, where everyone was talking about the extraordinary soirées offered by the Flea-tamer Leuwenhoek and about his alluring Dutch niece, Dörtje Elverdink. Skeptically and with condescension Pepusch had at last betaken himself to one of the soirées, and where he had come to mock, had stayed, as it were, to pray. Still more patently, however, the situation and characters of the Russian story reflect a parallel motif within the Tales of Hoffmann, namely the Olimpia episode from *Der Sandmann,* together with its Russian derivative, "Pogorel'skij's" *The Baleful Consequences of an Unbridled Imagination.* In *Der Sandmann* we have to do with a major episode when the charlatan Spalanzani encourages the infatuation of the over-sensitive hero with his daughter, the mechanical doll Olimpia; in *Meister Floh* the motif is introduced only briefly, in retrospect, and for wholly different purposes. It was Polevoj's initial error to make the two cases qualitatively identical. Hence he proceeded to give his personages the emotional values of the *Sandmann* characters while putting them through a story-evolution based on *Meister Floh.*

Antiox is thrown directly into a frenzy upon beholding Adelheid. The first time he attends an "evening" he hears her declaim the *Dedication* to *Faust,* after which he flees and cannot be found for three days. The second time he hears her declaim Thekla's song from *Wallenstein* – Polevoj cites the poem in Žukovskij's version, called *A Voice from that World* (Golos iz togo sveta) –, after which he weeps, curses Goethe, Schiller, and all poetry, denounces Adelheid as a cheap entertainer, vows he does not love her, and returns for a third "evening". This time, amid the "mad sounds" of a Beethoven symphony, he cries out: "It is she!", gazes rapturously at Adelheid, then registers despair upon seeing her flee from the room. Schreckenfeld diabolically invites him to come again, to come, in fact, to his intimate family circle.

Antiox becomes an almost constant inhabitant of the Schreckenfeld house, lost utterly in his love for Adelheid. He fights a duel to protect her honor and is then astonished to have her father demand that he marry her lest people misconstrue his motive in fighting the duel. Thereat Adelheid cries "Never!", and in a speech beginning: "Lofty souled, noble man, non-earthly creature, I am unworthy of you!", she explains that she has acted as a decoy for her father, who wishes to get Antiox's money. After a three-day anguish with repeated faintings, she dies, murmuring first "Dahin! Dahin!" and then "Kurz ist der Schmerz und ewig ist die Freude!" [10] A repentant Schreckenfeld then confesses his life story and evil purposes to Antiox. But Antiox, for his part, passes from a paroxysm of grief to unconsciousness, to a state of total apathy, to final madness. He dies, wasted and grey, on the first anniversary of Adelheid's death, breaking his year-long silence as he dies with the cry: "It is she!"

What Antiox suddenly realized that evening amid the mad sounds of the Beethoven symphony was that Adelheid was the other half of his soul. The girl was at first wholly bewildered when Antiox explained this point to her. He had once glimpsed her long ago, he said, in Italy, sitting on a cliff by the sea, her harp beside her, singing; and all around her there were cities amid laurels and citron groves. But antecedent even to that encounter, they had once lived together in a different world, a world where there were to be found the works of Shakespeare, Milton, Tasso, Firdausi. In fact, they had constituted a single creature there, until a demon named Schreckenfeld divided them into Antiox and Adelheid. Each sundered half retains dim memories of that time. The girl will recall the entire past when Antiox speaks the words: "I love you, Adelheid, half of my soul!" And when she replies: "I love you, Antiox!" the demon's spell will be broken forever. The demon is powerful, to be sure, but Antiox has read Jakob Boehme and Swedenborg and knows precisely how to deal with him. Possibly the soul-halves will need to die before reunion is feasible . . .

This uncommonly infelicitous narrative is derived from a wholly felicitous and major motif in *Meister Floh*. Recurring still to those

---

[10] "Dahin! Dahin!" is the refrain from Mignon's song, *Kennst du das Land?* "Kurz ist der Schmerz und ewig ist die Freude!" is the final line from Schiller's *Die Jungfrau von Orleans,* spoken by Joan of Arc as she dies.

same four or five pages of summary of antecedent action in the "Second Adventure" of that story, we discover that George Pepusch, upon meeting the beautiful Dörtje Elverdink, had a first glimmer of awareness of a previous existence in which they had both participated. Long ago, he recalls, in the Indian land of Famagusta, he was himself the Thistle Zeherit and Dörtje was simultaneously a princess and a tulip. That was in the morning time of the universe (as Schelling's philosophical system had postulated), when plants, animals, minerals, human beings, stars and clouds were all evolving, when all things were still free to alter their natures and become of whatever quality they would, before the arrogant and limited intellect gained control and confined all things in rigid patterns. In a delightful wooing scene between the modern parties, the realistic plane of consciousness is made to jostle crazily the plane of mythical, inner awareness. But Dörtje Elverdink is a volatile little creature. While pretending to understand everything that Pepusch-Zeherit is saying, her eye catches a passing soldier, and with a cry she is off in pursuit of the uniform, leaving the Thistle in a fury of disappointment.

The story proper of *Meister Floh,* in so far as it deals with George Pepusch, begins one evening in Frankfurt when the young man calls on Leuwenhoek and learns that Dörtje has run away. She has seen and gone in pursuit of Peregrinus Tyss, the actual hero of the story, and many will be the trials of Pepusch before he finds her and wins her for himself. Their wedding night restores them to their pristine selves. He, as the Thistle Zeherit, achieves the glorious form of the *cactus grandiflorus,* she becomes again the lovely tulip. Their passionate but unwise love brings them to full bloom at the midnight, when they perish together in a "Liebestod" amid clouds of fragrance.

In the Russian story Hoffmann's roguish humor has yielded place to prosaic lugubriousness and his staggering feats of fantasy to pedestrian invention. It was a serious error to conceive the vigorous, fiery-tempered George Pepusch in terms of the suffering Nathanael of *Der Sandmann.* George's other self and his pre-existence are real, whereas Nathanael's adventure was made up of the hallucinations of on-coming madness. It was a worse error to make Antiox a *schöne Seele* with Byronic trappings if he had to bear both George's vision and Nathanael's fate. Dörtje Elverdink has no place in Polevoj's scheme. Her headstrong vivacity would have exploded the plot at the outset. Her absence is filled by Adelheid, who is what the doll Olimpia would have been if a *schöne Seele* (and nothing more) had been breathed into her. As for

Schreckenfeld (preposterous name!), he is a feebler Spalanzani, rather than the amusing Leuwenhoek, a small-time operator of a semi-illegal nightclub with impotent magic and without the courage of his convictions. If he had a demon-role in "that other world", the motif is abandoned after a single mention. The interpenetration of two worlds, which is the very essence of *Meister Floh,* was beyond Polevoj's capacities to portray. He could handle only one world at a time. Ideologically, a silly and sentimental variation of Aristophanes's myth about the origin of love from the *Symposium* of Plato has been substituted for the Schellingian doctrine of the evolving universe. Yet beneath Polevoj's outlandish tale there may lie a subconscious allegory. In that troubled era of Russian life, when aesthetics alone was without harsh regimentation, the suppressed aspirations often found oblique expression in harmless fictions. There is no doubt that Antiox beheld some kind of ideal land, whether "Famagusta" or Italy, and yearned toward it with all his soul, and vague as it may have been, it bore little resemblance to the Russia of Nicholas I. It was madness so to yearn. Antiox perished mad. But, as the title of the story declares, the madness is blessed.

3. *THE PAINTER*

Four months after *The Felicity of Madness,* the May-June issues of *The Moscow Telegraph* carried the four installments of a new novelette by Polevoj entitled *The Painter* (Živopisec).[11] It presented the biography of an imaginary artist named Arkadij and his vacillations between two ways of life, the way of the "normal" man of the world and the way of the artist.

The slow narrative is given in first person as the account of a kindly old Mr. Mamaev, who, on the point of leaving his provincial home for a journey to Petersburg, was tearfully requested by his old friend, the provincial revenue collector, to seek out the latter's son, Arkadij, from whom there has been no news for over a year. With some difficulty Mamaev finally locates the young man in a rather luxurious studio of a great house on the Mojka. Arkadij is quite unlike the notion that

---

[11] *The Painter* (Živopisec), a novelette published in four parts in *The Moscow Telegraph,* May-June, 1833, No. IX, pp. 74—131; No. X, pp. 239—294; No. XI, pp. 396—448; No. XII, pp. 534—593. The story is dated at the end: June 10, 1833.

Mamaev had formed of him. He lacks the "Grecian countenance of Goethe", he lacks the "Germanic profile of Schiller", he lacks the "wildness of Hoffmann". He does not even look like an artist, but is a rather personable young fellow correctly dressed and with a mannered gesture of brushing his hair back off his forehead. The portraits about the studio are oddly assorted. Some indicate the inspiration of genius. Several repeat an over-sweet feminine likeness, which leads Mamaev to think "A woman has destroyed him". One represents an elderly society lady with ass's ears.

Arkadij gradually drops his hauteur and tells his life-story to the visitor. As a child he had made drawings, one of which, the copy of an ikon of the Madonna, caused his mother to believe that God had marked him for Art.[12] Before a spectacle of a sunset he had dedicated himself to that holy vocation. He studied under a saintly ikon-master and was very happy at his daily work of sacred representations. One day the Governor observed him and was so impressed that he made arrangements to adopt the lad unofficially into his family. For ten years Arkadij lived amid wealth and books. Suddenly the Governor died and his hateful heirs drove Arkadij away penniless. A faithful old servant supported him, procured clients for him to paint, and shielded him from the world. All this time he nourished the sweet dream of one day seeing Italy, the land of Art. The Academy authorities were considering granting him a scholarship for travel. Then he met Veren'ka, and forthwith left the Academy and forgot about Italy.

His love is honorable and all-engrossing, but Veren'ka seems to be giving at least half her time to another suitor, a wealthy lawyer and a Philistine. Arkadij works hard and prepares an exposition which he hopes will win Veren'ka admiration and love. With high hopes he leads her to view the canvases, *Jesus in the Desert*, *A Family Reading*, *The Knight's Farewell*, *The Oath of the Swiss Leaders* (after Schiller's *Wilhelm Tell*), and, above all, *Prometheus*. This last portrays an Aeschylean-Byronic Titan defying the Thunderer, his eyes full of prophetic vision, his wracked body flanked by a blood-thirsty eagle and a fierce Hephaestos, the grey sea behind them. Veren'ka turns

---

[12] The episode resembles an actual event in the life of Žukovskij. When Žukovskij was about six years old (1789) he drew the features of the Madonna on the floor, so that the serving girls, coming upon it, cried out that a miracle had happened. Though Salxa, his mother, clearly showed that the picture was Vasen'ka's doings, the tracing was allowed to remain. See: Carl von Seidlitz, *Wasily Andrejewitsch Joukoffsky, Ein Russisches Dichterleben* (Mitau, 1870), pp. 8–9.

her lorgnette upon the painting and shudders. ("She was a woman.")
Of the other works she remarks: "Charming, Arkadij", and "like
Mme de Staël speaking of Goethe or Werner." Her father is exclusively
concerned about the choice of frames, except for a complaint that the
artist has neglected native Russian themes for foreign subjects. Arkadij
rushes away in despair. He goes to Italy, vowing never to return.

For three years his letters come to Mamaev, then grow fewer, and
finally cease. A traveling Italian painter brings word of the death of
Signor Arcadio and delivers a "last picture". It is a scene of Christ
among the children; Veren'ka, idealized, is being blessed by the Saviour.
Arkadij himself sleeps beneath the myrtles of Italy.

Veren'ka marries the lawyer and has lovely children. Mamaev encounters them at a card party. Both seem prosperous and contented. At
a loge in the theatre he glimpses them again *en famille*. They form an
ideal bourgeois group.

The Russian critic Rodzevič has rightly identified *The Painter* as
an art-problem-story in the manner of Hoffmann's *Der Artushof*,[13]
pointing out that the doubts and questionings which torment young
Traugott, the painter-hero of that work, are paralleled in Arkadij's
debate with himself:

Do I really have within me something that sets me off from others?
Is there really within my soul some celestial fire? . . . If there is in me
nothing creative, constructive, I am not an artist. My dreams are the
unclear delusions of fever, the febrile ardor of an invalid who wants
to enter heaven. . . . Have I then erred in selecting an artist's life for
my field? Have I then erred in thinking that upon my head there
shone the flame of God's elect? . . .

Traugott, however, does not debate the issue so explicitly. The reader
discovers him at the beginning of the story, startled at his clerk's
desk by the remark of a mysterious acquaintance to the effect that he
may have the capacity to become a great painter. The young clerk
thinks of his distasteful job and of his suppressed desire to paint.
He turns over the drawings in his portfolio, seeking some confirmation
of his aspirations. In agitation he walks out into the country to think
matters over. Hoffmann presents a character in movement, not merely
an inner monologue.

Like Arkadij, Traugott is in love, or thinks he is in love, with a
mediocre Miss. The Christine Roos of the German tale is

[13]   S. Rodzevič, "K istorii russkago romantizma", *Russkij Filologičeskij Vestnik*,
LXXVII (1917), pp. 194–237; p. 207.

82 POLEVOJ, THE JOURNALIST

> ... a young lady of perhaps two-and-twenty, of medium height, well fed, with a round face, somewhat snub nose, friendly light blue eyes which smile right charmingly at everyone: "I am soon to be married!" — She has a dazzlingly white complexion, her hair is not too red — very kissable lips — a rather broad mouth ... Never has she had bad luck with an almond pastry, and her butter-sauce always obediently thickens because she never stirs it counter-clockwise, but always clockwise.

Veren'ka is a prissier, lorgnette-wielding version of Christine Roos, with all the humor omitted from her characterization. Arkadij is her pathetic and passive victim, whereas Traugott, having discovered an inspiring master of painting with a daughter who inspires love, quits Philistine Christine and her Philistine father without a qualm. Whereupon Christine finds herself another suitor and marries as quickly as possible. Subsequently, after Traugott has discovered his painting-master to be insane, he loses both father and daughter, for the old man's mania consists in frantic efforts to keep all suitors from Felizitas. The bereft hero follows the pair to Italy, only to find that the "Sorrento" to which they fled was not the Italian town near Naples, but an estate close to his native Danzig. By the time he has made the return journey and ascertained their whereabouts, he learns that the old painter has died and that Felizitas has married "a jurist from Marienwerder". Undaunted by his loss, Traugott goes back to Italy and to a third father-daughter pair. Once again the father is a painter, and the girl, whose name is Dorina, inspires his love. The story closes without revealing whether the new inspirations are genuine and final or merely another illusion.[14]

Illusion or reality, Traugott is inspired by the new love. He goes to Italy with joy. He does not die, but presumably has many a year of vivid life before him. He *is* a painter, and he will always paint, just as he will always be in love. Twice he escapes inspiration-destroying marital involvement with conventional young ladies, once with the out-

---

[14] Harvey W. Hewett-Thayer, *Hoffmann, Author of the Tales* (Princeton, University Press, 1948), pp. 203—204, discusses the ambiguous ending of *Der Artushof* and is of the opinion that Dorina will be an admirable wife for Traugott without impinging on his artist's career. If this interpretation is accepted, Dorina and her unnamed artist father mark a stage of just equilibrium between the extremes to which Traugott had strayed, first to the excessively Philistine Roos's, then to the excessively impractical and over-idealized Berklingers. The alternate interpretation would make Dorina a third and future disillusionment, to be followed presumably by others, as long as Traugott lived and aspired.

and-out Philistine Miss Roos, a second time with Felizitas Berklinger who seemed to be artistic but who, as soon as paternal constraint was relaxed, showed her true nature by marrying a provincial lawyer. The nature of Dorina is left a tantalizing mystery.

Arkadij, on the other hand, true to the *simplification* principle of the Russian Hoffmannists, loves only once. True to the *pessimistic* principle of the Russian Hoffmannists, the love destroys him. His escape to Italy and Art is an escape to mournful resignation and slow death. His "last picture" of an idealized Veren'ka among the children being blessed by Christ is both a pious canonization of a broken heart and a forestep to reunion of fleshless lovers after death in the manner of Klopstock.[15]

The mournful close of *The Painter* is not at all surprising, but Rodzevič holds [16] that it indicates that Polevoj was working not only on the basis of *Der Artushof,* but even more on the basis of *Die Jesuiterkirche in G.,* its pessimistic companion-piece.[17] The fact that the latter was available in Russian translation [18] probably is of no significance, but Arkadij's "last picture" does suggest the painting of the Virgin and St. Elizabeth which is completed, after long efforts, by Berthold, the hero of *Die Jesuiterkirche in G.,* just before his death.

It had been Berthold's destiny to go to Italy as a young man and to study painting under known masters. He saw only briefly and from a distance the beautiful woman who inspires his works, but later he came to know his Ideal personally and at length married her. No sooner married, however, than he discovered that all capacity to

---

[15] Klopstock found the idea in Young's *Night Thoughts* but more particularly in Elizabeth Singer's (1674–1737) *Friendship in Death,* which presented true lovers married after death. He used the motif in his ode *An Fanny* (Sophie-Marie Schmidt) in 1748 and in the episode of Semida and Cidli in *Der Messias.* This pair were lovers raised from the dead by Jesus. For the rest of their lives they follow the Master's teachings, postponing their union until they enter Heaven. It was in part by the reading of this passage from *Der Messias* that Klopstock wooed his second love, "Meta" (Marguerite Moller), in 1752 — and married her in 1754.

[16] Rodzevič, "K istorii russkago romantizma", *op. cit.,* pp. 205–206.

[17] The artist problem of conventional life versus life for Art had already been announced in the closing pages of *Die Fermate,* which was written January 16 to February 3, 1815. The theme was developed in optimistic vein in *Der Artushof,* written February 17 to March 6, 1815, and in pessimistic vein in *Die Jesuiterkirche in G.,* written late in 1815 or early in 1816. *Rat Krespel,* written in September 1816, also harkens back to the same problem.

[18] "Iezuitskaja cerkov'" appeared in *The Moscow Messenger,* No. VI (1830).

paint had deserted him. Neither the devotion of his wife Angiola, nor his own enduring passion for her, could console him for the loss of Art. When she bore him a son, he became furious, cursed his wife in a violent scene, and left her. The reader receives the impression that he murdered both wife and child. Years later, when the narrator of the tale is speaking to Berthold — who is now engaged in decorating the Jesuit church in G(logau) —, he asks him point-blank whether he did murder them. With horror Berthold disclaims such an act. Subsequently, the narrator learns, Bethold was reconciled with his family, finished his great painting, and disappeared from G. His hat and cane were found on the bank of the river O(der). Apparently he had committed suicide.

Since *The Painter* omits almost all narrative matter, it is difficult to say which of Hoffmann's art-problem-tales was the more important source for Polevoj. Probably both were important to him. It was the problem analysed in both that concerned him, not the plot of either one. Indeed, the element of plot is very tenuous in *The Painter*. The largest part of the work is commonplace biography told in retrospect. The outcome is tersely reported by the Italian traveler. Only the episode of Veren'ka's visit to the exposition of paintings constitutes action with characters in conflict, and this episode does not occur until the fourth installment of the work. Polevoj seems to have been unable to present complex action such as the suspenseful and psychologically valid alternation of Traugott between his "two worlds", the world of Christine Roos and her business-man father and the world of Felizitas Berklinger and *her* mad artist father. With Hoffmann the action was the problem in operation. With Polevoj there has been substituted a slow-paced enumerative chronology with pauses for head-on monologue debates by the hero of the subject which is in the author's mind. *The Felicity of Madness* had shown Polevoj baffled by Hoffmannian story-technique. In *The Painter* he chose to deal with Hoffmann's thought alone and let the story be. His model was more elusive than he had believed.

4. *EMMA*

As further substantiation of Polevoj's concern with the companion works, *Die Jesuiterkirche in G.* and *Der Artushof,* there is the fact that he followed up *The Painter* with a companion piece of its own, entitled *Emma*, six months after its predecessor.[19] The parallels and alternation, however, are along wholly different lines. In the new story a young heroine replaces the young hero caught between the conflicting forces of convention and Ideal.

The setting is the old German Suburb of Moscow before its destruction by the fire of 1812. Two houses once stood there side by side, one a fine mansion inhabited by Prince S***, the other a charming cottage reminiscent of a scene from the novels of August Lafontaine. In the latter lives an elderly German couple whose pious "Gothic" faces gaze with contentment upon three grandsons, who look as though they had stepped out of a painting by Greuze, and upon a young lady granddaughter, Emma. They are all German-speaking, devoted Lutherans, but unstintingly loyal to the Tsar. From her friend "Fanny" — Klopstockian nickname for Feodosija Gottliebovna — Emma learns that the son of Prince S*** was brought home some months ago as a raving madman. Doctors call his case hopeless.

Seated amid the flowers of the garden one summer's day, Emma is startled by the sudden appearance of young Prince Paul S***. He has eluded his keepers, climbed the garden wall, and is coming toward her like a wild beast. At sight of her he stops, clasps his hands over his heart, falls to his knees, and implores her not to leave him. "Like one of Klopstock's immortal spirits" she stands over him till his pursuers arrive. The doctor, who is "a disciple and friend of the great Mesmer" and who could have cured "that fool Werther", proclaims that a straitjacket and cold water over the head will do for this fellow. At his words the patient becomes savage again. But the doctor is a shrewd man. He observes Emma's strange effect upon his patient and persuades her to undertake the young man's cure.

Emma's life among the wealthy, Orthodox, aristocratic family is a troubled one. Her patient worships her as an angel, it is true, but his hoity-toity mother resents the intruder in spite of her son's betterment, while the servants gossip that Emma is a sorceress. Eventually Paul is able to reenter society and to pursue his courtship of Moina, a wealthy and prominent society girl (whose name comes out of Ossian). Moina's presence brings Emma to the realization that she herself is in love

[19] *Emma*, a novelette in 17 chapters, published in four installments in *The Moscow Telegraph*, January-February, 1834; Chapters I—III in No. I, January, pp. 72—127; Chapters IV—VI in No. II, January, pp. 241—286; Chapters VII—XIII in No. III, February, pp. 407—453; Chapters XIV—XVII in No. IV, February, pp. 574—612.

with Paul, and that her love is not reciprocated. The crafty Princess-mother offers her an eligible suitor in one Colonel Dobrov, but Emma confides to Fanny in a letter that she is about to die. And die she does, of a broken heart, converted, however, to Orthodoxy on her death-bed. In 1812 Paul "wrenched himself loose from the toils of his charmer, Moina", went to the defense of the Fatherland, and was brought down by a French marauder's bullet. By coincidence, his body was buried, amid the confusions of war, in the very grave of "that young German girl that lived with the Princess, was converted, and died here".

Though no plot-outlines show relationship between *Emma* and *Die Jesuiterkirche in G.*, Rodzevič sees in the spurned Emma a reminiscence of Angiola, the spurned wife of Berthold, as well as a further reminiscence of Röschen, bookbinder Lämmerhirt's charming blue-eyed daughter in *Meister Floh*.[20] Neither claim seems cogent. Emma's prototypes are clearly Schiller's heroines, Amalie (*Die Räuber*) and Luise (*Kabale und Liebe*), as well as Thekla (*Wallenstein*), with whom she declares in Chapter IX that she has a special affinity. Her poor-governess-type role suggests a post-Hoffmannian heroine such as will presently appear in the novels of Charlotte and Anne Brontë.

Nor does the theme of Mesmerism relate the Russian story to Hoffmann in any but the most general way. All three things belonged simply to a certain area of common interest. Besides, Emma's influence upon Paul is not mesmeric so much as it is the effect of a *schöne Seele* upon a rabid spirit. There is more of Klopstock in it than of Hoffmann. Polevoj was veering rapidly away from the Hoffmannian course he had set.

5. *ABBADONNA*

Only remote echoes of Hoffmann are to be heard in the full-length novel which Polevoj published in 1834 with the title *Abbadonna*.[21] Though Klopstock's repentant fallen angel Abbadona (with one n) was male,[22] the reference here is to the beautiful actress Eleonore, mistress of Baron Kahlkopf but profoundly in love with the poet hero.

[20]   Rodzevič, "K istorii russkago romantizma", *op. cit.*, p. 210.
[21]   *Abbadonna,* a novel in four parts, published in book form (Moscow, 1834).
[22]   The most celebrated figure in *Der Messias* is Abbadona, the repentant rebel angel, odious to himself, rent with the bitterness of not being loved, yearning for God from the depths of hell. At his reappearances in Cantoes II, V, IX, and XIII, sentimental readers wrote Klopstock begging him to save Abbadona in

The latter, whose name is Wilhelm Reichenbach, is confronted with the dilemma of having composed his drama *Arminius* — Klopstockian title! — under the inspiration of the gentle bourgeoise, Henriette Schulz, but of having it produced at the instigation of Eleonore. Moreover, Eleonore's influence over Baron Kahlkopf makes her virtual ruler of the *Residenzstadt,* and to follow her imperious will can lead to fame and wealth in addition to serving the cause of Poetry. Belinskij observed immediately after the publication of the book that this quartet of characters recapitulated under new names the principal personages of Schiller's *Kabale und Liebe:* Reichenbach-Ferdinand; Eleonore-Lady Milford; Henriette-Luise Müller, and Baron Kahlkopf-the President. In so far as the story deals with the milieu of the theatre, it borrows details from Goethe's *Wilhelm Meister.* The poet's name, for instance, as Kozmin points out,[23] undoubtedly comes from Goethe's hero, while Eleonore has traits of Wilhelm Meister's actress-inamorata, Marianne.

The 1835 reviewer for the *Literary Gazette* found that the book bore resemblances at some points to *Kater Murr.* The reigning Prince, for instance, is described as not infrequently attending the theatre,

... pleased that this school of morals cost him nothing yet delighted all his subjects, and that, as to his father, it brought him fame as a protector of the arts. Moreover, he too displayed his talent by composing an entr'acte.

The bumblingly stupid ruler reminds one of Prince Irenäus, ruler of Sieghardtsweiler, who himself once wrote a poem on the idyllic life *procul negotiis.* Pointed satire of court life at various intervals through the book, the same reviewer claimed, repeatedly recall the malicious wit with which Hoffmann had portrayed Sieghardtshof. The reviewer was quite right in making these observations, but the passages in question are incidental details, and the plot and characters of *Abbadonna* owe extremely little to *Kater Murr* or to any other work of Hoffmann.

Critics and public alike praised the novel highly in 1835. Only the censor was unhappy. The German *Residenzstadt* setting did not obscure the fact that the unflattering portraits of foreign rulers and courtiers might, if transposed to Russian scenes, display uncomfortable simi-

---

the end; theologians forbade him to do so, saying that such a redemption would shatter Christianity. Klopstock made God pardon him. Žukovskij made a translation in 1814 of Abbadona's speech during the infernal debate of Canto II, lines 627–830.
[23]   Kozmin, *op. cit.* (see footnote 4 above), p. 165.

larities to local persons and conditions. The book was, in short, both daring and fashionably Romantic.

Publication of the second edition in 1841 evoked quite different responses. The *Literary Gazette* was hostile now, as was *National Notes,* and Belinskij, who had praised the serious parts in all sincerity in 1835, now found only the comic parts readable at all. Five years of public life, he said, equalled fifty years of an individual's life, and the public was no longer interested in the poetic tribulations of characters like Wilhelm Reichenbach.

Such thorough reversal of opinion on one and the same book within a five-year interval is striking confirmation of the headlong speed with which Romanticism was going out of fashion in 1841. The attacks saddened Polevoj greatly, coming as they did when everything in his life was going wrong. The five years remaining to him were to recoup neither his journalistic fortunes nor his literary fortunes, any more than they were to bring him back to health or financial prosperity. At age forty-five he was, literarily speaking, a superannuated man. His works were ridiculed, his models were relegated to the Limbo of authors of past eras. Hoffmann along with the rest. A new age was urgently demanding new things. There was no place for him.

At age fifty he died. Most of his creative writings died with him. Lacking the graceful charm of "Pogorel'skij", they were composed with tremendous enthusiasm but small art. His Hoffmannism was undoubtedly broader and deeper than "Pogorel'skij's", and certainly more ambitious, but he lacked the talent to apply it. His primary service to Russian Hoffmannism was his publication of translations. His greatest achievement was his magazine, *The Moscow Telegraph.*

PRINCE ODOEVSKIJ, THE PHILOSOPHER

When Prince Vladimir Fëdrovič Odoevskij gathered up three volumes of his writings in 1844 and published them as *The Works of Prince V. F. Odoevskij* (Sočinenija Knjazja V. F. Odoevskogo), he was doing himself an injustice. He was but forty-one years of age and his career was by no means at an end. Yet, of the vast array of projects in his notebooks, ranging from almost completed stories to the merest outlines and in some cases to bare titles, very little was to be realized as completed works in the years that remained until his death in 1869. The title was further a misnomer in that numerous short pieces, published in various magazines, were passed over. They remain scattered still, presenting, along with the bulk of the manuscript notebooks, a complex problem for a scholar who would assess his total work.

Not dilatoriness, but a sombre sense of duty hindered Odoevskij's literary fulfillment. His career in government service was a lifetime progression from heavy to ever heavier responsibilities because his sense of duty forced him to commit his energies to their fullest capacity in every position to which he was called. From 1826 onward we find him successively as secretary of censorial committees, director of the Department of Spiritual Affairs for Foreign Confessions, member of the imperial chancellery, director of the Imperial Public Library and of the Rumjancevskij Museum, and finally senator in 1861. His private charities to individuals, to the poor, the sick, the orphaned, and the homeless, were such that in the end he exhausted his large fortune and died poor. No philanthropic enterprise ever went without his support, and not merely his financial support. He personally founded and organized the Society for the Enlightenment of the Poor in St. Petersburg, and as he said somewhat ruefully, the nine years from 1846 to 1855 which he devoted to that organization consumed his literary career "with nothing left over". As part of that project he created the children's tales which continued in use as school texts into the twentieth century. For himself he asked little. Nor was he concerned with his thousand-year-old ancestry, more illustrious than that of the

Romanovs and extending to Rurik himself. The "Prince" of his title had been handed down from Kievan chieftains.

Born July 30, 1803 in Moscow, he lost both parents at a very early age, both his commoner-mother and his father who was the director of the Moscow division of the national bank. An uncle reared him and sent him to the Noble Pension of the University of Moscow. Preexcellence there in his studies won him the gold medal upon completion of his course in 1822. For four years thereafter he flung himself with ardor into the studies of literature and philosophy. We have already seen him as prime mover in the circle of the Moscow Schellingians. His desire was to be a universal man. Philosophy he conceived as the crown of knowledge, a guide to all departments of character, informing all the rest with significance and awareness. His conscience compelled him to give his best energies to government service; his heart bade him devote much of his time to charitable work; his passionate interest in music he felt bound to relegate to the status of a hobby; his literary career, which he longed to make paramount in his life, was realized almost in spite of himself, and the three volumes of the 1844 *Works* represent a significant and enduring contribution to Russian letters. Earnest, kindly, sombre-dispositioned, an aristocrat in fact and by conviction, Prince Odoevskij stands as a kind of human monument to his caste, exemplar of the conscience, humility, and thirst for knowledge that marked that Petrine society at its best, and wholly without the ugly elements that brought that society to its collapse in 1917.

Almost from the beginning of his career as a writer, Odoevskij had toyed with the notion of associating heterogeneous productions in a general frame-tale where a group of speakers might exploit the philosophical implications of the various stories. As early as the preface to his little volume of *Variegated Tales* (Pëstrye Skazki) in 1833 he had announced such a work, to bear the title of *The House of Madmen* (Dom sumasšedšix), and at least five pieces are known to have been designated for inclusion in it. Both plan and component works belong to the years 1831–1835, the heyday of Russian Romanticism — and of Russian Hoffmannism —, but only belatedly, in 1844, when the Romantic movement was clearly an abandoned cause, did the plan come to fulfillment in the altered form and with the new title of *Russian Nights* (Russkie Noči). These occupy the entire first volume of the *Works*.[1] Included in the new form are the five previously designated

[1] See: P. N. Sakulin, *Iz istorii russkago idealizma: Knjaz' V. F. Odoevskij, myslitel'-pisatel'*, Vol. I, Part II (Moscow, 1913), pp. 202–250. Pp. 207–212

pieces, all but one of which, the essay called *Who are Madmen?* (Kto sumasšedšie?), had been published separately between 1831 and 1835. At the time of their separate publication they had been termed Hoffmannian; upon their reissue as sub-stories in *Russian Nights* the claim was made anew, by no less a critic than Belinskij, as well as by others, and the whole frame-tale organization was judged to be in the manner of *Die Serapionsbrüder*. The earlier collection of 1833, *Variegated Tales,* had likewise been deemed Hoffmann-like, and to Odoevskij's name there clung all his life the sobriquet assigned to him by Countess Rostopčina: "Hoffmann II".

---

list the component parts of *Russian Nights* as follows:

1. Rostislav's fairy-tale in the frame-tale conversation of the "First Night" was originally an independent and unpublished piece entitled *Children's Fairy-tale for Grown-up Children* (Detskaja skazka dlja vzroslyx detej). (See Sakulin, pp. 169—170.)

2. The essay *Who are Madmen?* (Kto sumasšedšie?), now presented by Faust in the "Second Night", was originally intended as the *Introduction* to *The House of Madmen* (Dom sumasšedšix); previously unpublished.

3. *Opere del Cavaliere Giambatista Piranesi,* now part of the "Third Night", republished, with very slight textual variations, from *Northern Flowers* (Severnye Cvety), 1832.

4. The following subsections of the "Fourth Night": a) *The Brigadier* (Brigadir), republished from the anthology *New Colony* (Novosel'e), Part I (SPb, 1833). b) *The Ball* (Bal), *ibid.*, 1833. c) *The Avenger* (Mstitel'), previously unpublished, figured originally as a section of the unfinished story *Jantina* (1836), with the title of *An Apology for Poetry* (Apologetika poèzii). (See Sakulin, pp. 94—98.) d) *A Corpse's Mockery* (Nasmeška mertveca), republished from Maksimovič's *Dawn for 1834* (Dennica na 1834-ij god) (Moscow, 1834). e) *The Last Suicide* (Poslednee samoubijstvo), previously unpublished. f) *Cecilia* (Cecilija), previously unpublished.

5. *The City without a Name* (Gorod bez imeni), now part of the "Fifth Night", republished from *The Contemporary*, Vol. 13 (1839).

6. *Beethoven's Last Quartet* (Poslednij Kvartet Betxovena), now part of the "Sixth Night", republished from *Northern Flowers for 1831* (Severnye Cvety na 1831 god), (SPb, 1831).

7. *The Improvisor* (Improvizator), now part of the "Seventh Night", republished from Baron Rozen's *Halcyon for 1833* (Al'ciona na 1833-ij god), (SPb, 1833), with the note: "From the book entitled *The House of Madmen* to be published in the near future."

8. *Sebastian Bach* (Sebastijan Bax), which now comprises the entire "Eighth Night", republished from *The Moscow Observer* (Moskovskij Nabljudatel'), May, 1835, Part II, pp. 55—112, with date of 1834 and signature of "Bezglasnyj", and with the note: "From the unpublished book, *The House of Madmen*".

9. The following unpublished pieces, now included in the *Epilogue:* a) a note of comment on President Van Buren's inaugural address of March 4, 1837, intended for *The House of Madmen*; b) a note about the regeneration of Europe, originally intended for the *Epilogue* to *The House of Madmen*; c) a note of reply to Čaadaev's first *Lettre philosophique* as published in *The Telescope* (Teleskop), 1836; intended for the *Epilogue* to *The House of Madmen*.

In preparing a second edition of his frame-tale collection in 1862 Odoevskij added an extra foreword entitled *Notes to Russian Nights* (Primečanie k Russkim Nočam),[2] but this interesting piece was not printed until the next edition in 1913, long after his death. Here we read:

Many people have found, some to my credit, others to my discredit, that in *Russian Nights* I tried to imitate Hoffmann. This accusation does not disturb me too much. There has never been in the world a writer, small or great, who did not willingly or unwillingly echo the thoughts, words, procedures, etc. of others. This is inevitable in the harmonious relationship that naturally exists between people of all epochs and of all nations. No thought is born without participation in the evolution of antecedent thought, either of one's own or of other people's. Otherwise an author would have to reject his capacity to receive impressions from what he reads and sees, i.e. to reject his right to feel, and consequently to live. Naturally I am not the least offended when they compare me with Hoffmann; on the contrary, I take the comparison as a compliment, for Hoffmann will always remain a man of genius *sui generis,* like Cervantes, like Sterne. Nor is there any exaggeration in my words, if genius is equivalent to invention. Hoffmann invented a special kind of the marvelous (čudesnoe). I realize that in our century of analysis and doubt it is rather dangerous to speak of the marvelous. Nevertheless this element exists even now in art. ... Hoffmann discovered the single thread by which this element could be introduced into the literary art of our time. His marvelous always has two sides, the one purely fantastic, the other real, so that the haughty reader of the XIXth century is not expected to believe unconditionally in the marvelous occurrences narrated to him. Within the limits of the tale everything is presented whereby the occurrences may be explained very simply. In this way one may have his cake and eat it too. The natural inclination of man toward the marvelous is satisfied, and at the same time the searching spirit of analysis is not outraged. To reconcile these two antithetical elements was the work of a genuine talent.

But meanwhile I did not imitate Hoffmann. I know that the very form of *Russian Nights* recalls the form of Hoffmann's creation, *Serapien's Brüder* (sic). Likewise the conversation between the friends, likewise the various narratives introduced into the conversation. But the fact is, that at the time when *Russian Nights* was taking form in my mind, i.e. in the 'twenties', the *Serapien's Brüder* were wholly unknown to me. It seems that this book did not then even exist in our bookstalls. The only work of Hoffmann which I had then read was *Das Majorat,* from which apparently there is not the slightest trace in my book.

[2] *Kn. V. F. Odoevski: Russkija Noči,* ed. S. A. Cvetkov (Moscow, 1913), pp. 13—22; pp. 13—16.

With so utterly honest a man as Odoevskij there can be no doubt of the truth of this statement, which, on the face of it, would seem to preclude any influence whatsoever from Hoffmann. Was Odoevskij self-deceived, or were his contemporaries, Belinskij included, and all subsequent critics, in error? The matter will require scrutiny.

1. *OPERE DEL CAVALIERE GIAMBATISTA PIRANESI*

Readers of Hoffmann will recall that the very first of the famous *Tales* was the brief *Ritter Gluck,* composed in 1808 when the author had passed his thirty-second birthday and published in 1809. Its unnamed narrator is described as sitting in the Berlin Tiergarten one sunny afternoon, presumably in 1808, listening to a park-band grinding out a sentimental waltz. All at once a stranger, near by but hitherto unperceived, complains aloud at the sorry music. A conversation is struck up. The stranger is perhaps fifty years old, of odd appearance, and a musician of rare sensitivity, a composer, in fact, though he claims to have abandoned composition now. His long overcoat, opened for an instant and then hurriedly closed again, covers an eighteenth century costume. He requests the orchestra to play Gluck's overture to *Iphigenia in Aulis,* then returning to his seat, proceeds to direct the musicians and to play with them as though his table were a keyboard. When the piece is concluded and conversation reopened, a chance remark by the narrator sets off an extraordinary tirade from the stranger, in which he describes the anguish of the disembodied spirit amid the realm of inspiration. He portrays regions of terrifying emptiness where rays of tone and waves of melody beat upon him, where Tonic and Fifth appear as mailed giants marching against him, and where a great eye evokes music from a mighty organ. Suddenly, without farewell or apology, he walks off in the midst of his narrative. By chance the narrator meets him again on the way home, but their second conversation is cut off almost as abruptly as the first, when, after some talk of Mozart, the narrator makes an innocent reference to Gluck. A third encounter, again by chance, occurs some months later outside a theatre where Gluck's *Armida* is in performance. This time the stranger invites the narrator home, where, he says, he shall *really* hear *Armida.* In a back street they enter an unimpressive house, climb several flights of stairs, and emerge into a dusty but elegant room decorated in the taste of the eighteenth century. The host takes down a volume of Gluck's

works, seats himself at the piano, and plays *Armida,* requesting his
guest to turn the pages at proper intervals. The narrator is amazed to
see pages of totally blank staves and to hear the music played splendidly but with the oddest alterations from the original score. The rapt
musician sings the vocal parts as he plays the altered and intensified
music. When he has finished, the narrator asks in wonder: "Who are
you?" Laying his finger to his lips, the host withdraws to an inner room
where he is absent for some time, and when he returns he is dressed
in full court costume of the eighteenth century. With a strange smile
he announces: "I am the Chevalier Gluck."

The story which occupies the "Third Night" of Odoevskij's *Russian
Nights* is entitled *Opere del Cavaliere Giambatista Piranesi.* A middle-
aged bibliophile is telling a group of persons about an adventure which
befell him in Naples when he was young. In a book-shop one day his
eye caught sight of a curious customer, an elderly man in old-fashioned
French dress and powdered wig, minutely examining the drawings in
a folio edition of the works of the architect Piranesi. (A sentence which
appears only in the 1832 printing lists "Hoffmann's tales and the novels
of Nodier" among the books on the shelves of the shop.) The narrator
peers into the book himself and finally asks the gentleman if he is a
lover of architecture. The old man closes the volume and with a pitying
glance says that he is. The narrator reopens the volume, whereat the
stranger in terror begs him to close it. An impulse of generosity causes
the narrator to offer the old man money to buy the book. A great deal
of money is needed, says the old man, for Mt. Etna must be linked to
Mt. Vesuvius by a huge triumphal arch to serve as entrance-way into
the palace he means to build. He then introduces himself as Giambatista Piranesi, author of the folios open before them. But, the narrator
objects, Piranesi died in 1778. (Hoffmann had assumed that *his* readers
would understand that Gluck was long dead, even if they did not recall
the specific year 1787.) Lies and nonsense! retorts the old man, who
now in rambling discourse recounts his life. Originally a pupil of
Michelangelo, that artist had sent him out into the world lest further
study should make him merely an imitator of his master. Since that
day he has wandered the earth, often penniless. Once he met the
Wandering Jew, of whom he declares all reports to be malicious gossip.
He has drawn up fabulous plans for buildings, but emperors and kings,
popes and cardinals, have all rejected them. Just now, from that opened
book, he clearly saw a church built in the middle of the Mediterranean,
one of whose pillars shook its shaggy head at him. Sadly the narrator

gives him a ducat. The old man pockets it eagerly and explains that it is something towards the ten million ducats he is collecting in order to buy up Mont Blanc, which must be razed lest it block the view from his new palace. Therewith he hurries away.

With the substitution of an architect for a musician, and with characteristically Russian reduction to a single episode, Odoevskij has retold *Ritter Gluck*. Characteristic darkening has also made the central figure a hopeless lunatic and poor, while Hoffmann's hero lived in physical comfort, was actually possessed of genius, and from his illusion of being Gluck derived both self-respect and a certain happiness. Critics rightly termed the story Hoffmannian both in 1832 and in 1844.

2. *BEETHOVEN'S LAST QUARTET*

A somewhat more elusive instance is presented by *Beethoven's Last Quartet* (Poslednyj Kvartet Betxovena), the tale which occupies most of the "Sixth Night". At head of the text stands an epigraph from *Rat Krespel*, one of the *Serapionsbrüder* stories which appeared in separate Russian translation in 1830. The rather imperfect translation of the passage is subscribed simply "Hoffmann".[3]

In the spring of 1827 certain musical amateurs are playing over the latest-printed Beethoven quartet and are bewildered and disappointed by the dissonances and unfamiliarly abrupt turns of the music. Unexpectedly the aging, deaf composer enters, listens for a moment, then withdraws to a corner of the room and weeps. A young girl, later identified as a faithful pupil and named only Luiza, comes, takes him by the hand, and leads him home like a child. The core of the story is the long monologue which Beethoven addresses to Luiza, who herself

---

[3] The text from *Rat Krespel* reads: „Nicht einen Augenblick zweifelte ich daran, dass Krespel wahnsinnig geworden, der Professor behauptete jedoch das Gegenteil. 'Es giebt Menschen', sprach er, 'denen die Natur oder ein besonderes Verhängnis die Decke wegzog, unter der wir andern unser tolles Wesen unbemerkbar treiben. Sie gleichen dünn gehäuteten Insekten, die im regen sichtbaren Muskelspiel missgestaltet erscheinen, ungeachtet sich alles bald wieder in die gehörige Form fügt. Was bei uns Gedanke bleibt, wird dem Krespel alles zur Tat.' " The epigraph in Odoevskij's version, whether translated by him or another, reads: "I was sure that Krespel had gone mad, but the Professor asserted the contrary. 'With some people,' said he, 'nature or special circumstances have torn away the veil behind which we quietly occupy ourselves with various extravagances. They are like those insects from which the anatomist removes the membrane and thereby exposes the movement of their muscles. What with us is only thought, is action with Krespel.' "

does not speak again, once they have arrived at his poorly furnished room. The monologue is climaxed by the illusion of the sudden restitution of his hearing. Rushing to the window, he leans out to hear an orchestra playing his music for the final scene of *Egmont*. He stands in ecstasy, recalling the whole dramatic finale of the play. That evening at a splendid Minister's ball a voice is heard to remark: "What a pity! Theatre Music Director Beethoven has died, and they say he doesn't have enough to bury him." But the voice is lost in the crowd. Everyone is listening to two diplomats "who are talking about some quarrel or other that has taken place between someone or other in the palace of some German Prince or other".

The staccato ending is typical of Odoevskij, as is the indignation at unrecognized genius. The static delivery of the monologue is likewise typical, for Odoevskij frequently slighted narrative elements to concentrate on the essential message of his writings. What narrative features the story does have, however, bear a striking resemblance to *Ritter Gluck*! Again the process of simplification common to Russian Hoffmannists has reduced the three encounters of the German characters with their conversations about music to a single episode, that of the quartet-playing amateurs, which is here left as a loose end. The sentimental figure of the girl Luiza, whose sole function is to listen, corresponds to Hoffmann's narrator, who also listened, but who also observed and had emotions of his own. A journey on foot to "an old stone house" located "at the end of the city" brings Beethoven and the girl home, just as the former pair had arrived at a back street and an unimpressive house. In both cases the pairs had mounted dark staircases to upper storeys and an artist's quarters. Again the darkening process common to Russian Hoffmannists has made those quarters a "small stuffy room divided by a partition" (a typically Russian feature!) instead of the dusty elegance of the "Chevalier Gluck's" apartment. In a Russian tale *Beethoven* must live in penury, while Hoffmann's musician, who only *thought* he was Gluck, might live in the charmed mystery of simulated courtly splendor. As for the monologue itself, it corresponds to that tirade about the realm of inspiration which the "Chevalier Gluck" delivered at a different point in Hoffmann's story, but which is here transposed to form the very heart of Odoevskij's work. Beyond the fact, however, that both deal with artistic inspiration, there is no resemblance between the two passages.

The Russianized Beethoven speaks of a symphony that has just come into his mind during the walk home. He will write it with such harmonies as will confound the carping professors of Harmony as well as the pedantic conductors who think him senile. It will be based on "a chromatic melody of twenty kettle-drums", it will contain chords "of a hundred bells" — for bells may "successfully be used in a quiet adagio" —, and in the finale there will be "a battle of drums and rifle fire". (The notion seems to look forward to Čajkovskij's *1812 Overture!*) Herewith Beethoven walks to the piano, no string of which remains unbroken, and plays imagined music, just as the "Chevalier Gluck" had played on his restaurant table as if it were a keyboard. Abstruse fugues in five and six voices form under his hands, until one (soundless) chord makes him pause. It is the seventh chord, to which he dreams of adding many, many more tones. The train of thought carries him to Goethe and to Mephistopheles's *Song of the Flea,* to Michelangelo and the statue of Moses, and finally back to Goethe and the *play* of *Egmont.* Death comes to him in a transport of joy as he visualizes the final action of the drama. In a total and deliberate confusion of the arts, a favorite Lovers of Wisdom concept, the author, whose own inspiration is Beethoven's *Egmont* music, makes the character Beethoven assume the heroic stance and destiny of Goethe's dramatic figure.

The results of Odoevskij's efforts are more bizarre than pleasing, and his Beethoven is neither humanly nor musically acceptable. Nevertheless, the story represents the influence of Hoffmann, whether written directly from *Ritter Gluck* or only from a submerged memory of *Ritter Gluck.*

3. *SEBASTIAN BACH*

Probably because it deals with a musician-hero, critics also tended to see the influence of Hoffmann in the story *Sebastian Bach,* which occupies the entire "Eighth Night" of *Russian Nights.* The original publication date of 1835 removes this work somewhat from the core-period of Russian Hoffmann-mania, 1830—1833, where the former two stories fell, and of Hoffmann there is indeed no trace.

Written as a glorification of Bach at a time when, as a footnote explains, that composer was all but unknown in Moscow, the story is told by a fifty-year-old gentleman who stresses the fact that an artist's true biography is to be read in his artworks alone. For all of that, his narrative is made up largely of external facts, beginning with the prosy statement: "The Bach family made itself known in Germany around the middle of the XVIth century." Some effort is made to depict Bach as one member of a whole clan of artists, all of whose lives were marked with spiritual harmony. The childhood of the composer is recounted, including the inevitable episode of the forbidden music copied in secret from his stern guardian-brother. A vision of choiring angels is vouchsafed to the youth when he falls asleep inside the organ of the Eisenach church during a nocturnal visit of exploration. For a time the vision is negated by a pedantically rationalistic teacher, but it is revived under the influence of his next teacher, the wise, good, poetic-souled Johann Albrecht of Lüneburg, whose long speech about the *language* of music sounds rather like Wackenroder's essay *Von zwei wunderbaren Sprachen*. The latter third of the story strays into mere enumeration of Bach's travels and successes, with a hasty but approving glance cast at his tranquil marriage with Albrecht's daughter Magdalena. A protracted final episode introduces the dangerous charms of the traveling Venetian musician, Francesco Cesti, who by his music and by his handsome presence brings Magdalena to the verge of a purely spiritual adultery. He leaves the household in good time, however, and Magdalena recovers from her heart's distraction, while Bach adapts Cesti's new *canzone* to make parts of the *Well Tempered Clavichord*. Old age and peaceful death conclude his life.

Any source in Hoffmann's works is out of the question, but the reference to Wackenroder provides the clue to the real source. Not only is Albrecht's doctrine of the language of music a free adaptation of *Von zwei wunderbaren Sprachen,* but the figure of Albrecht himself is conceived in terms of Wackenroder's portrait of Albrecht Dürer in one of his contributions to *Phantasien über die Kunst,* the essay entitled *Schilderung wie die alten deutschen Künstler gelebt haben, wobei zu Exempeln angeführt werden Albrecht Dürer nebst seinem Vater Albrecht Dürer dem Alten*. The attempt at a depiction of the inner artist's life of the young Bach, in turn, owes much to the first of the two pieces which Wackenroder wrote under the title of *Das merkwürdige musikalische Leben des Tonkünstlers Joseph Berglinger,* which Odoevskij's close personal friend and fellow Slavophile, Ševyrëv, had translated for the *Moscow Telegraph* (IX) in 1826 under the title: *Remarkable and Musical Life of the Artist Joseph Berglinger* (Primečatel'naja i muzikal'naja žizn' xudožnika Iosifa Berlingera) (sic). The translation of 1826 repeated the common error of the time of attributing these works to Tieck, who edited them in 1799 and in 1814 and who was, in fact, co-author of the volumes. Odoevskij's story, it may be remarked, is rather heavy-handed by comparison with the "Giotto-esque" impressionism of Wackenroder.

4. *THE IMPROVISOR*

With *The Improvisor* (Improvizator), the tale of the "Seventh Night", the problem of the artist is approached in different terms. The story relates the misfortunes of Cipriano (Kiprijano) a young poet who, in despair at his artistic failures, has recourse to the mage Segeliel' and receives from him the gift of omniscience. The pact concluded, Cipriano finds himself able not only to write poetry but to improvise it on the spur of the moment. In fact, he gives public performances at which he dictates and simultaneously recites verses of the most varied kinds, tender, passionate, humorous, satirical, so that different sectors of his audiences are at one and the same time moved respectively to tears, ardor, laughter, and rage. But while he may command all emotions in others, Cipriano himself remains utterly impassive. Omniscience has withered all poetic feeling in him. Affairs have already reached this stage when the story begins, and the opening section describes one of Cipriano's improvisations. The compact with Segeliel' and the disastrous revelations to the hero's all-seeing eyes are presented only in retrospect. In the final paragraph the hitherto unmentioned narrator states that he came across Cipriano on the estate of a remote landowner, where the unfortunate youth filled the office of jester. With tears Cipriano recounted to him his life story, adding that his bitterest cross was the fact that everyone laughed at his one precious possession, his hapless but wholly sincere early verses to his beloved.

Hardly a narrative at all, but rather the analysis of a certain situation, *The Improvisor* produces an effect unlike that of a Hoffmann story. The characters, however, of the young poet and the half-supernatural mage are patently Hoffmannian types. The poet's beloved Charlotte — a German name — can hardly be reckoned a character since she appears only in a single paragraph of indirect report. If this pair of figures, poet-hero and villain mage, be dipped for a moment, as it were, in a chemical wash to remove the coating of sorrow and evil from them, they will be seen to approximate the male principals of *Der goldene Topf,* the student Anselmus who aspired to Art, and the potent master of the land of Art, Archivarius Lindhorst.

Anselmus was there portrayed in his struggle to become a poet. Against him the forces of Philistinism waged furious battle to make of him a conventional husband, bread-winner, government official, and man of common sense, but through the power of love he won his way to the enchanted land of poetry, to "Atlantis", where he was happy in a state which stolid burghers were pleased to name "madness". His apprenticeship to poetry and wonder was served in the fantastic house of Archivarius Lindhorst. There, amid speaking birds and moving flowers, in rooms where every object was enchanted and every orna-ment was a symbol full of meaning, he went daily to copy magic manu-scripts, many of them in the finest Arabic script, which Lindhorst took down for him from the shelves of his library .The lore of these manu-scripts was the lore of Beauty.

Cipriano also aspired to poetry and in all good faith went to Segeliel' for enlightenment. What he received was soul-destroying scientific knowledge in intolerable excess. Indeed, he actually witnessed the mass of it as it formed to invade his mind. Segeliel, after pronouncing the fateful spell over him, with one hand placed on the poet's head and the other upon his heart, had caused the youth to step out of the room. Then he had cried: "Pepe! The frieze cloak!" — "Ahu!" had come the cry from all the shelves of the library "as in the 2nd act of *Freischütz*". Cipriano, peeping through the keyhole, had then beheld all the books on all the shelves in motion:

... from one of them leaped out the figure 8, from another the Arabic Alif, and then the Greek delta: and more and more, until finally the room was filled with lively figures and letters. They stooped con-vulsively, grew longer, swelled up, interlaced their awkward legs, jumped and fell. A countless number of dots circled around them like infusoria in a solar microscope, and an old Chaldean polygraph beat time with such force that the frames rattled in the windows ...

In countless permutations these characters penetrated his mind until he "knew all, understood all", and could not endure the knowledge.

The Anselmus-Lindhorst pair, however, is not the sole example of poet-client and master-mage in Hoffmann's works. *Klein Zaches* offers their parallel in the student Balthasar and Prosper Alpanus, whose common opponent, the repulsive dwarf Zaches, had been endowed with magical powers whereby all other persons' achievements seemed to be his. It was to seek help against this "omniscient" little monster that Balthasar came to Prosper Alpanus' country villa, and in that ideal mansion he beheld a collection of books whose illustrations came alive and moved in miniature forms about the marble table-top. For Prosper Alpanus, like Lindhorst, was a mighty wizard and a profound knower of Nature. And all the servants in his mansion were enchanted animals.

In short, we are confronted with one of Hoffmann's doublet-motifs, and the sparseness of Odoevskij's scenario, indeed the near-absence of any scenario at all, makes it uncertain which story, *Der goldene Topf* or *Klein Zaches,* was the model. Segeliel' could be with equal plausibility an evil transformation of either mage. All three, Segeliel', Lindhorst, and Prosper Alpanus, inhabit apparently conventional mansions which are in reality arenas of magic; all three control mysterious libraries that determine the heroes' fates; all three are at war with society, the latter two contending against Philistinism, the former against all spiritual order; all are far-traveled, Lindhorst to "Atlantis", Segeliel' and Prosper Alpanus to "India"; all impart their vast lore to selected clients; all are bestowers of the gift of poetry upon youthful aspirants.

But before we seek to account for the wholly evil nature of Segeliel' in the face of these supremely benevolent mages, still another Hoffmann analogue suggests itself. When Cipriano begins to sense the full horror of omniscience he rushes to his dear Charlotte for consolation. To his horror he finds that his microscopic vision beholds his beloved as a grotesque anatomical conglomeration: her lovely eyes are a kind of *camera obscura* device, her lovely complexion is a mere sheath over reticulated nerves and veins, her very heart is a machine. In *Meister Floh* Peregrinus Tyss receives from Master Flea a tiny microscopic lens which enables him to read the thoughts of interlocutors. Near the end of the "Third Adventure" (chapter) he applies the lens to his eye while in conversation with the deceitful Mr. Swammer.

Behind the cornea of Swammer's eyes he perceived curious nerves and filaments, whose wondrously tangled course he was able to follow far into the brain and to discern Swammer's thoughts.

The thoughts prove to be very different from the honied sentiments being voiced by Mr. Swammer. A chapter later Peregrinus applies the same lens to observe the little lady, Dörtje Elverdink:

As usual, (he) saw beyond the cornea the strange network of nerves and veins which penetrate into the depths of the brain. But through that network were intertwined brightly shining silver threads a hundred times more delicate than the most delicate of spiderwebs, and precisely these strands, which seemed to be endless, as they branched forth out of the brain into Something inaccessible even to the microscopic eye, entangled thoughts of a more sublime kind with others of a variety more readily comprehensible . . .

It may be mentioned further that the first application of the lens to Peregrinus' eye had transformed Master Flea himself from a tiny dot into the scaly monster which seventeenth century microscopes first revealed to human sight and the labeled diagrams of which served as the basis for Hoffmann's description of his insect "character". Thus Cipriano's horrendous vision of Charlotte seems to be a transformation, appropriately realistic and pessimistic, of a motif from *Meister Floh*.[4] If this conclusion is correct, Odoevskij displayed more interest in the great Märchen as a group than had been shown by other Russian Hoffmannists.

Meanwhile the conversion of benevolent to evil mage remains unaccounted for. Such a reversal is characteristically Russian, to be sure, but one wonders whether some specific work was used in combination with the sources mentioned. The malignant nature of Coppelius in *Der Sandmann,* for example, could have been attributed to the Lindhorst-Alpanus figure to give a result very like Segeliel'. Yet recollections of *Melmoth the Wanderer* (see pp. 147-148 below) would have done the same, and it is further necessary to recall that later in *Russian Nights* Segeliel' is identified with Satan himself. Again the static quality of *The Improvisor* makes a final demonstration impossible, so that only the provenience of mage and poet-client as types is certain.

5. WHO ARE MADMEN?

The four works just considered, it will be recalled, were all originally intended to form part of a collection to be named *The House of*

---

[4] By virtue of his orientation toward German Romantic ideologies, Odoevskij was understandably antipathetic toward classical French literature. His political and social conservatism made him dislike the contemporary French Romantic writers even more. Yet, as Sakúlin, *op. cit.,* p. 380, points out, there is the following astonishing parallel between *The Improvisor* and Eugène Sue's *La Salamandre. Roman maritime*, 1832, p. 50: "Pour un moment, il devint comme ce fou dont parle je ne sais quel poète, qui, possédé par le démon du savoir, ne voyait plus la peau délicate et rosée de la femme, ses yeux purs et transparents, sa chevelure de soie . . . non, cette ravissante enveloppe lui échappait . . . mais de son regard aigu et acéré il découvrait les veines sanglantes qui se croisaient sous cette peau, les nerfs qui agitaient ces yeux, les muscles rouges qui faisaient mouvoir ce corps. Horreur! Là il ne voyait plus qu'un cadavre animé." Published as it was in 1832, Sue's novel could have been known to Odoevskij, though his dislike of this author in particular makes it seem problematical that the parallel is anything more than a coincidence.

Madmen, and for that unrealized project a foreword was prepared, entitled *Who are Madmen*? An essential segment of that foreword passed, like the stories, to *Russian Nights,* where it is given as part of the frame-tale discussion of the "Second Night". There we are confronted with the earnest question of what *is* the difference between madness and genius, and, through Faust, the principal speaker of the frame-tale quartet of speakers, Odoevskij proposes that there is in reality very little difference. How is distinction to be made, for instance, between a lunatic who fancies that he is stationary and that all objects move about him, and Ptolemy who declared the earth was stationary amid moving planets? Columbus' America was considered the dangerous delusion of a maniac, as was Harvey's circulation of the blood, as was Fulton's claim for the use of steam power. So too with all poets, for they must seek Truth through "magic exaltation" (magičeskaja vostoržennost'), and, as one of Faust's friends remarks: Humani generis mater nutrixque profecto *dementia* est.

Very much the same point is made by Serapion-Brother Cyprian at the very opening of *Die Serapionsbrüder,* less by head-on "philosophical" debate than by that untitled story of Count P.** who dwelt in the forest near the south German city of "B." (Bamberg), claiming he was the very Serapion who suffered martyrdom for his Christian faith under the Emperor Decius and calmly demonstrating to his would-be rescuer that the latter could not *prove* the claim to be false. The brethren were much impressed by the tale and named their club for its hero. That opening story of the four-volume collection also permitted Hoffmann to state the "Serapiontic principle" upon which so many of the subsequent stories depended, the principle of irony and of the "felicity of madness".

We are strongly tempted to say at this point that *The House of Madmen,* planned 1831—1835, was conceived as a "philosophical" variant of *Die Serapionsbrüder,* with frame-tale speakers, with story insets about "madmen", and with *Who are Madmen*? for its foreword, this last being both by contents and by position the equivalent of the story Cyprian told about "Serapion". The following chronology of events suggests that the project was abandoned and merged with the separately planned *Russian Nights,* presumably for being too obviously Hoffmannian, in the latter 1830's when Hoffmannism was so rapidly declining in prestige: (a) in 1836 *The Moscow Observer* printed *Russian Nights. First Night,* essentially identical with the final text of 1844, and followed it with the words "To be continued"; (b) evidence shows that in 1837 Odoevskij was still planning *The House of Madmen* separately; (c) some time around 1840 a junction of the two projects was made, with both sections of frame-tale debates and story-insets transferred to *Russian Nights*. Against such a conclusion stands the emphatic disclaimer already quoted from the author's foreword to the second edition of *Russian Nights* (1862; first published 1913). Before forming a final opinion on this matter it is desirable to consider the *Russian Nights* collection itself.

6. *RUSSIAN NIGHTS*

The frame-tale. — The preface to the 1862 reissue of *Russian Nights* states that the frame-tale was conceived in the 1820's as the equivalent of the ancient Greek chorus in a new art-form which should be an adequate synthesis of the inadequate modern drama and the inadequate modern novel. In meditation upon the rise and fall of nations throughout history, Odoevskij conceived four elements which must coexist in any durable culture: Knowledge, Art, Love, and Faith. In history he felt he discerned how each of these four elements had been preponderant in turn: Knowledge in pre-Homeric times, Art from Homer to Christ, Love from Christ to the present, and Faith in the era now beginning. The predominance of Faith in the new era explains the concern of the frame-tale speakers with "the new science" and "the new art". The author's manuscript Notebook No. 24, page 79, lists five proposed frame-tale speakers together with the aspect of life which each was to embody: Faust-Knowledge, Viktor-Art, Vjačeslav-Love, Vladimir (the author's own given name)-Faith, and "I"-"Russian skepticism". The completed *Russian Nights* omits the "I" and makes the four remaining characters embody somewhat different concepts: Faust is a "mystic"; Viktor, his most frequent challenger, is a rationalist ("Condillacist"); Rostislav (formerly named Vladimir) is a Schellingian (as Odoevskij himself had been); and Vjačeslav is a genial Voltairean. The philosophic issues which arise claim to deal with the nature of Man, in which context Viktor is a "utilitarian", an admirer of Adam Smith, and a Westernizer, while Faust — who most often speaks with the author's voice — is a Slavophile. The nine "Nights" of readings and debate culminate in the Epilogue, which is an impassioned plea for the Slavophile vision of Russia as the bearer of highest culture to coming ages.

The story insets. — About half of the total of story insets in *Russian Nights* is composed by the five pieces transferred from the abandoned project of *The House of Madmen:* (1) *Who are Madmen?* (Second Night), which is at the very least analogous to the Serapion story at the head of the *Serapionsbrüder* collection; (2) *Piranesi* (Third Night), which is certainly derived from *Ritter Gluck*; (3) *Beethoven's Last Quartet* (Sixth Night), which also betrays influence from *Ritter Gluck;* (4) *The Improvisor* (Seventh Night), whose major figures are surely adapted from *Der goldene Topf* or from *Klein Zaches* or from both; and (5) *Sebastian Bach* (Eighth Night), which we feel is related to Wackenroder without any perceptible admixture of Hoffmann.

Six short pieces, all significantly less fantastic and more "social" in quality, are read aloud by Faust from a notebook entitled *The Economist* in the course of the Fourth Night: *The Brigadier* (Brigadir), in which a ghost laments a life lived with no emotions whatsoever; *The Ball* (Bal), which contrasts grandiose concert music with simple, devout prayer; *The Avenger* (Mstitel'), which sketches aspects of a man given to Byronic Satanism; *A Corpse's Mockery* (Nasmeška mertveca), which confronts a heartless lady with her suicide lover; and *The Last Suicide* (Poslednee Samoubijstvo), which presents a vision of Malthus' over-populated earth transformed into a single vast megapolis where "benevolence became libertarianism, mockery of life the customary greeting, and love a crime"; and *Cecilia* (Cecilija), a brief sketch about the consoling power of music and a tribute to its patroness-saint. This last suggests a Hoffmann affinity but no Hoffmann influence, while the five other pieces are remote from Hoffmann's manner.

The longer tale of the "Fifth Night", *The City without a Name* (Gorod bez imeni), is concerned with a future time when disaster has wrecked a "city without a name" that had been founded by Jeremy Bentham and which had existed solely according to the principle of utility. Aagain the topic is wholly alien to Hoffmann.

The Epilogue. — In the closing pages of the "Ninth Night" the central figures from all the story insets are brought together in the presence of a High Judge to whom each must make a final statement of intention and error. There "Piranesi" admits that he so intensely cultivated the self that he lost sight of humanity; Bach negated the self utterly for the sake of Art; Beethoven attempted to found the soul of man in tone and failed from the incommunicability of emotion (!); Cipriano bartered his very life for knowledge, only to perish from it.

When Segeliel' is brought in he defies the court's jurisdiction and asserts that nothing exists except the ego. To him the Judge replies: "Defendant! Thou concealest thyself from me. I see thy symbols — but thee, thee I do not see. Where art thou? Who art thou? Answer me!" Whereat a "Voice in Bottomless Depths" cries: "For me there is no adequate expression!" In short, Segeliel' is Satan, or at least a major fallen angel. (Data pertaining to an unfinished story called *Segeliel'* of 1832 clearly show him to be derived from Klopstock's Abbadona via Žukovskij's translation of the "Abbadona episode" from *Der Messias.*) Whether this Last Judgment scene formed part of the plan for *The House of Madmen* is unknown.

Surveyed then in its totality, *Russian Nights* is an impressive if tendentious prose poem of fundamentally political nature in advocacy of Slavophile doctrines and Belinskij was in error in terming it Hoffmannian. Its quality as a miscellaney is emphasized by the inclusion in the Epilogue of such items as a refutation of Čaadaev's famous *Première Lettre Philosophique* of 1836 and a comment on President Martin van Buren's Inaugural Address of March 4, 1837. Odoevskij's remarks of 1862 relative to the non-Hoffmannian evolution of the work are no doubt perfectly true, but within the miscellaney there were included in 1844 those five components from the abandoned *House of Madmen,* four of which we agree with Belinskij in identifying as Hoffmann-inspired. Indeed, we feel that the over-all plan of that earlier frame-tale work *was* an imitation of *Die Serapionsbrüder,* even if *Russian Nights* was not. In his foreword of 1862 Odoevskij may have felt that the *Russian Nights* context had so altered the *House of Madmen* components that they were no longer connected with the Tales of Hoffmann; or perhaps he simply did not remember their influence upon him in the early 1830's, three decades previous, though it is somewhat odd that he should so well recall his plans of the 1820's and be so vague as to his literary procedures of the 1830's. In any case, a certain fraction of the final work is of Hoffmannian origin, more than the 1862 foreword would seem to allow but less than Belinskij's opinion claimed.

7.   *VARIEGATED TALES*

The composition of those Hoffmannian segments of *Russian Nights* dated from the early 1830's, as we have said. Contemporaneous with them was Odoevskij's smaller collection of 1833, entitled *Variegated Tales* (Pëstrye Skazki). In the original printing [5] this charming little book is rarely prized as the first Russian work to appear in de luxe form for the public trade. Taking the adjective of the title literally, the title page prints its lines of text in rainbow hues and each letter of the prominent word SKAZKI (Tales) in a different color. Excerpting the book for Volume III of the *Works* of 1844, Odoevskij condescended to *Variegated Tales* as a mere jest providing opportunity for experiment with fine editions and with the novel idea of woodcut illustrations. Actually, the little pieces are more durable than some of the author's more sombrely ambitious works.

Two whimsical prefaces open the 1833 version, one by the "Editor", V. Bezglasnij, and one by the "Author", Irenej Modestovič Gomozejko — both pen names of Odoevskij —, and following these there is a frame-tale entitled *The Retort* (Retorta), which, with the *Epilogue,* encloses eight other short stories.[6] The narrator of *The Retort* is pictured as a guest at a splendid ball. Stepping to the window for a breath of fresh winter-night's air, he is puzzled by a large expanse of shiny glass opposite him. It looks like a mirror, yet he knows no mirror can be so large. He goes to the door to investigate, but again he is confronted by the shiny wall. Presently he perceives that the entire house with all its dancing and card-playing guests, and himself, is contained within a

---

[5] *Variegated Tales* with a word in jest, collected by Irinej Modestovič Gomozejko, Master of philosophy and member of various learned societies, edited by V. Bezglasnyj (St. Petersburg, 1833). (*Pëstryja Skazki* s krasnym slovcom, sobrannyja Irineem Modestovičem Gomozejkoju, Magistrom filosofii i členom raznyx učënyx obščestv, izdannyja V. Bezglasnym, Sanktpeterburg, 1833.)

[6] The contents of the little book are as follows:

(a) *Editor's Preface* (Predislovie Izdatelja).

(b) *Author's Preface* (Predislovie Sočinitelja). 1. *The Retort* (Retorta), 2. *The Tale of the Dead Body that Belonged to No One Knew Whom* (Skazka o mërtvom tele neizvestno komu prinadležaščem). 3. *The Life and Adventures of One of the Local Inhabitants in the Glass Jar, or the New Jocko* (*A Classical Tale*). Žizn' i poxoždenija odnogo iz zdešnix obyvatelej v stekljannoj banke, ili Novyj Žoko (klassičeskaja povest'). 4. *The Tale about how Collegiate Councillor Ivan Bogdanovič Otnošenie was Unable to Offer Holiday Greetings to his Superiors on Easter Sunday* (Skazka o tom, po kakomu slúčaju Kolležskomu Sovetniku Ivanu Bogdanoviču Otnošeniju ne udalos' v Svetloe Voskresenie pozdravit' svoix načal'nikov s prazdnikom). 5. *The Igoša* (Igoša). 6. *Just a Tale* (Prosto skazka). 7. *The Tale of How Dangerous it is for Girls to Walk in Groups on the Nevskij Prospekt* (Skazka o tom, kak opasno devuškam xodit' tolpoju po Nevskomu Prospektu). 8. *The Same Tale, Only Reversed* (Ta že skazka, tol'ko na izvorot). 9. *The Wooden Guest, or The Tale of the Awakened Doll and the Nodding Gentelman* (Derevjannyj gost', ili Skazka ob očnuvšejsja kukle i Gospodine Kivakele). 10. *Epilogue* (Epilog).

glass retort. An imp out of hell has scooped them all up, put them into his bottle, and is bringing the bottle down over a flame preparatory to distilling society. When the narrator manages to scramble out of the neck of the retort, he is seized by the five-year old imp, whose tail has barely sprouted, and tossed by him into a Latin dictionary, where, wriggling and crawling on a journey more arduous than Captain Parry's, he meets fellow captives. From each of these he hears a story which now will be retold.

The section of the 1844 *Works* captioned *Excerpts from Variegated Tales* omits both prefaces and this frame-tale, as well as item 3, which is a grotesque autobiography of a spider, item 6, called *Just a Tale* (Prosto skazka), and item 10, the Epilogue. The sad trials of the spider with poverty, love, and above all his cannibalistic father, show Odoevskij in a satirical vein, his target being, as the subtitle ". . . or The New Jocko" indicates, those orang-utan extravagances of Parisian Romanticism which "Pogorel'skij" had taken seriously enough to imitate them in *The Journey by Stagecoach*. The satirical animal-autobiography suggests an imitation of the feline autobiography by Hoffmann's Philistine Tom-cat Murr, all the more so because in 1836 Odoevskij published, under the pseudonym of "Uncle Irenej", a rather mediocre fairytale for children, entitled *Letters to a Very Dear Uncle, Mr. Kater von Murr, from his Dutiful Nephew Kotovas'ka* (Pis'ma k ljubeznejšemu djadjuške Gospodinu Kateru fon Muru ot ego počtitel'nago plenjanika Kotovas'ki). Relegated to a wholly different section of the 1844 *Works* is item 5, *The Igoša*, a most interesting story of a small boy's irrational fancy as he adapts a half-understood anecdote of his father's to create an imaginary scapegoat, the "Igoša", for his mischievous actions. The remaining five items are reproduced in the *Works* in a new order.

No. 4, *The Tale about how Collegiate Councillor Ivan Bogdanovič Otnošenie was Unable to Offer Holiday Greetings to his Superiors on Easter Sunday,* presents, with a wit to rival Gogol's, a forty-year-old official in the minutely ordered round of his small existence. On Easter Eve his invariable Saturday night card game produces such extraordinary hands that he fails to hear his mother's warning about the advanced hour. Not even the three shots fired by the dawn cannon are heard by the intent players. When finally they sense the Easter dawn and blow out the candles, a fearful shock tumbles them from their seats. The playing-card Queens sit in the straight chairs, the Kings in the armchairs, the Aces on the divans, and the Jacks (valets) parade about the room. Ivan Bogdanovič's mother returns from Mass to find her son and his guests stunned and sprawling in various attitudes upon the floor.

No. 2, *The Tale of the Dead Body that Belonged to No One Knew Whom,* is a highly amusing portrait of a slow-witted rural clerk baffled by a problem unanticipated by any manual of instructions. A traveler, so cold one night that he was afraid his soul would freeze, slipped out of his body, piled the body into the carriage, left the horse to find its own way, and hurried on ahead to the inn to get warm. Horse, carriage, and "corpse" went somehow astray, and the disembodied spirit has come to the clerk for legal assistance. The spectral visit proves a dream, but an unidentified frozen corpse *was* buried by the local officials.

No. 7, *The Tale of how Dangerous it is for Girls to Walk in Groups on the Nevskij Prospekt,* is an allegory. Eleven pretty girls on a stroll with their nurses enter a store and purchase expensive trinkets. Upon leaving, the nurses, who can count only to ten, fail to notice that one girl has been left behind. This unfortunate, tarrying, is captured by the wicked sorcerer who makes girls into mannequins. At thirteen o'clock, when all the mannequins come to life, up pops a brainless French Head from the powder-box, up springs a delicate German Nose from the tobacco-box, and an English Belly emerges from the soda-water bottle. At the sorcerer's directions this trio now concocts an unholy brew in a retort, into which they throw several novels by Mme de Genlis, Chesterfield's *Letters,* Italian trills, new contradances, and other items, spiced finally with handfuls of Petersburg air with bits of conversation in it and a sheaf of diplomatic correspondence. They extract the Slavonic Beauty's heart, steep it in the brew, and replace it. Then, with a little *rouge végétal,* some *lait de concombre,* a mouth-shaping machine, and tight-laced corseting, she becomes a perfect doll. A young man admires her, buys her, finds out that she is alive, and falls in love with her. Try as she will, however, she cannot learn to speak except in the words of others. She grows ill-tempered, and finally her tantrums about clothes so distress him that he throws her out the window.

No. 8, *The Same Tale, Only Reversed,* is an essay which serves as a miniature frame-tale to introduce No. 9, *The Wooden Guest, or The Tale of the Awakened Doll and the Nodding Gentleman.* A Hindu sage, finding the inert doll, breathed into her the poetry of Byron, Deržavin, and Puškin, and brought her to life. She married a monster on whom she had taken pity, but he was so stupid that he could only nod his head at whatever she said. He smoked a pipe and often asked about horses. She pined away for grief, and in the end the ill-tempered boor threw her out the window.

Polevoj's unexpectedly hostile review in the *Moscow Telegraph* attacked *Variegated Tales* as cold allegories of dull ideas while purporting to be works in the new fantastic vein that required the reader to think and feel as a poet; they fell far short of Hoffmann, "the loftiest model in this genre". This over-harsh judgment was offset by the review in Baron Rozen's *Northern Flowers,* one of the organs of the Franco-British school of Russian Romanticism, which was full of praise for these "original tales so vividly reminiscent of Hoffmann".[7] Belinskij, writing of *The Igoša,* remarked that "we have reason to think a great influence from Hoffmann was exerted on the fantastic orientation of our gifted author". No one of these contemporary critics makes the relationship to Hoffmann specific. Equally vague are later critics: König (1862), who cites *Variegated Tales* as evidence of Odoevskij's Hoffmannism;[8] N. Putjata (1874), who claims (wrongly) that these imitations of Hoffmann "first acquainted the Russian public with that original writer".[9] Even the meticulous Veselovskij in his book on western influences in Russia states categorically that Odoevskij was "the masterful successor of Hoffmann by virtue of *Variegated Tales* and *Russian Nights*",[10] but he cites no examples.

Affinities with Hoffmann do exist in *Variegated Tales,* but of an odd sort. Anselmus in the "Tenth Vigil" of *Der goldene Topf* found himself contained in a glass bottle, with other prisoners in other glass bottles aligned on the same shelf, though the circumstances were very different from those of *The Retort;* Tom-cat Murr wrote his ironic autobiography in *Kater Murr,* but it is a far cry from the career of Odoevskij's spider; the opening pages of *Der Sandmann* vividly tran-

---

[7] See Sakulin, *op. cit.,* pp. 32—35 for a description of the press reactions to *Vagiegated Tales.*

[8] König, *Literarische Bilder aus Russland* (SPb, 1862), pp. 153—156; pp. 154—155. "For some time (Odoevskij) wrote fantastic tales in the manner of Hoffmann, in which he showed himself an imitator of him in form rather than content." Cited by Sakulin, *op. cit.,* p. 348.

[9] N. Putjata, "Kn. V. F. Odoevskij", in *Russki Arxiv,* 1874, Kniga I, p. 259. "(Odoevskij) published his *Variegated Tales* and by their imitation of Hoffmann first acquainted the Russian public with that original writer." Cited by Sakulin, p. 348.

[10] Veselovskij, *Zapadnye Vlijanija v Novoj Russkoj Literature,* p. 235. Cited by Sakulin, p. 348.

scribe a small boy's fears, and monstrous distortions inspired by the evil Coppelius haunt his dreams, but the armless, legless Igoša is the waking invention of a mischievous little boy and, though wicked enough, has nothing of the evil horror of Coppelius; the infernal spell of the playing cards is a motif in Hoffmann's *Spielerglück* as well as in that section of *Die Elixiere des Teufels* where Medardus plays faro at court, but in both cases the infernal spell is the daemonic extension of human passions and brings the characters under the control of awesome Powers of Evil; the mechanical doll Olimpia in the central episode of *Der Sandmann* was, in part, the author's satire on heartless salon belles, but the illusion of her womanhood was of far more complex significance than the nationalistic allegory of the doll-*like* Slavonic Beauty in the Nevskij Prospekt store.

Story-wise there are no parallels with Hoffmann's works at all, for even in these anecdotal pieces Odoevskij dwells on analysis rather than on narrative. His typical procedure is to begin with a generalized essay on manners, out of which the anecdote emerges by way of example. The point of departure in most of these pieces is a topic, a motif, a situation, isolated from its original Hoffmannian context and dwelt upon for its own usefulness in making plain an issue in morals. The sheer number of these motifs is significant in a book of such small compass, but what is even more significant is the fact that all of them occur in works of Hoffmann that had recently been translated into Russian and hence were popularly known in the early 1830's. This profusion of Hoffmannian motifs in *Variegated Tales* is, moreover, contemporaneous with the plan and partial writing of *The House of Madmen*. Decidedly, Odoevskij was *now* familiar with more than *Das Majorat,* whatever may have been the case in the 1820's when *Russian Nights* was first conceived. The treatment accorded these numerous motifs in *Variegated Tales* is entirely independent and the results far more pleasing than the author in later years was willing to allow.

8. MISCELLANEOUS WORKS

Of Odoevskij's miscellaneous tales for which Hoffmann has repeatedly been cited as the inspiration, the odd double story *Salamandra* [11] offers

[11] *Salamandra,* as printed in Volume II of the *Works* of 1844, under *Domestic Conversations* (Domašnye Razgovory) and with date of 1841, consists of two parts:
  1. *The Southern Shore of Finland at the Beginning of the XVIIIth Century* (Južnyj Bereg Finljandii v načale XVIII stoletija), first published in V. Vla-

the least justification for the claim. A scene with a pair of alchemists at an eerie forge-fire in *Der Sandmann* and Archivarius Lindhorst's dual role as human being and Salamander Prince in *Der goldene Topf* are the only points of contact with Hoffmann's Tales.

More defensible is the claim made for *Sylphida*,[12] though, as in the case just referred to, no one of the critics whom Sakulin lists as making the claim saw fit to specify a source. This miniature epistolary novel of 1837 details the adventures of young Mixail Platonovič who goes to the country to claim the estate of a deceased uncle and there becomes simultaneously engrossed in a pretty neighbor girl, Katen'ka, and in his late uncle's cabalistic library. For a time the latter interest prevails and the hero becomes, in everyone's opinion, "mad". He is cured, however, by a regimen of hot baths, wine, and roast beef, and in the end happily marries Katen'ka. It is his invocation of water-spirits that introduces a vaguely Hoffmannesque quality. Daily he drinks water that has stood in the sunlight, as one of his uncle's books had prescribed, and into which

---

dislavlev's almanac *Morning Dawn* (Utrenjaja Zarja), 1841, as an independent story. Its later joining with the second story was an afterthought.

2. *Elsa* (El'za), originally entitled *Salamandra*, was written in 1838 and published as an independent story in *Notes of the Fatherland*, 1841, Part III, pp. 1—38.

The first story relates the adventures of a Finnish war-orphan boy, Jakko, who followed Peter the Great to Russia and became rich and famous. His return home to fetch his sister Elsa, however, brings him misfortune. Not only is Elsa wretchedly homesick in Russia, but strange dream-trances cause her to be feared as a witch. She mysteriously disappears in the midst of a flood in Petersburg, but Jakko discovers that she returned to her peasant village and married her fellow-countryman Jusso.

The literary connections are patently with Puškin's romance *The Negro of Peter the Great*, with Walter Scott's novels, and with the Songs of Ossian.

In the second story, Jakko, now married to a nagging Russian wife, has come upon evil days since the death of Peter the Great and is seeking his fortune through alchemy. In his laboratory forge-fire Elsa appears to him in the form of a salamander and promises to come to him soon with help. She comes presently in human form, destroys both Jakko's wife and his wealthy patron,

The first story relates the adventures of a Finnish war-orphan boy, Jakko, palace burns mysteriously, killing all inhabitants.

Sakulin, *op. cit.*, p. 349, cites three critics, each of whom mentions *Salamandra* as evidence of Odoevskij's Hoffmannism without adducing any specific source: Nikolaj Mizko, *Stoletie Russkoj slovesnosti* (Odessa, 1849), p. 328; N. F. Sumcov, *Knjaz' V. F. Odoevski* (Xar'kov, 1884), p. 25; and I. A. Kubasov, *Kn. V. F. Odoevskij*, pp. 55—56. The only possible connection would be with *Der goldene Topf*, where Archivarius Lindhorst is a Salamander-Prince and where there is vengeance by fire, but the connection is tenuous.

[12] *Sylphida* (Sil'fida), first published in *The Contemporary*, 1837, No. 1, with censor's date of Nov. 11, 1836; republished in Volume II of the *Works* of 1844, under *Domestic Conversations*.

a turquoise ring has been cast. The ring dissolves, blue and golden
sparks fill the water, a rose forms, and amid its unfolding petals is seen
a water-sprite. What Mixail Platonovič ultimately beholds in the "sun-
water" is a series of visions of a land of beauty and wisdom and poetry.
His utter abstraction as he contemplates the water indicates how near
the nixie is to possessing him entirely when his rationalistic neighbors
and friends intervene to "rescue" him.

Plausible analogies can be made with *Der goldene Topf*, with Mixail
Platonovič standing between the "real" Katen'ka and the "unreal" nixie
much as the student Anselmus stood between the Philistine Christine
Roos and the gold-green Serpentina, daughter of the master-mage
Archivarius Lindhorst. Lack of an Archivarius Lindhorst equivalent
makes the analogy less certain, however, and certainly the outcome of
the story is the reverse of Hoffmann's. Odoevskij, basically a realist
and a pessimist, longed for "Atlantis" and the enchanted marine vision
of *Sylphida*, but he felt such longing *was* a sort of madness and that
the grim here-and-now must be faced with a will born of sad resignation.
Hence Reason and roast beef win the day in this pleasantly light tale
which Sakulin rightly cites as the author's best work in the fantastic
genre. Literarily the story makes free combinations of motifs. The uncle-
nephew detail echoes *Eugene Onegin*, while the water-sprite herself
was probably inspired by Fouqué's *Undine*, which appeared in Russian
translation in 1831 and in Žukovskij's verse adaptation in 1833—1836.
Fragments of a story by Odoevskij, entitled *Undina*, have been preserved.

Finally, Sakulin himself adduces parallels between Hoffmann's
Christmas tale for children, *Nussknacker und Mausekönig* — the basis
for Čajkovskij's *Nutcracker Suite* — and Odoevskij's (uncollected) story
of 1840, called *Kosmorama*.[13] The title refers to a magic toy, a "cosmorama", the gift of eccentric Dr. Bin to the five-year-old Volodja.
The latter, after forgetting about the toy for many years, rediscovers
it in adulthood, to behold in it revelations of himself and of the universe.
Dr. Bin does indeed resemble the half-charming, half-eerie Pate Drosselmeier and the latter's gifts of mechanical toys to children in *Nussknacker und Mausekönig*, but the revelations of the cosmorama, in so
far as we learn of them, are figments of a philosophy to which Schelling contributed considerable but Hoffmann nothing at all.

The greater parts of Volumes II and III of the works collected in

---

[13] *Kosmorama*, 1839, published 1840 in *National Notes*, Vol. VIII. See
Sakulin, *op. cit.*, pp. 82—90; p. 85.

1844 have not been brought into the present discussion for the simple reason that they are totally unaffected by Hoffmann. Their range is wide: from the lurid Italian tale *Imbroglio* to the haunting Christian legend of *The Inevitable House* (Neobojdënnyj dom), which was appropriately dedicated to Žukovskij, and from the experiment in controlled pedagogy of *The Black Glove* (Čërnaja Perčatka) to the uncharacteristically glib journalism of the haunted-house-tale *The Ghost* (Prividenie). Certain aspects of Odoevskij's work are not represented at all in the 1844 volumes, for example, his early historical novels about the Italian Renaissance. More regrettable is the omission of his unfinished Utopian romance, *The Year 4338* (4338-oj god), which tells of a time when the "Deichers" (Germans) are remembered for a few fragments of Goethe, when the English have auctioned off their islands to Russia, when the bankrupt Americans have sold their cities and for lack of other business opportunities have taken to private piracy in China, when China itself has "awakened" and is to Russia what Russia once was to nineteenth century Europe, and when Russia, with supreme culture, manufactures the world's airplanes, electric intercontinental subways, artificial sunlight, "elastic glass" garments, etc., etc.[14] From a strictly literary point of view, Odoevskij's most successful stories are those dealing with high life and his own aristocratic class. The most distinguished of these, the justly admired *Princess Mimi* (Knjažna Mimi), written as early as 1834, portrays unforgettably a self-appointed watchdog of society's morals who destroys romances she is too old to share. In the midst of the Romantic movement the story is a triumph of realism, and indeed the whole course of Odoevskij's evolution as a writer may be described as a slow extrication from introspection and fantasy and a gradual emergence as a social critic.

The influence of Hoffmann on Odoevskij, so broadly claimed by critics, proves upon examination to be elusive. This is not to say that it is non-existent, but it is less prominent than has been alleged. He scarcely deserved being labeled "Hoffmann II". The borrowings are numerous but tiny; treatment of them is original and interesting but static, "philosophical", contemplative, and didactic. From non-Hoffmannian matter he made *stories*; on isolated Hoffmannian motifs he made "meditations"; he never wrote a Hoffmannian *story*. And in the end, like all other Russian Hoffmannists, he abandoned Hoffmann for realism.

---

[14]   See Sakulin, *op. cit.*, pp. 179—200.

V

PUŠKIN, THE INDEPENDENT GENIUS

The great Puškin was born in Moscow but by far the larger part of his life, exiles and travels apart, was centered in Petersburg. From the newer capital he viewed the Russian literary scene in its broadest aspects, maintaining friendly relations with most of the writers in the older city, yet holding aloof from their ideologies. Toward Polevoj, it is true, he felt a certain hostility, though he admired *The Moscow Telegraph* and acknowledged the general superiority of Moscow journals over their Petersburg counterparts.[1] With Prince Odoevskij his relations were more cordial. Of the young Muscovites of the middle 1820's there were two who, had they lived, might have enlisted his more active sympathy for their intellectual position: Venevitinov, who died young, and Küchelbecker, who passed into the living death of Siberian exile after 1825. The latter, transformed to some degree, entered the poem *Eugene Onegin* under the name of Lenskij, the hero's friend. From the portrait there given of him may be deduced what Puškin thought of the Germanizing enthusiasts of his time. Chapter II introduces Lenskij as a handsome youth just returned from the

---

[1] In an article written between 1833 and 1835 but left an unpublished fragment, Puškin wrote: "Moscow journalism beats the journalism of Petersburg. Ševyrëv, Kireevskij, Pogodin, and others have written several essays worthy of standing alongside the best articles of the English *Reviews,* whereas the Petersburg journals judge of literature as of music, of music as of political economy, i.e. at random and any old way, sometimes appositely and keenly, but for the most part superficially and shallowly. German philosophy (he adds), which found in Moscow perhaps too many young adherents, would seem to be beginning to yield to a more practical spirit. None the less, its influence was salutary: it saved our youth from the cold skepticism of French philosophy and took them away from the high-flown and harmful dreams which had such an awful influence on the finest flower of the preceding generation." The succeeding paragraph mentions a most interesting essay, written by a friend who was a "great melancholic", comparing the two capitals. The essay has been unfortunately lost. See A. S. Puškin, *Polnoe Sobranie Sočinenij v šesti tomax* (Moscow-Leningrad, 1935), Vol. VI, edited by Ju. G. Oksman, p. 182, under the editor's title of: *Putešestvie iz Moskvy v Peterburg.*

University of Göttingen in "misty Germany", a disciple of Kant, a devotee of Goethe and Schiller, rich, idealistic, chaste, sentimental, impractical, immensely likeable, and a trifle absurd. As Professor Karpovich once wrote: [2]

By education and natural inclination alike, Puškin in many respects belongs more to the eighteenth century than to the nineteenth century. Unlike so many of his contemporaries, he remained totally unaffected by German idealistic philosophy and allied tendencies in European Romanticism. Even when he spoke of philosophy in history, what he meant was "philosophy" in the sense of Voltaire, not of Schelling.

French models of the eighteenth century were the first models for his writing. English models, notably Byron and Scott, superseded them. Yet in 1834, in the heyday of Russian Hoffmannism, he composed the extraordinary story, *The Queen of Spades,* the uniqueness of which among his works strikes even the most casual reader. In actual fact, however, it was not his first essay in the Hoffmannian genre. Known chiefly to scholars and not included in most editions of his works, there is a predecessor story dating from as early as 1829. Its title is *The Lonely Cottage on Vasil'evskij Island* (Uedinënnyj domik na Vasil'-evskom ostrove).

1. *THE LONELY COTTAGE ON VASIL'EVSKIJ ISLAND*

Puškin had been long dead before the first mention of his authorship of this story was made by Mme A. P. Kern in her memoirs, published in 1859. Only slight attention was given to her statement at the time. Mme Kern, whose recollections tended at moments to be somewhat impressionistic, wrote:

When he [Puškin] decided to be nice, nothing could compare with the brilliance, pungency, and charm of his talk. In one of those moods he gathered us into a circle and told a tale about a devil who rode in a cab to Vasil'evskij Island. The tale was written down from his very words by a certain Titóv and put, apparently, in *Snowdrop* (Pods-nežnik). Puškin was delightful beyond description when he undertook the theme of entertaining and diverting society.

Actually the story was printed, not in *Snowdrop* — Mme Kern had become confused as to flowers —, but in pages 147—217 of the "Prose"

[2]   Michael Karpovich, "Pushkin as an Historian", *Centennial Essays for Pushkin* (Cambridge, Mass., 1937), pp. 185—186.

section of the almanac for 1829, issued as an annual supplement to
Boron Del'vig's magazine, *Northern Flowers* (Severnye Cvety). No
mention was made of Puškin. The piece was signed with Titov's regular
nom de plume: "Tit Kosmokratov".

Not until 1879, fifty years after the publication of the story, did Titov
himself clarify the matter. In a letter to A. V. Golovnin, former
Minister of Popular Education, he made a formal declaration about
the connection between Puškin and "Tit Kosmokratov":

The Lonely Cottage on Vasil'evskij Island: — In a strictly historical
sense this is not a production of Kosmokratov at all, but of Aleksandr
Sergeevič Puškin, who masterfully related this whole devilry of the
lonely cottage on Vasil'evskij Island late one evening at the Karamzins',
to the secret agitation of all the ladies, among whom was Ekaterina
Nikolaevna [Karamzina], who was adored by Puškin himself and by
all of us, and who later became the wife of Prince Pëtr Ivanovič
Meščerskij. The Apocalyptic number 666, the gambler devils who
wagered hundreds of souls on a card and who had horns itching
beneath their tall wigs — the honor of all these inventions and of the
principal thread of the narrative belongs to Puškin. Sitting in the same
room, Kosmokratov overheard. Going home, he could scarcely sleep
all night, and some time later he committed it to paper from memory.
Not wishing, however, to disobey the Old Testament commandment
'Thou shalt not steal,' he went with his notebook to Puškin in the
Demuth Hotel, prevailed upon him to listen to it from beginning
to end, and made use of many of his often memorable corrections.
Then at the urgent desire of Del'vig, he submitted it to *Northern
Flowers.*

The surrender of a literary idea to another writer was not unusual with
Puškin, whose generous nature sought the enrichment of Russian
letters rather than mere personal glory. Puškinian anecdotes, as is well
known, underlie both Gogol's *Inspector General* and his *Dead Souls.*
The aspiring young author of the present instance, Vladimir Pavlovič
Titov, alias "Tit Kosmokratov", was not wholly unworthy of the favor
bestowed upon him. Born in 1807 of an ancient noble family, he had
acquired an unusually fine command of classical languages and literatures at the Noble Pension of the University of Moscow. From 1824 to
1828 he served among the "Archive Youth", where he was a close
friend of Venevitinov, Ivan Kireevskij, M. P. Pogodin, and others. The
latter, as editor of *The Moscow Messenger,* had accepted various
articles from Titov for publication. At Princess Volkonskaja's salon
he had become acquainted with Puškin, with whom he came in contact
again in 1828 when he moved to Petersburg. His literary aspirations

brought him too little success to be persevered in, and during the 1830's he gradually came to realize that government service offered the only practical career for him. By 1839 he was Consul-General of Wallachia and Moldavia. Upon his death in 1891 his appointments had included ambassadorships to Turkey, supervision of the education of the imperial family, and presidency of the Department of Civil and Religious Affairs. To his wide acquaintance he was known as a learned and likeable man. The poet Tjutčev admired him greatly. Posterity, ironically, remembers him as the amanuensis-preserver of an early prose tale of Puškin.

The question remains as to why Puškin should have abandoned this particular story at all. The critic Michael Gorlin has made a plausible suggestion.³ Observing that relatively few supernatural elements mark *The Queen of Spades,* Puškin's only comparable work, he deduces that the author was dissatisfied with the too great abundance of them here and hence was inclined to scrap the story. As it stands, the story is undoubtedly faithful to the scenario of the tale presented by Puškin at the soirée in the home of Historian Karamzin's widow. That it was "written down from his very words", as Mme Kern's memoirs claim, may be doubted somewhat in view of certain stylistically naive passages, but there is no cause for doubting Titov's word that Puškin reviewed the completed manuscript. We may proceed with confidence on the assumption that *The Lonely Cottage on Vasil'evskij Island* is a work of Puškin's and a most interesting experiment of his in the Hoff-mannizing manner. ⁴

The story, unavailable in translation, may be summarized as follows:

In a humble cottage on Vasil'evskij Island, one of the several islands at the mouth of the Neva which comprise parts of Petersburg, lives a genteel widow with her pretty daughter Vera. At irregular intervals they are visited by their cousin Paul, a frivolous young man whom the widow has discounted as a possible husband for Vera. For his part,

³ Michel Gorlin, "Hoffmann en Russie", *Revue de Littérature Comparée,* XV (1935), pp. 60—76; p. 70.
⁴ The text may be found, as edited by Professor S. A. Vengerov, in *Biblioteka Velikix Pisatelej: Puškin* (Petrograd, 1915), Vol. VI, pp. 181—192. Professor Vengerov's notes, pp. 192—194, include the quoted passages from Mme Kern and Titov as well as other information pertinent to the establishment of authenticity. The publication in 1912 of the memoirs of Baron Del'vig, editor of *Northern Flowers,* removed the last possible doubts about the work. See also the article by V. Pisnaja in *Puškin i ego Sovremenniki, XXXI—XXXII* (1927), pp. 19—24.

Paul is principally concerned with the round of pleasures through which he is being guided by his friend Varfolomej (Bartholomew). From the start of the story hints are dropped that indicate that Varfolomej is really a devil in human form on assignment from hell to encompass the ruin of this young scapegrace.

One Sunday, after a riotous Saturday night and after oversleeping the time for Mass, Paul decides to visit his relatives. Unexpectedly Varfolomej appears and insists on coming along. Reluctantly Paul agrees, stipulating that his friend is to lay no snares for Vera's innocence. The girl's first impression is that Varfolomej is an evil man, but as the day wears on he wins the sympathy of both mother and daughter. Other visits follow. And when Varfolomej observes that Paul is becoming all too virtuously interested in his cousin, he urges him to see a bit of high society before committing himself to a life of domesticity.

At a soirée in the home of Countess I., Paul finds the *haut monde* fascinating, obtusely failing to see that the guests are disguised devils. Great wigs cover their horns, full Turkish trousers conceal their malformed legs, and not one of them removes his gloves for fear of revealing his claws. Paul falls madly in love with the Countess, until one evening he overhears her laughing with a particularly odious guest and sneering at his poor pronunciation of French. Furious, Paul leaves vowing never to return.

Meanwhile Varfolomej has captured all of Vera's affections. When Paul indignantly challenges him on this score, the two get into a quarrel. Paul raises his hand to strike his opponent. Instantaneously a mysterious force hurls him across the room and knocks him unconscious. When he revives, he is furious both with his friend and with the Countess, whom he suspects of complicity in his discomfiture.

A tender note from the Countess, however, brings him back to her that very evening. Such is his ecstasy that he wholly disregards a quarrel among the lady's card-playing guests over the number of souls that has been staked. He lives in restless anticipation of a rendezvous which the Countess has promised for eleven o'clock the following night.

The ardent beginning of that tryst is interrupted almost at the outset by an unknown caller who asks to see Paul. When Paul emerges, the caller has vanished. A second and a third knock disturbs the lovers until the young man pursues the retreating figure out of the house and into the snowy night. His quarry eludes him completely and he finds himself knee-deep in snow at a cross-roads outside the city.

Out of nowhere a cab appears. Paul hails it. He rides on and on, coming to no familiar landmark. Suddenly he notices that the cab-number is 666, the number of the Beast in the Apocalypse. He questions the driver but gets no response. Angrily he brings down his cane on the fellow's back. There is a sound of bones striking against bones. The driver turns. His face is a death's-head. In terror Paul makes the Sign of the Cross, whereat a wild laugh is heard, cab and driver vanish, and Paul is left alone in a strange rural spot.

He awakes to find himself in his own bed, tended by his old serving man. Fever and delirium torment him for three days, then he begins to recover. Just then the old cook from Vera's house arrives with word that disaster has come upon the lonely cottage on Vasil'evskij Island.

In the interim much has happened. Vera's mother has been taken ill. Varfolomej has tended her kindly, even supplying her with medicines. Vera began at last to suspect that her mother's illness was fatal and asked Varfolomej whether they had not better send for a priest. He postponed such a step as harmful to the widow, whose disposition had remained cheerful in her sickness. One evening, the same evening as Paul's rendez-vous with the Countess, he left the cottage in search of medicines and on his return learned that a priest had been sent for in his absence. He was furious, but the old woman died before the priest could come. The old servant recalls that she was herself tending the corpse when a profound sleep overcame her. Just afterward Varfolomej attempted, first by persuasion, then by force, to make Vera yield to his passion. The girl fainted, uttering a cry to God for protection as she fell. When the servant roused to her senses, the house was on fire. No water could quench the flames. Before the fire brigade could help it, the cottage burned to the ground with the widow's corpse inside. The priest took Vera and the servant to his own house and has now sent the latter in search of Paul.

Varfolomej vanished without a trace. Paul comforts Vera with the thought of their future happiness together, but the girl withers and dies before the springtime arrives. After her burial Paul withdraws to a remote country estate where he secludes himself like a hermit, dying in the prime of his years.

The framework of *The Lonely Cottage on Vasil'evskij Island* was borrowed, as Gorlin has shown,[5] from Hoffmann's *Datura fastuosa,* which had been translated in *The Moscow Telegraph* in 1826 as *The Botanist* (Botanik). With a thoroughness that negates all possibility of spur-of-the-moment invention on Puškin's part, the outline of the original has been stripped of all the rich and curious detail that made its excellence, with the result that the two works are utterly unlike in tone and manner.

Datura fastuosa was composed by Hoffmann at intervals between January 1818 and July 1821 by way of fulfillment of a promise made to Adalbert von Chamisso, the author of *Peter Schlemihl,* to write a "botanical novel".[6] In fact, Chamisso, who later became Assistant

---

[5]   Gorlin, "Hoffmann en Russie", *op. cit.,* p. 69.

[6]   *Datura fastuosa:* proposed in outline by Chamisso before 1815; written at intervals between January 1818 and July 1821; published a few months after Hoffmann's death in *Taschenbuch für das Jahr 1823. Der Liebe und Freundschaft gewidmet* and again in 1825 in *Die Letzten Erzählungen;* translated as *The Botanist* (Botanik) in *The Moscow Messenger* 1826; used by "Pogorel'skij"

Director of the Berlin Botanical Garden, had himself suggested the outlines of the story before he set out on his three-year journey around the world (1815–1818). The tale thus contrives to place the characters in a "botanical" atmosphere and to establish certain subtle parallels between them and the flowers by which they are surrounded.

A summary of this fine, though neglected, work of Hoffmann will be helpful:

Upon the death of Professor Helms, a botanist, his majestic and beautiful widow, aged in her sixties, warns the student Eugenius that gossipers are speaking evilly of his continued presence in the household after the Professor has died. When he protests that she and her fourteen-year-old adopted daughter Gretchen are his only family and that the greenhouse is his very life, the widow proposes that his only course is to marry her. She hastily adds that they would, of course, continue to live together as mother and son. Despite warnings from his friend Sever against the match, Eugenius marries the widow Helms and lives in perfect tranquillity. He even fights a duel with a loud-mouthed defamer. Sever concludes he has underestimated his friend.

Happiness continues unmarred until Eugenius becomes the crony of a café acquaintance named Fermino Valies, a Spaniard, and a smooth-tongued rascal. Hints are dropped that he may be a devil in human form.

On an evening stroll Eugenius chances upon a fine house with a magnificent garden of rare plants, including a *datura fastuosa* that far surpasses the paltry specimen in his own greenhouse. The next morning a black servant of Valies brings an invitation to visit this very house and garden, which are the property of Angelo Mora, another Spaniard and Valies' master. A kind of fever besets Eugenius all day until it is time to go. At dusk Valies meets him and presents him, not to Mora, but to a ravishingly beautiful Countess Gabriella, apparently Mora's daughter. With her Eugenius strays about the garden in a state of ecstasy. That night erotic dreams confuse his sleep with alternating images of a nameless bride he once saw, of Gretchen, and of Gabriella.

The next day Eugenius' wife, who abhors Valies, receives from him the gift of a *datura fastuosa*. Not long afterward Eugenius himself receives from him a subtle poison which, if placed in the blossoms of the plant, will kill a human being without leaving a trace. For Valies' study includes elaborate chemical equipment and the owner is expert in the mixing of drugs. Soon Valies arranges a midnight rendez-vous between Eugenius and the Countess Gabriella in the conservatory, where there is a great, night-blooming *cactus grandiflorus*, — a plant

---

in 1828 to make the character of Venturino in *The Baleful Consequences of an Unbridled Imagination;* it will be used again, in all probability, by Dostoevskij in 1848 as partial source for *A Christmas Tree and a Wedding.*

which, to judge from *Meister Floh,* connoted to Hoffmann self-annihilating passion. From this rendez-vous Eugenius returns home in frenzy, quarrels with his wife, strews the poison in the blossoms of the *datura fastuosa,* and rushes back to Gabriella.

He arrives to find her in the passionate embrace of Fermino Valies. A scream of rage breaks from him, then he mysteriously sinks to the ground. He wakes to find himself lying in the street, alone. Rushing home to remove the poison from the flowers, he finds that happily neither his wife nor Gretchen has touched them. He loads his pistols and sets out to kill Valies and Gabriella. They, however, have both been arrested, Valies as a disguised Jesuit spy, Gabriella as an Italian carnival dancer impersonating a noblewoman. Their purpose with Eugenius was apparently blackmail.

Some time later, the ailing elderly wife of Eugenius dies, and when Gretchen is about to depart to live with other relatives, he suddenly realizes that he loves her. They are happily united in marriage.

As might be expected, the unique "botanical" features of the story have disappeared in the Puškin-Titov transformation. The setting has been shifted from the genteel upper-middle-class professorial establishment in the midst of an unnamed city — patently Berlin — to the remoter sections of Petersburg. In her new guise as Vera's widowed mother, the widow Helms lacks the striking matronly dignity and mysterious sympathy that made her an extraordinarily attractive character, and has become a colorless woman, a little vain, a little stupid, careless about religious matters, and with just a suggestion of skittishness.[7] Gretchen's transformation is even more regrettable, for Hoffmann's deft portrayal of precocious adolescent love, however briefly conveyed, was a stroke of genius as well as a startling anticipation of twentieth century psychology. Vera is simply an ingénue without a jot of individualization. Pious, sweet, and passive, she could be transferred to hundreds of inferior stories without modification. Nor has Eugenius fared well in the transformation process. Hoffmann had depicted him, as he had Gretchen, with profound insight. He was a youth of sound and noble instincts, coming late to maturity. The very essence of the story was his slow approach to awareness through perils which he saw, dealt with in his own way, not without determination, yet understood only after he had eluded them. He was a most interesting variant of the "wise fool". Paul, however, is

---

[7] Vengerov, *op. cit.,* p. 194, points out Puškin's fondness for the sentimental theme of the old widow with the simple, beautiful daughter dwelling in a humble cottage. The situation recurs in *The Little House in Kolomna* (Domik v Kolomne), 1830, and in *The Bronze Horseman* (Mednyj Vsadnik), 1833.

merely vapid and obtuse. He passes through the most suspicious events and among the most unlikely persons without a glimmer of perception, and at the same time has none of the inner purity and strength that made Eugenius remarkable.[8] Even Fermino Valies, who is far from being one of Hoffmann's most successful creations, has been rendered into a mediocrity, for if Varfolomej is a devil in human form, surely he has been recruited from among the Infernal Privates and detailed to a fool-proof mission. The stock role of the siren Gabriella is reenacted with slight modifications by the Countess I.

Yet here are the five principals of Hoffmann's cast, together with much of the narrative matter originally assigned to them. Paul is now a comparative stranger to Vera's mother, their family connection being merely a device to facilitate the author's purposes, and the whole interesting reversal of the January-and-May theme has been eliminated. Varfolomej is no longer a chemist devil, but apparently he has an acquaintance who fits the description. He still furnishes drugs for Vera's mother, though it is never explicitly said that they are poison or that she dies from their effects. He still exerts the powerful force that can hurl an opponent into insensibility, and he still operates in collusion with an alluring Countess to destroy the innocence of unsuspecting young men. Fermino and Gabriella had been lovers, but such a connection between Varfolomej and the Countess I. is left as an unconfirmed suspicion in the mind of the dull Paul. But these are differences of detail. Up to the final disasters that sweep these puppets from the stage, they proceed through the same pattern as the characters of *Datura fastuosa*.

If Puškin's adaptation reduced the unique to the commonplace, *The Lonely Cottage on Vasil'evskij Island* is redeemed by two memorable episodes which have no counterpart in *Datura fastuosa*: the episode of Paul's ride in the cab with the death's-head and the scene of the gambler devils at Countess I.'s soirée. For neither of them has Gorlin advanced any explanation. The fact is that both represent grafted episodes from another Tale of Hoffmann, *Die Abenteuer der Sylvester-*

---

[8] The critic Tit Levit lays stress on the undistinguished nature of Paul, claiming that it unites him with other Puškinian heroes. Hermann in *The Queen of Spades* will be an average man, and Eugene Onegin, who in 1829 had already run half of his history, had already set the Puškinian pattern. The mediocrity, Levit further claims, distinguishes Paul from the unusual and gifted heroes of Polevoj and Odoevskij. See Tit Levit, "Gofman v Russkoj Literature", an essay in *E. T. A. Gofman: Sobranie Sočinenij*, edited by Z. A. Veršinina (1930), Vol. VI, pp. 336–370; p. 344.

nacht, or more specifically from Part IV of that work, the celebrated
Geschichte vom verlorenen Spiegelbild, familiar to opera-goers through
its rearrangement as Act II of Offenbach's *Contes d'Hoffmann.*

This was the woeful narrative of Erasmus Spikher, the man who sold
his mirror-image to the devil, in all too patent imitation of Peter
Schlemihl's sale of his shadow to the Man in Grey. Hoffmann admired
Chamisso's fairy-tale enormously and, indeed, brought Peter Schlemihl
himself briefly into an earlier chapter of the present tale. Spikher, aged
twenty-seven, had bidden farewell to his loyal wife and his little son
and had come to Italy, the land of his heart's desire. In Florence he
had fallen among high-living companions and formed a liaison with the
beautiful courtesan Giulietta. His conscience and the warnings of his
good friend Friedrich that Giulietta is dangerous, prompt him to quit
Florence and its temptations, but he is induced to remain by Dr. Dapertutto, a scarlet-clad persuader with unequivocal allegiance to hell.
Rivals contest for Giulietta's favors, until one day Erasmus murders one
of them. With horror he realizes that he must now flee the country. But
how is he to exist without Giulietta? At this point the evil courtesan
proposes to keep his mirror-image with her. Erasmus consents, and
directly his reflection in the mirror before which they are standing
leaves the glass and walks, independent of him, into Giulietta's arms.
Erasmus rushes away from the house. Just then he is seized and forced
into a cab.

The voice of a fellow-passenger speaks to him from the cab's dark
interior, speaks at length and with extraordinary knowledge of the
hero's connection with Giulietta and of the murder of a few
minutes ago.

"You are, moreover, a very nice young man", the voice observes, "and
astonishingly inclined to pleasant pranks, the like of which please us
very much, Giulietta and me. I found that a first-rate German kick in
the neck. The way that amoroso's tongue hung blue as a cherry out
of his gullet — it looked very funny, and the way he moaned and
groaned and couldn't die straight off — ha — ha — ha —".

The voice suggests that all reprisals for the murder can be eluded if
Erasmus is willing to countenance certain "operations" with his mirror-
image. Just then some passing torches illumine the cab and Erasmus
beholds Dr. Dapertutto as the speaker. He leaps out of the vehicle and
starts for Germany. It is only at the end of the story, when Dapertutto
and Giulietta seek out Erasmus in Germany and attempt to destroy his

wife and son, that the agents of Evil are dispersed by an invocation to the powers of Good. At the crucial moment Erasmus' wife calls upon the Saviour's name and the infernal pair vanish amid screams, rustlings of raven-feathers, and a cloud of stinking smoke.

Dapertutto is loquacious during that cab-ride, in contrast to the stubborn, and far more effective, silence of the death's-head who drives Paul about the streets of Petersburg. More effective too is the violent end of the episode when Paul's half-inadvertent making of the Sign of the Cross overturns the ghostly cab and makes the devil vanish amid hellish laughter. This is an improvement both on the tame close of Erasmus' ride and on the dispersal of the fiends when his wife cries: "In the Saviour's name!"

It will be noted also that the details of the scene have become much more specifically Christian and theological than in the original. The Russian Hoffmannists usually had recourse to Christian symbolism when conflict was involved between Good and Evil. Thus, not only does the cab bear the Apocalyptic number 666, but is has come to fetch an unrepentant mortal just when his sin lies heaviest upon him. Yet, short of actual death, a sinner is always capable of contrition. The very thought of God, merely the Sign of the Cross, can, and in this instance does, save him, breaking and scattering the engines of Satan. The experience is a spiritual crisis, and Paul's torments of conscience follow directly in the form of fever and illness unto death.

In purely poetic terms, the scene has been given a completely new quality. In place of the scarlet and black coloration of Hoffmann's scene — night, torches, Dapertutto's crimson garb — and the rich connotations of the Italian setting, Puškin has substituted a grey mysteriousness of snow and winter's moonlight. The source for his changes is not far to seek. It is indicated when the text says: "The moon in the manner of Žukovskij dimly lighted the travelers through the scudding clouds." A triple complex of poems underlies that statement. First, in chronological order, is Gottfried August Bürger's famous ghost-ballad *Lenore* of 1774, which Žukovskij translated once (1829) and imitated twice.[9] The earlier and closer imitation was the epoch-

---

[9] The subject matter of the poem is actually of Scottish origin and is represented by the ballad *Sweet William's Ghost* in Bishop Percy's celebrated anthology of 1765, the *Reliques of Ancient English Poetry*. With this poem Gottfried August Bürger blended elements of native German folk poetry to make his own ballad, *Lenore*, in 1774. In this form it enjoyed a European reputation and inspired, among other imitations, Sir Walter Scott's ballad *William and Margaret*, 1796. Žukovskij's imitation, *Ljudmila*, 1808, is one of

making ballad *Ljudmila* (1808). Its heroine, upon learning that her beloved has perished in the wars, despairs of happiness, rejects all consolation, and cries aloud that God is unjust. That night her lover's ghost comes and carries her away on his swift horse — "the dead ride swiftly" — to his "narrow home" in the grave. The poem concludes with a stern warning against the blasphemy of decrying God's dispensation. More conciliatory and less harshly just is the tone of the second imitation of 1811, entitled *Svetlana*. In this poem the beloved has been absent for a year, though not to the wars, and no word has come from him. Alone before her mirror at midnight. Svetlana beholds him enter and declare that he has come to take her to be married at once. Through the night they fly in a sleigh, snow whirling about them and misty moonlight above. They arrive at a hut almost buried in snow. Suddenly horses, sleigh, and bridegroom all vanish into the night, leaving the girl terrified and alone in the snow. Making the Sign of the Cross and murmuring a prayer, she enters the hut. The interior is arranged as for a funeral. Her beloved lies on a bier, dead. All at once the corpse eerily stirs. Just at that moment Svetlana awakes. She is in her own room before her mirror. Dawn is breaking. All has been a dream. Sleigh-bells are heard. She looks. It is her lover, alive and well, come to make her his bride. Puškin's admiration for this particular ballad had already been demonstrated in 1826 when he developed aspects of it to make a large part of Tatjana's famous dream-sequence in Chapter V of *Eugene Onegin* (stanzas XI-XXI).

Here in Žukovskij's *Svetlana* are to be found the sleigh-cab which appears out of nowhere at midnight to carry its occupant through snow and misty moonlight to strange places, the mysterious vanishing of the vehicle, the making of the Sign of the Cross, and the (apparent) presence of death. In the closely related *Ljudmila* are to be found another midnight departure, in this case on horseback, with a rider who is a death's-head and who makes no reply to the heroine's frightened questions.

---

the important documents of Russian pre-Romanticism, while his second imitation, *Svetlana,* 1811 (possibly an error for 1814), was of hardly less importance. "Svetlana" was Žukovskij's nickname in the Arzamas society. Lines 267–268 of *Svetlana* serve as the epigraph to Chapter V of *Eugene Onegin.* During the 1820's Žukovskij abandoned poetry temporarily, and when he resumed writing, precisely in 1829, he began his second period with a translation of Bürger's *Lenore,* as though this poem were the touchstone of his poetic productivity. It is possible that the fresh experience with this subject is directly related to the formation of *The Lonely Cottage on Vasil'evskij Island.*

The episode of Paul's nocturnal ride is a fine bit of Puškinian imagination. Its excellence increases as we distinguish how it was suggested by a slight passage in *Die Abenteuer der Sylvesternacht* and then blended with Žukovskian balladry to make an entirely new and striking creation. What is less happy is its imperfect jointure with the scenario adapted from *Datura fastuosa,* for, memorable as it is, it remains poorly integrated with the complete story. Mme Kern remembered this episode when the rest of the tale had been forgotten.

Quite as excellent and more familiarly Puškinian by their quick humor are the episodes in the Countess I.'s salon. The gambler devils who wager hundreds of souls on the draw of a card are a delightful invention and an amusing travesty of Russian aristocrats staking their "souls", that is to say their peasants, in reckless card games. Delightful too is the invention of their costume: trousers of the infidel Turk to conceal their devilish conformation, wigs over their horns, gloves over their claws. The counterpart in the *Sylvesternacht* was more subtly but less directly humorous, namely that "elegant old German costume" which the youth of the late eighteenth century fancied was historical, national, manly, and anti-French. Its wearers, in Hoffmann's story, were presented pseudo-rationalistically as Teutonic cavaliers reveling, each with his *donna* by his side, amid the orange trees, jasmin, and mandolins of a Florentine garden by night. Puškin removed the scene within doors, yet, oddly enough, the Countess I.'s divan room retains some aspects of the bower which was its predecessor. It not only doubles as divan room and orangerie, but myrtle trees line its walls and candelabras glow amid the branches, replacing the torches of the original.[10] In both stories there is an attempt to present a haunt of voluptuousness, Hoffmann conceiving his Florentine garden in terms of a lush Renaissance painting, Puškin showing his siren's rooms as tongue-in-cheek exaggerations of wealthy Petersburg interiors, particularly the quarters of seductive ladies.

In their respective settings, Paul and Erasmus Spikher pay adoration to a ravishingly beautiful lady of absolutely no virtue and each is plagued with a swarm of rivals. Paul's opponent is a swaggering fellow with a physical deformity which earns him the nickname of "Crook-Leg". The Countess finds him none the less attractive and with him indulges in mockery of Paul's spoken French. Paul, humiliated and

---

[10] Similar "residues" mark Dostoevskij's adaptations of Hoffmannian material. See Passage, *Dostoevski the Adapter* (University of North Carolina Press, 1954), pp. 72, 78, 89—90.

jealous as he overhears their interchange, feels an impulse to attack
"Crook-Leg" forthwith, but swallows his pride and leaves the salon
abruptly. Erasmus Spikher's Italian rival, on the other hand, is repulsive not only in appearance and manners but unforgivably insulting
in speech as well. His slurs against Germans in general and Erasmus
in particular are made openly. With greater violence than Paul exhibits,
Erasmus challenges him directly to cease his remarks or be thrown into
the garden pond. The Italian draws a knife. Then it is that Erasmus
administers that "first-rate German kick in the neck" which Dapertutto finds so admirable from his point of view and which kills the
aggressive opponent.[11] The murder is followed by that frenzy of passion
in which the hero willingly surrenders his mirror-image to Giulietta.
When she vanishes directly thereafter, he flees from the house and
into that cab in which he rides with Dapertutto through the dark
streets.

An interval of absence in both stories keeps the heroes from their
temptresses. When Paul returns to the Countess I., it is first for a
reconciliation and then for that ill-fated rendez-vous interrupted by
the supernatural visitor. The next encounter between Erasmus and
Giulietta occurs in far-away Germany after the wandering husband has
rejoined his family. Her appearance is preceded by that of Dapertutto,
who promises to bring the lady, to restore the lost mirror-image, and
to cure all of the hero's troubles if he will administer to his wife and
little son a few drops of the liquid that is contained in the little phial
now offered by the tempter. Death will ensue painlessly and instantaneously and only a pleasant scent of bitter almond will indicate their
passing. Briefly Erasmus is tempted to free himself by this means of his
encumbering family in order to rejoin Giulietta in a passionate freedom,

---

[11]   Given the nature of Hoffmann's narrative art and the composition of over
sixty stories in little more than a decade, it is not surprising to find variants
of motifs from work to work. Thus, in *Die Fermate,* which otherwise does not
resemble Puškin's story in the least, there is an episode which actually parallels
this adventure of Paul's more closely than does the passage from *Die Abenteuer
der Sylvesternacht.* The young musician-hero of *Die Fermate,* Theodor by name,
is traveling with two Italian musicians, the sisters Teresina and Lauretta, and
is in love now with the one, now with the other. One day he overhears both
sisters malign him and his musicianship for the enormous amusement of a
visiting Italian tenor. Together they sing one of Theodor's compositions for the
guest, parodying Theodor's mannerisms heartlessly as they sing. In a cold fury
the hero leaves their company and takes the next stage-coach home. An acrid
farewell note explains his departure. Years later he encounters the sisters again
and is cordially welcomed as if no difficulty had ever arisen.

but the temptation fails and all ends well, except for the fact that the hero's mirror-reflection must still be sought for all about the world. With the motif of the proffered poison — in this case specifically prussic acid — may be seen the link between the plot outlines of *Datura fastuosa* and the *Sylvesternacht*. In both Hoffmannian stories the poison is accepted by the hero from the hands of devilish villains, is almost administered, but in the end is rejected before any harm is done, whereas the potions provided by Varfolomej, whether poison or something else, are definitely administered and serve the devil's purposes.

Precisely at this stage Puškin's narrative begins to head for a tragic close. By the end, all the characters have wretchedly perished, Vera's mother by fire, Vera herself by wasting disease, Paul in madness, while the supernatural Varfolomej has vanished without a trace. The "lonely cottage" itself has been obliterated. The excess of catastrophes, in marked contrast to the happy ending of *Datura fastuosa* and the moderately happy ending of *Die Abenteuer der Sylvesternacht,* led Gorlin to see the influence of a third tale of Hoffmann, *Der Magnetiseur.* This was the early story (1813; published 1814) that had appeared in *The Moscow Messenger* in Venevitinov's translation two years previously (1827) and which "Pogorel'skij" was to imitate in his novel-fragment, *The Hypnotist,* a year later (1830). Its catastrophe-piled ending seems to have outweighed, among the Russians, the optimistic endings of dozens of Hoffmann's other works. The story relates the sinister destruction by the evil hypnotist Alban of a whole family. His ultimate motivation is unclear. Though we know him to have been thwarted in his love for the girl Maria, his hatred seems to have been directed long years previously to an attempted murder of her father, the Baron. All his actions are the expressions of a never wavering malignity. In rapid succession in the final two pages of the work, we are informed that Maria unexplainably collapsed at the altar at the very moment of pronouncing her vows and died in the arms of her beloved Hipolyt; that Hipolyt was subsequently killed in a duel; that Maria's brother had fallen in battle; that her father died of grief; that even Bickert, the old family friend, has died alone and broken hearted; and that Alban disappeared without a trace.

In support of Gorlin's claim may be adduced the scene in which Varfolomej exerts some quasi-hypnotic force upon the corpse of Vera's mother in an effort to compel the dead woman to order her daughter to submit to his passion. On the other hand, there is the puzzling fact that practically all Russian Hoffmannizing works after 1829 will, regardless of author and regardless of optimism of the source, be marked by similarly tragic endings. The present story cannot possibly have established a precedent, and it seems odd that *Der Magnetiseur,* plus perhaps *Der Sandmann,* should have sufficed to modify the whole course of Russian Hoffmannism after "Pogorel'skij". Nevertheless, in the case of *The Lonely Cottage on Vasil'evskij Island* Gorlin's proposal appears to have considerable plausibility.[12]

In 1829 the cult of Hoffmann in Russia was just beginning to assume major proportions. Puškin, sensitive to every literary stimulus, must have felt an impulse to try his hand at the genre. By temperament he found it essentially unsympathetic. He understood it imperfectly. An omnivorous reader, he was not likely to miss the 1826 translation of *Datura fastuosa,* much less his friend Venevitinov's version of *Der Magnetiseur.* The recent publication of the first volumes of Hoffmann's "complete" works in the French of Loève-Veimars may have supplied him with *Die Abenteuer der Sylvesternacht.* Association of any piece of German literature with Žukovskij was all but inevitable with Puškin. Working fairly close to the models in the unfamiliar and not wholly congenial genre, he planned *The Lonely Cottage on Vasilevskij Island.* The imperfect blending of the separate elements suggests that the scenario was experimental. It is plausible, though beyond proof, that he had already rejected it in his own mind as too obviously derivative and too far short of his own high standards to be completed for publication. On the spur of the moment, perhaps as a gesture of teasing the romantic ladies, he used it as an impromptu entertainment at Mme Karamzina's evening party. His ingratiating personality and his narrative gift undoubtedly lent it a charm which the printed page will never convey. Mme Kern remembered the telling and the teller rather than the story itself. But "Kosmokratov overheard". To the ambitious amateur Romanticist it was an improvisation of genius. Puškin was too conscious an artist not to know the imperfections of his scenario and too generous a man not to make a gift of it to an amateur so fervent as to record it from memory. He resigned the work to "Kosmokratov": his own masterpiece in the Hoffmannizing manner would come later.

[12]   Gorlin, "Hoffmann en Russie", *op. cit.,* p. 69.

2. *THE QUEEN OF SPADES*

Neither the *Tales of Belkin* nor any other of Puškin's prose works in the early 1830's suggests that his coolness to German literature had altered. Amid the ever increasing number of translations from Hoffmann and from other German authors, with popular enthusiasm for such works at its peak, and with native imitations of them appearing left and right, from Polevoj, from Prince Odoevskij, and most recently from Gogol', he could hardly have escaped discussions of the subject. Certain it is that his library contained the entire set of the Loève-Veimars *Œuvres Complètes,* the last volumes of which were published in 1833.[13] Some time in that same year, for reasons unknown, he reversed literary directions and set about writing a story of his own in the German Romantic genre. It was completed and published in 1834 with the title of *The Queen of Spades* (Pikovaja Dama).

The product is unique in Puškin's career, unique amid the works of Russian Romanticists, unique amid all Romantic literature. A double paradox applies to the story. First, it is a Romantic tale told in the style of Voltaire; second, it is a Romantic tale in which all the Romantic motifs are either spoofed or made to serve as symbols for a realistic purpose. A captious anti-Romantic could easily demonstrate, for instance, that no apparition of the old Countess's ghost need be literally credited, any more than it must be believed that her corpse winked at Hermann from its coffin: these were illusions of his deranged mind. No mysterious power directed him to her house: to have come upon it accidentally while walking in the streets was the most natural of coincidences. His amazing winnings, first of 47,000 rubles and on the following evening of 94,000, by betting each time on a single card, were matters of luck, while his loss of a fortune by the same process on the third evening confirmed that he had no magic. Luck varies unpredictably, that is all. There may never even have been any secret formula of three winning cards, either with Hermann or with the old Countess. Tomskij's anecdote about his grandmother, related in Chapter I, is offered as entertaining gossip. Its actuality is never substantiated. It is distinctly possible that it never happened. Its details are left extremely vague in an atmosphere of a life-time ago in the remote and now defunct Versailles court. And as for the Count de Saint Germain, the reader can be sure of nothing about him (though he was a historical

---

13   Levit, "Gofman v russkoi literature", *op. cit.,* p. 345.

personage). The author smilingly passes in review a whole series of Romantic possibilities — that he was the Wandering Jew, that he was an alchemist, that he was a spy, as "Casanova states in his *Mémoires*" —, but none of these identifications is accepted seriously. His dealings with Tomskij's grandmother suggest a Melmoth-like sale of the soul to Satan for money, or more specifically the escape of the original seller from his bargain by transfer of the Satanic bond to another party who is in turn desperate for money.[14] But not for a moment does the author become really engaged in this lugubrious theme. We never discover what the Count de Saint Germain told Tomskij's grandmother, or whether he told her anything, or whether she ever really consulted him in her plight. The whole episode is a delicious *canard*. Puškin's eyes must have twinkled as he wrote it.

Yet the story is by no means a parody of Romantic themes. On the contrary, it is serious and profound. Its essence is the struggle between a mind and an idea. Hermann's mind is taut with strain before the story opens. From genteel poverty and obscurity he aspires to Napoleonic grandeur. Regularly he attends card parties, hungrily watching money won and lost, yet never dares touch a card. At such a party he hears Tomskij tell of how his grandmother gained possession of an infallible formula for winning. *The idea enters his mind*. He conceives and carries out an elaborate plan of making love to the old Countess's protégée-companion, Lizaveta Ivanovna, and of arranging a tryst with her for the sole purpose of getting a secret interview with the old woman and forcing her, at gun point if necessary, to disclose to him her magic formula. *The idea obsesses him*. The old woman dies of fright, having disclosed nothing, and Hermann spends the rest of the night confessing his whole conduct to Lizaveta Ivanovna, not from remorse at the Countess's death, not from remorse at the girl's deception, but in dejection that the secret should have died with its owner. *The idea has exterminated all humanity in him*. That night the Countess's ghost comes to him and surrenders the secret that the living woman withheld. *The idea has triumphed over reason and sanity*. Triumphantly Hermann goes to Čekalinskij's gaming salon on three successive evenings, wins twice, and loses everything on the third evening. The trey had won, the

---

[14]   It is Hermann in his confrontation of the old Countess (Chapter III) who says, referring to the secret: "Maybe it is connected with some terrible sin, the loss of eternal bliss, some bargain with the devil...", and in his feverish excitement adds: "I am ready to take your sins upon my soul."

seven had won, but instead of the supreme ace there turned up the Queen of Spades, with the face of the dead woman, to undo him utterly. *The idea, in total possession of his mind, compels the acting out of the obsession, even to disaster.* The terse epilogue states that Hermann lies in the Obuxov Hospital, cell No. 17, repeating interminably: "Trey, seven, ace! Trey, seven, Queen!" *The idea has eaten away the last remnants of his mind.* Like the seed or spore of a parasitic vine, the idea had dropped into the susceptible decay of some gnarl or bruised bark of the tree of him, and there it had grown relentlessly, choking the tree gradually, drawing the substance of the tree's life into itself, until at last there remained only a fallen trunk covered and spun over with luxuriant tendrils of parasitic growth. A human mind has been reduced to a single thought fixed permanently on the exacerbated nerve of consciousness: "Trey, seven, ace! Trey, seven, Queen!"

Whence Puškin took such a conception is unknown. Probably from no one book or person. The precise formulation of the concept may well have been his independent creation, but the general notion would have been impossible without at least indirect contact with the ideologies of German Romanticism.

It may be safely asserted that underlying all German Romantic thinking was the eighteenth century discovery of hypnosis by Franz Anton Mesmer (1734—1815). The phenomenon revealed aspects and depths of the human personality unsuspected by the rational mind, and at the same time Mesmer himself was led by it to a belief in a universal, all-pervasive force in the atmosphere that sustained life. The hypnotic agent might extract such quantities of this force as his subjects possessed and arrogate them to himself until he might become the equal of God, who was simply a spirit endowed with this force to a transcendent degree.

Upon his hypnosis the German Romantic philosophers erected a vast edifice of thought, which conceived of the life-force as an emanation from God, operating through innumerable permutations toward an ultimate synthesis *in* God. Man's external life was a superficial matter, just as the rational mind that perceived it, was a superficial organ. Within man lay the unconscious — in modern terms "subconscious" — unfathomable, "sidereal" self, which, mute and inert as it was, nevertheless was in immediate contact, outside of time, with the omniscient universe and evolving with the evolving universe toward that ultimate synthesis in God. But how was insight to be gained into the "sidereal self"? Hypnosis, which temporarily removed the obstacle of the conscious "Adamitic self", was one means. But the sidereal self expressed itself spontaneously on occasion, in dreams, for instance, and in abnormal states of all kinds: madness, hysteria, fixation, somnambulism, and in the creations of artistic genius. But, as Franz von Baader asked, what would happen if the sidereal self were perverted to evil? What if, for example, it came under the domination of an evil hypnotist? To answer that question Hoffmann wrote his tale, *Der Magnetiseur* (The Hypnotist) (1813), in which Alban is just such an evil man. His explicitly stated plan is to deflect the rays of life-force which proceed from other human beings toward God, and absorb them into himself in order to become himself *like* God.

Ramifications of Romantic theory about the nature and operations of the sidereal self are very extensive,[15] some of them reaching down through the nineteenth century to emerge as the doctrines of Freud and the tenets of modern psychology. Literary exploitation of the theory began simultaneously with its elaboration, and no author made more frequent or skillful use of it than Hoffmann. Puškin, reading widely in his works as he may, indeed must, have done, would have come across many a parallel to the motifs that occur in *The Queen of Spades*. In *Der Sandmann,* for instance, of which two Russian translations had been printed (1830 and 1831), the hero Nathanael, whose mind is predisposed to madness, falls prey to a fixed idea that finally destroys him. In *Die Elixiere des Teufels* a mysterious power guides the steps of the monk Medardus from the moment of his flight from his monastery until his return, after many wanderings, to the place of origin. A similar power guides Hermann on what he fancies is a random stroll through the streets of Petersburg. Coming to a certain house and asking a policeman who lives there, he is informed that it is the home of the Countess who possesses the secret of the cards. The hero of *Das öde Haus* (translated into Russian in 1831) was drawn by a kind of magnetic attraction to the deserted house of the title, which was next door to a confectioner's shop, as the Countess's house seems to be. The same deserted house shelters an aged and unhappy woman with whom the hero will be confronted during the story. Mysterious old men like Saint Germain, with benevolent or malign wisdom, comprise one of Hoffmann's most numerous and most characteristic categories of personages,

[15] For a brilliant exposition of German Romantic ideology, see Ricarda Huch: *Ausbreitung und Verfall der Romantik* (Leipzig, 1902), particularly the chapters, *Romantische Aerzte,* pp. 273–305, and *Die Nachtseiten in der Literatur,* pp. 224–238.

while dreams involving the fantastic transformation of symbols may be found in numbers of Hoffmann's tales.[16]

One of the forms that may be assumed by the sidereal self in a state of daemonic possession is mania, the compulsive repetition of action for which there is no rational justification. To Hoffmann, gambling was a mania, and with it he associated an eerie contact of the soul with malignant forces outside of man and impossible to identify exactly. The subject formed the basis for his tale *Spielerglück* (1819), which had been translated in *The Messenger of Europe* in 1823. His biographer, Walther Harich, makes the claim that this was the first story in world literature to deal with the theme of the compulsive gambler.[17]

It is a miniature *roman à tiroirs* which presents the lives of three daemonically possessed gamblers. First — and this section is slightly modified autobiography — Baron Siegfried, an attractive young man,

---

[16] Amid the concise Voltairean prose of *The Queen of Spades* there is one passage that seems oddly at variance with the surrounding text. This is the passage in Chapter VI where the obsession with the three cards luxuriates into fantastic dreams in Hermann's mind: "'Trey, seven, ace' were perpetually running through his head and continually on his lips. If he saw a young girl, he would say: 'How slender she is! quite like the trey of hearts.' If anybody asked: 'What is the time?' he would reply: 'Five minutes to seven.' Every stout man that he saw reminded him of the ace. 'Trey, seven, ace' haunted him in his sleep and assumed all possible shapes. The trey bloomed before him in the shape of a magnificent flower, but the seven was represented by a Gothic portal, and the ace became transfigured into a gigantic spider." Elaborate dream sequences are to be found in too many of Hoffmann's works to permit the singling out of any one of them as a parallel, though Severin's hallucinatory impressions in *Aus dem Leben dreier Freunde* and the final chapter of *Meister Floh* may be cited as striking examples. None, however, is more striking than the dream-phantasmagorias experienced, or rather endured, by Medardus after his repentance and confession (*Die Elixiere des Teufels*, II, 2, *Die Busse*). Among horrendous spectres out of his past life there appear "heads creeping about on grasshopper-legs that grew from their ears ... ravens with human faces ... Belcampo with a loathsome lizard-face sitting on a revolting winged dragon ... tiny ants with dancing human feet ... horse-skeletons with glittering eyes ... a rider with a gleaming owl's head astride it, the rider's armor being a bottomless goblet and his helmet an inverted funnel..." (Hoffmann's source of inspiration was apparently the paintings of Hieronymus Bosch.) It would be tempting to see in the grotesqueries of Medardus' visions a source of inspiration for Hermann's dreams, were it not for the fact that the magnificent dream-phantasmagoria of Chapter V of *Eugene Onegin*, composed in 1826, already contained such elements at a time when influence from *Die Elixiere des Teufels,* or any other work of Hoffmann's, seems all but impossible.

[17] See: *E. T. A. Hoffmann. Das Leben eines Künstlers,* dargestellt von Walther Harich, 2 vols. (Berlin, 1920), Vol. II, p. 201.

never plays faro, though his friends all urge him to join them at the game. Finally, when they taunt him with niggardliness, his pride drives him to play. He is troubled, however, whenever he plays by the presence and persistent stare of a certain old man, the Chevalier Menars. Questioning him at last, he hears his life story.

Menars had, in his youth, been averse to gambling, then taunted by friends into trying it. He won. Gradually he became a compulsive gambler, until a disastrous experience befell him. There appeared one evening to play against him a certain old man named Francesco Vertua, who was noted as a pitiless miser and usurer. Vertua's presence in the gambling salon amazed everyone. His frantic excitement amazed them even more. For three successive nights he played, losing each time, and on the third evening lost everything on the turn of a Queen, — whether of Spades or of some other suit is not specified. Vertua admitted that his ruin went beyond his money losses to include the possessions of his daughter Angela. Menars took pity on him, persuaded him to accept money from him, and eventually fell in love with and married Angela.

The life of Vertua, which is next related, shows him to have been, like the other two, a spectator coaxed to play and then becoming a habitual gambler. He had once abjured cards after a rival had tried to murder him, but the fabulous unbroken luck of Menars, which is the talk of the city, has goaded his jealousy into returning to the green tables to beat him. The attempt ended in disaster. As for Menars, he was not sufficiently warned by his father-in-law's experience. His mania continued and increased in intensity, bringing him even to the point of mistreating his wife Angela. A childhood sweetheart of Angela's arrived in the city, himself also a gambler. A bitter hostility developed between the two men. The newcomer challenged Menars to play for higher and higher stakes, the last stake being the possession of Angela herself. Menars lost, the fatal card being a Queen, but when the pair came to confront Angela herself, they found her dead.

A series of literary, as opposed to ideological, parallels between *Spielerglück* and *The Queen of Spades* suggests some link between the two works: the young man averse to gambling who becomes disastrously involved in play; the sacrifice of a young woman's love to the mania; the use of the cabalistic number three and the fateful appearance of the Queen to precipitate the player's undoing.

Gambling, with its eerie association with evil powers outside of man, also constitutes one of the worldly experiences of the runaway monk

Medardus in *Die Elixiere des Teufels*. In Part I, Section 4 of that novel, Medardus, traveling under the pseudonym of "Mister Leonhard", sojourns at the court of a certain Prince. The Prince is fascinated by faro and has established his own gambling salon, to which he urges Medardus to come. The ex-monk accepts the invitation, plays, and loses consistently. Suddenly, with a tactlessness that would have ruined a man not under the aegis of an Evil Power, he requests the Prince to let him play unwatched, since his presence brings him bad luck. The Prince wrily withdraws. Medardus selects a card at random.

It was the Queen. — It may well be absurd to say that in that pale, lifeless face-card I fancied I discovered the features of Aurelie [the heroine of the novel]. I stared at the card and could scarcely conceal my inward excitement. The call of the banker to know whether bets had been made roused me from my stupor. Without reflecting, I drew from my pocket the last five louis-d'ors that I still had with me and staked them on the Queen. She won, and now I staked again and again on the Queen, higher and higher as the winnings increased . . .

He quits the table at last with some two thousand louis-d'ors but haunted by the feeling that he "was but the passive instrument which (an alien) Power was using for purposes unknown to him". The ever-lasting mirroring of Aurelie's image could, he feels, be nothing else but an infamous lure to evil deeds.

Puškin, himself an inveterate gambler, may well have found this episode memorable. That Medardus' Queen was the Queen of Hearts and brought him luck, while Hermann's card was the Queen of Spades and brought him disaster, would be no more than consistent with the transformation of Hoffmannian optimism into the pessimism of his Russian counterparts.

No possible claim, however, can be advanced that the episode from *Die Elixiere des Teufels* or even the tale *Spielerglück* contributed anything more than a small fraction of the total substance of *The Queen of Spades*. That was Puškin's independent and brilliant creation. In contrast to all other Russian Hoffmannists, including himself as co-author of *The Lonely Cottage on Vasil'evskij Island,* he did not develop his Hoffmannizing story out of a disengaged episode from the German source, nor by *contaminatio* of episodes from two or more sources. Rather, he read with extraordinary insight quantities of Hoffmann's productions and worked himself back to the plane from which Hoffmann worked, which may be termed the general plane of German Romanticism. With uncanny empathy, the like of which is to be encountered almost nowhere else in literature, he entered into the spirit of Hoffmann, deduced the principles of Hoffmann's craft, and, in a medium which he could not love, wrote as Hoffmann might have written.

Except for *Spielerglück,* no single story can be adduced as a direct source for *The Queen of Spades.* What is interesting, however, is that the *area* of Hoffmann's work can be identified from which Puškin made his deductions. It is essentially the area represented by the Russian translations up to 1833: *Spielerglück* itself, translated 1823, for the gambler hero, his undoing by the fateful Queen, and the motif of the innocent girl sacrificed to gambling mania; *Der Sandmann,* translated 1830 and again 1831, for the theme of fixation and progressive madness; *Das öde Haus,* translated 1831, for the motif of daemonic attraction to a certain house where there lives an old woman with a secret; *Der Magnetiseur,* translated 1827, for the figure of an evil man with aspirations to superhuman goals; *Aus dem Leben dreier Freunde,* translated 1831, for dream-phantasmagorias (life of Severin) and for an elderly female ghost (life of Alexander). Here probably should be added two other tales in which ghosts appear, *Eine Spukgeschichte* and the splendid *Das Majorat,* translated 1825 and 1830 respectively. Their presence reinforced the notion that a Hoffmannian tale ought to have a ghost in it. The only appropriate but untranslated item was *Die Elixiere des Teufels,* upon an episode from which Puškin's friend Gogol' was building his own story, *The Portrait,* simultaneously with the composition of *The Queen of Spades.* Puškin's conception of Hoffmann seems not to have extended to the musical tales, the art-problem-tales, or the great *Märchen* and *Kater Murr.*

In its finished form *The Queen of Spades* was immediately recognized as a story in the German vein, in Hoffmann's vein. Puškin surely intended it as such. The opening page announces the hero as a German. A rejected fragment informs us that the heroine was intended to be called Charlotte Müller.[18] Hoffmannian motifs abound, in marked contrast to his normal prose manner. Yet the story is all Puškin's. The marriage of eighteenth-century elegance and wit to such subject matter could have been achieved by him alone. Most striking of all is the realism hooded within the husks of Romanticism. Hermann's madness is real and the supernaturalisms are his delusions. There is no hint of madness as an ironic escape from hateful reality. Hermann's madness

---

[18]   See A. S. Puškin, "Polnoe Sobranie Sočineni", *op. cit.,* Vol. IV, p. 595.

is also symptomatic of a nascent opinion in the Russia of 1834: pseudo-Napoleons are mad, along with pseudo-Byrons. For all the concessions apparently made to the current vogue, the work urges toward the age of Realism, which is only about to be born.[19]

[19] Proceeding on the analogy of the mediocre heroes, Paul and Hermann, Levit (*Gofman v russkoi literature, op. cit.,* p. 345) argues for the addition of Adrian Proxorov, hero of *The Undertaker,* among Puškin's Hoffmannian figures. *The Undertaker* (Grobovščik) (also translated as *The Coffin-Maker*) is the third of the *Tales of Belkin,* published 1830. Hardly more than an anecdote, it relates how Adrian Proxorov, an undertaker, became irritated at a party when guests made jokes about his occupation, particularly by the toast proposed by certain merchants: "To our customers!" Not to be outdone, Adrian invokes all *his* customers, inviting them to visit him. He arrives home to find his room full of these customers, all very lively and loud despite the fact that they have just come from their graves in various states of physical decay. At the crisis of the confusion Adrian awakes to find that all has been a nightmare brought on by his hosts's wine. Except as a kind of parody, this subject can bear no relationship to Hoffmann, who avoided physical horror and who never undercut his established mood by reducing it to a mere dream, alcoholic or otherwise. In *Die Brautwahl,* for example, only Vosswinkel, the lowliest Philistine, suggests such an explanation for the hero's misadventures on the night of the autumnal equinox. Levit's formula: "an ordinary man foolishly evokes the world beyond the grave" brings the story only to the remotest edge of Hoffmann's sphere.

VI

GOGOL', THE MORAL ARTIST

In February of 1829 Greč's magazine *The Son of the Fatherland* printed, under the title *Italia,* a lyric poem full of Germanic *Sehnsucht nach Italien* patently derived from Goethe. No author was mentioned. The poem caused no comment.

Five months later there appeared a pamphlet in the bookshops of Petersburg bearing the caption *Hans Küchelgarten. An Idyll in Scenes. Composition of V. Alov* (Ganc Kjuxelgarten. Idilija v kartinkax. Soč. V. Alova). In platitudinous verses that strove to sound like Žukovskij's, the poem told of a German youth named Hans Küchelgarten who was bored with his tranquil lot and with his sweet fiancée, the grand-daughter of a pastor. He went out into the world to "serve the Good" but returned after a few years, disappointed though rich, to marry his faithful Luiza. The girl's name, along with a fair amount of the poem's contents, had been taken from Voss's famous idyll *Luise* (1795). The concluding lines constituted a hymn to Goethe and to Germany, "the land of thought and merry fantasy". A note in the pamphlet stated that "the editors" were "proud to reveal a youthful talent's work to the public". The public was apathetic. Only a few copies were sold. Two reviews, one of them in *The Northern Bee,* agreed that the poem was worthless. Shortly thereafter, all copies of the pamphlet disappeared from the book stalls: "the editors" had bought them up and destroyed them.

In February of 1830 *National Notes* carried a markedly Romantic prose tale with the lengthy superscription: *Bisavrjuk, or The Eve of St. John the Baptist. A Little Russian Story (from folk tradition) related by the sacristan of the Church of the Intercession* (Bisavrjuk, ili Večer nakanune Ivana Kupala. Malorossijskaja Povest' [iz narodnogo preda-nija] rasskazannaja d'jačkom Pokrovskoj Cerkvi). The author was unidentified. The story might or might not be a Ukrainian folk tale; it certainly had a plot remarkably similar to that of Ludwig Tieck's *Liebeszauber,* which by coincidence had appeared that same year in Russian translation as *The Magic of Love* (Čary Ljubvi) in Raič's magazine *Galatea*. The resemblance was pointed out the following year in an article by Nadeždin, editor of *The Telescope*.[1]

Ukrainian again in subject was the chapter of a historical novel called *The Hetman* (Getman), which was begun — and never continued — in the annual almanac of Baron Del'vig's *Northern Flowers*, December 1830. The signature in this instance was "oooo".

Two chapters of another unfinished Ukrainian tale, *The Terrible Boar* (Strašnyj Kaban), were published by the *Literary Gazette*, anonymously, in January of 1831.

The same issue carried an article by "G. Janov" called *Some Thoughts on the Teaching of Geography to Children*.

The public could hardly be expected to divine that a single personality comprised these anonymities together with "V. Alov", "oooo", "G. Janov", and even "the editors" of *Hans Küchelgarten*. Yet a single, very persistent and very ambitious, young author with a decided penchant for German-type Romanticism was here at work and cautiously testing public taste from behind a series of masks. The results of these tests were threefold: they annihilated the bad lyric poet straight off, they left undecided the pedagogue, and they gave encouragement to the fictionalist who dealt in Ukrainian local color. In August of 1831 the young author made a new bid for fame by publishing a set of four Ukrainian tales under the general title of *Evenings on a Farm near Dikan'ka* (Večera na xutore bliz Dikan'ki). Still cautious, he signed the collection "Rudi Pan'ko, Beekeeper". Three of the tales were new; the fourth, now called simply *St. John's Eve* (Večer nakanune Ivana Kupala), proved to be a revision of the Tieck-inspired *Bisavrjuk* of the previous year. The author's pretensions to erudition caused the addition of a Foreword containing a glossary of Ukrainian terms. Such success attended the book that a second volume was brought out in March of 1832. Its pattern duplicated the first: a Foreword followed by four tales. One of the tales, Ukrainian or no, combined, under the title of *A Terrible Vengeance* (Strašnaja Mest'), the plots of two short stories of Tieck, *Karl von Berneck* and *Pietro von Albano*.[2] Public favor made

---

[1] See *Sočinenija N.V. Gogolja*, edited by N. Tixonravov (Moscow, 1889), Vol. I, p. 256, where the source of Gogol's story is identified as Tieck's *Liebeszauber*, one of the tales from the collection *Phantasus*, 1812—1816, the translation of which as *The Magic of Love* (Čary Ljubvi) was printed in Raič's *Galatea*, 1830, No. 10—11. Nadeždin's article is cited as that in *The Telescope* (Teleskop), 1831, No. 20, p. 653. (*The Telescope*, published 1831—1836, carried on the editorial policies of the defunct *Moscow Messenger*.)

[2] See Stender-Petersen, "Gogol und die deutsche Romantik", *Euphorion*, XXIV,

the twin volumes the talk of Petersburg and the "Ukranian tale" a genre of Romanticism unto itself. The finest of the series was yet to come. In April of 1834 "Rudi Pan'ko, Beekeeper" issued the masterful *Story of how Ivan Ivanovič Quarrelled with Ivan Nikiforovič* (Povest' o tom, kak possorilsja Ivan Ivanovič s Ivanom Nikiforovičem). But not until the publication of the two-volume miscellaney, *Arabesques* (Arabeski) in January of 1835 did the author officially disclose his true identity, which had long been an open secret, as Nikolaj Vasilevič Gogol'.

The Gogol' family were old Ukrainian rural gentry, educated provincials with a tradition of tranquil life on their modest estates. The writer's great-grandfather had been a priest, and both grandfather and father had studied in seminaries. The latter was a well-read man who knew Latin and wrote unpublished and unperformed comedies. As a child, Nikolaj Vasil'evič had displayed no remarkable aptitude for learning. During his seven adolescent years at the *gymnasium* in provincial Nežin, 1820–1827, he passed his courses with mediocre and less than mediocre marks. Only in religion did he excel. Fellow-students remembered him as easy-going, witty, talented in mimicry, drawing, and amateur theatricals. His letters to his mother, both before and after his father's death in 1825, reveal a personality more complex, or at least more puzzling. In long and pompous periods they dwell on egotistic self-analysis interspersed with rather patronising dictations to that naive woman about how to conduct her life and affairs. Above all, they are characterized by many references to and invocations of the deity. Affected as these passages sound, they were sincerely intended, and in them may be seen anticipations of the religious melancholia which ultimately destroyed the artist in him and placed him during the last ten years of his life in a grey twilight between the day of sanity and the night of madness.

In December of 1828, four months before his twentieth birthday, he set out, wide-eyed with idealism, for Petersburg, where he expected to "serve the Good" as a functionary in the government and to find glory, power, and wealth. A blue suit with brass buttons had been ordered from the best tailor in the capital. The capital, however, met him with indifference. The weather was miserable, the government offices politely declined the offers of his services, and the rooms which

---

3 (1922), pp. 628–653; pp. 635–637. See also Jeanette Eyre, *Gogol and German Romanticism,* Susan Anthony Potter prize essay in Comparative Literature, Radcliffe College, 1937 (unpublished), p. 30. Tieck's *Pietro von Albano,* translated as *Petro Apone,* appeared in *The Moscow Messenger* in 1828.

he shared with friends commanded uninspiring prospects of a side-canal. Literature, which was to have been his recompense, proved no less of a disappointment. Crushed with mortification after the *Hans Küchelgarten* fiasco, he took the only money available — money his mother had sent him to be paid against a mortgage on the home estate — and fled to Germany. The Baltic made him sea-sick; Lübeck and a few other German towns made him heart-sick. *North* Germany, at least, was not the "land of thought and merry fantasy". Upon return, he determined to become a painter. During the winter of 1829—1830 he attended art lectures at the Petersburg academy, writing his mother meanwhile for the loan of money and asking her, with only vague explanations of his reasons, for details about Ukrainian folklore. Actually, he was writing his story *Bisavrjuk,* which he was presently able to sell to *National Notes.* The winter of privation, with nothing sturdier than a top-coat all that cold season, forced some kind of employment upon him, and by spring he had obtained a berth in the Lands Administration office at a very unidealistic salary. He was to spend only a year in this milieu of Akakij Akakievič Bašmačkin. Literary friends rescued him by getting him appointed to a professorship in history at the Patriotic Institute, the Empress' school for young girls. (He wrote his mother that the Empress herself had requested him to accept the post.)

His literary efforts, however, were meeting with success. That same spring (1831) editor friends presented him to that redoubtable salon mistress, Aleksandra Osipovna Rosset, whose position as protégée of the imperial family gave her extraordinary influence and prestige.[3] Mme Rosset took an immediate interest in the awkward young man and directly took steps in his behalf. Her devotion to him, maternal in part and in part based on the vanity of being a patroness of genius, was to endure as long as he lived. She it was who introduced him to Žukovskij and Puškin, obtained for him a tutorship to young Prince Vasilščikov, and arranged for Grand Duke Michael to attend a soirée at

---

[3] This remarkable lady, whose maternal grandfather was French and whose father was a Swiss named Joseph de Rosset (or Rossetti; Russianized as Osip Ivanovič Rosset), married Nikolaj Mixajlovič Smirnov. As Mme Smirnova, she enters the annals of Russian literature at more than one point, most notably perhaps as the character of Stavrogin's mother in Dostoevskij's *The Possessed.* When the censor forbade Gogol's *The Inspector General* in 1836, it was she who coaxed Nicholas I into playing Louis XIV to Gogol's *Tartuffe,* with such success that the Tsar heard a reading of the play and ordered it to be put into rehearsal at once.

which the aspiring young author gave a reading from his Ukrainian tales. The private success of that reading was followed in a few months by the public success of the printed stories.

For three years Gogol' continued to exploit the precious vein of Ukrainian ore, aware that sooner or later it must be exhausted. Its limitation worried him. He knew he was able to write splendidly once he had a subject, but he also knew he was lame at inventing story-outlines. His artistic procedure was the elaboration of minutiae. From trivial details he could construct paragraphs and pages of brilliant description or delicious humor or pathos to mist the eyes of many a reader. But to find a point from which to begin, there was the difficulty. In October 1835, when he had decided to write for the theatre, he urged in a letter to Puškin: [4]

... Be a good fellow and give me some subject or other, comic or not, a true Russian anecdote. My hand trembles with eagerness to write a comedy. If I don't do so, time will pass, I shall do nothing, and then I don't know how I shall get out of my present situation. All in all, I have nothing but the miserable 600 rubles from my university appointment. Give me a subject and I shall at once write a five-act comedy which, I assure you, will be devilishly funny ...

Puškin furnished the anecdote, and *The Inspector General* was produced from it, just as at a later time Pushkin furnished him with another story situation out of which *Dead Souls* was produced. His manipulations of story-outlines from Tieck have already been mentioned.[5]

---

[4] Cited by Boris de Schloezer in *Gogol,* No. 37 of the series *Le Roman des grandes existences* (Paris, 1932), p. 115. Biographical information has been drawn from that book.

[5] Tieck's reputation in Russia had spread rapidly since 1817 when Žukovskij first proposed translating tales from *Phantasus.* A number of these did appear in Russian journals in the latter 1820's, particularly in *The Russian Messenger.* Selections were made only from Tieck's early Romantic works; his contemporary "Dresdener Novellen" held no interest for Russians. It is interesting to observe the shocked reactions of Russians like Prince Vjazemskij to Küchelbecker's *Mnemosyne* article of 1824, in which he related his interview with Tieck in Dresden in 1820 and quoted the doctrinaire Romantic notions he heard on that occasion: condemnation of Klopstock and Wieland, praise of Novalis, and the statement that "People usually place on the same level the great Goethe and the immature Schiller." Prince Vjazemskij wrote A. I. Turgenev that Küchelbecker's article was "a heavy beery ecstasy". These views as of Jena, 1798—1801, never found acceptance in Russia, nor did Tieck ever command the prestige as critic that he enjoyed as author. See Percy Matenko, "Tieck's Russian Friends", *PMLA,* LV. 4 (December 1940), pp. 1129—1145.

With fame now seized in 1831—1832, there was the problem of holding the elusive captive. More Ukrainian tales were forthcoming: *How the Two Ivans Quarrelled* in 1834, and then in 1835 the fine collection called *Mirgorod. Stories serving as a continuation of Evenings on a Farm near Dikan'ka.* But a new vein of ore had to be found, and what source offered more likely success for one of his affinities with German Romanticism than the Tales of Hoffmann which were now at the peak of their Russian and their European popularity? Thus, in 1833—1834, while Puškin was composing *The Queen of Spades,* he began a Hoffmannizing tale of his own, entitled *The Portrait* (Portret).

1. *THE PORTRAIT* (1835 version)

The story, as originally written in 1833—1834 and published in *Arabesques* in 1835, is divided into two parts.

Part I relates the history of a young painter named Čertkov who one day at an auction spends his last fifty rubles for a portrait of a sinister old man with fierce and life-like eyes. Once hung on his wall, the picture so fascinates him that he is obliged to cover it with a sheet in order to divert his mind from it. During a state of half-dream between sleep and waking he beholds the sinister old man descend from the picture and speak to him, promising wealth and fame if Čertkov will but renounce his pursuit of great Art. The young man dismisses the experience later as a hallucination. On the following day the landlord comes with a policeman to confiscate Čertkov's belongings for unpaid rent. Just as the policeman lays hands on the portrait, a hidden spring in the frame ejects a roll of gold coins. Himself aghast, Čertkov pretends equanimity, pays the rent with the gold, and sends the landlord and the policeman away.

Soon afterwards a lady appears. She has brought her daughter to be painted by the "famous" artist Čertkov. Again suppressing astonishment, he sets to work at once. The clients' second visit surprises him in contemplation of his representation of Psyche. With delight they praise his excellent likeness of the lady's daughter and the rapid skill that completed it earlier than all expectation, pay him handsomely, and leave.

Fame comes directly to Čertkov. Aware that his art is the sorriest hack-work, he nevertheless revels in the wealth it brings. One day he comes upon a great painting by a true and dedicated artist. The sight awes him. He hurries home to attempt something genuine himself. But he can produce only the cheap and tawdry. In fury, he exhausts his wealth buying up all the great paintings he can find, ripping them to shreds one after one. His fury becomes mania, his mania becomes fever and delirium. He dies, raving about the picture of an evil old man which he says is hanging on the wall, but no such picture is there.

Part II opens with another auction scene. With a cry of "Ah, there it is!" one customer picks up the portrait of the sinister old man and proceeds to relate its history to the curious by-standers.

The speaker's father, who had been an artist, was summoned one night to the death-bed of a feared and hated old money-lender named Petromixali, who demanded to have his portrait painted immediately. The artist set to work, contrived the fierce eyes of his subject, but refused to continue when he beheld the eyes come to life on the canvas. Petromixali explained that he had made a pact with the Evil One, but that he could escape hell for long ages yet if his portrait could be painted to hold half of his self in this world. He died at the stroke of midnight. The artist retained the unfinished picture.

One day he began his confession of the incident to the priest. At that precise moment his wife choked on some needles she had in her mouth and died on the spot. On another occasion he began his confession anew, and one of his children fell from the window where it was leaning and was killed. The artist retired to a monastery; his only surviving son, the present speaker, went to the Army.

Years later the son visited the holy place, and there, before a picture of the Blessed Virgin which he had just completed, the father managed to relate the entire story of Petromixali. Petromixali was Antichrist himself, seeking to invade God's world by supernatural means. But if on the fiftieth anniversary of his death some one would recapitulate his story, his evil force would be dissipated forever.

The fiftieth anniversary coincides with the moment of the auction, and even as the speaker concludes his tale, the form of the old man vanishes from the portrait and only an insignificant landscape is left.

The ultra-Romantic matter shows Gogol' still fascinated by the elements of horror, fate, hereditary guilt, witchcraft, and evil enchantment which he had found in Tieck's *Liebeszauber* and *Pietro von Albano.* Yet Belinskij cited *The Portrait* as a story à la Hoffmann and over-harshly denounced it as a poor imitation.[6] Hoffmannian it is, but with a very clever admixture of other materials, and much ingenuity has been expended on determining its origins.

The classical story of Pygmalion's statue was a legend of wish-fulfillment, quite at variance with the modern motif of the picture-come-to-life, which is a variation of the theme of the Double. In its crudest form it is simply a ghost-motif, and as such had been used by many an author since Horace Walpole's proto-Gothic romance, *The*

---

[6] Belinskij, *Sočinenija* (Moscow, 1891), Vol. I, p. 493.

Castle of Otranto (1765), had brought the quaint old ghost of Alphonso the Good down from Alphonso's portrait and caused it to stalk past the terrified members of the household. Hoffmann, too, used the motif in different forms. Stender-Petersen proposed *Aus dem Leben dreier Freunde* (translated 1831) as the source for Gogol's tale,[7] but his proposal carries little conviction since in that story Alexander merely recognizes the identity of the old woman's ghost by its resemblance to her portrait. With more plausibility, Čudakov suggested [8] *Der Artushof,* where the old painter Berklinger and his "son" (actually his daughter Felizitas in boy's clothing) do descend from the murals of the ancient Arthur's Hall in Danzig to enter the action of the story. But the story itself bears no other resemblance to Gogol's. Better still was the same scholar's proposal of Washington Irving's *The Adventure of the Mysterious Picture,* from the collection usually known as *The Traveler,* which had appeared in Russian translation in the journal *Athene* in 1829. Irving's story concerns a guest at a fox-hunting party who spends the night downstairs for inability to sleep in his assigned room, where a sinister portrait hangs on the wall. The sympathetic host explains that the portrait is a picture of a murdered man painted by the murderer, not from observation of the corpse, but from the image in his haunted memory. The translation of the American story should probably be regarded as a contributory source for Gogol'. At least it formed part of the literary atmosphere in which Gogol' wrote.

The fierce, glittering eyes of Petromixali, however, have a different origin, as Šljapkin discovered,[9] namely Charles Maturin's celebrated *Melmoth the Wanderer* (1820), which soon after its publication was translated into Russian and enjoyed great popularity in Russia through the Romantic age.

In Chapter I of that prodigious tale, young John Melmoth is summoned to the deathbed of a miserly uncle. After the old man's death his will is found to contain directions to "destroy or cause to be destroyed" a certain portrait representing a sinister old man with extraordinarily fierce and evil eyes and bearing the legend "J. Melmoth, 1646". The nephew rips the picture to shreds and burns it on the grate.

[7] Stender-Petersen, *op. cit.,* p. 646.
[8] Čudakov, "Otnošenija tvorčestva Gogolja k zapadno-evropejskim literaturam", *Kievskie Universitetskie Izvestija,* 1908; cited by Gorlin, *N. V. Gogol und E. T. A. Hoffmann,* Inaugural-Dissertation (Berlin, 1933) (Teildruck), p. 9.
[9] Gorlin, *N.V. Gogol und E. T. A. Hoffmann, op. cit.,* p. 17, says: "Die Ehre, das Urbild des geheimnisvollen Porträts gefunden zu haben, gehört Šljapkin", and refers to *Literaturnyj Vestnik,* 1902.

That night, as he sleeps, the original appears to him in a dream and John awakes to find his wrist black and blue "from the gripe of a strong hand". That same night brings an unexpected guest, a young Spaniard named Moncada, who for three and one-half volumes of narrative reveals the horrendous life of the original Melmoth of 1646. At the price of his soul that individual had compacted with Satan for more-than-human knowledge and for a life-span of a century and a half. A clause of the infernal compact permitted Melmoth's withdrawal, provided he could persuade another to accept the bond voluntarily, and many were the desperate individuals whom Melmoth succored in direst need, yet not one of them ever accepted his "unspeakable condition" for total rescue from their assorted plights. Late in Volume IV Moncada is interrupted by the arrival of the Wanderer himself. The hundred and fifty years are up this midnight and he has come to spend his final hours on his ancestral domain. He must now meet the terms of the bond. In the morning the two young men follow his footsteps from the house to the edge of a high cliff overlooking the sea. There the footprints end.

Here, then, in Maturin's popular and current novel are the originals of Gogol's portrait of the sinister old man with the fierce eyes and the explicit compact with Satan, together with the terms for its transfer, for of Petromixali we read:

... he sometimes gave money gratis, not seeking for its return, but making such a demand that everyone fled from him in horror, and even the most talkative women could not bring their lips to repeat it.

Here, too, is a strong contributory factor in the make-up of Odoevskij's Segeliel' in *The Improvisor* and (apparently) of the Count de Saint Germain in Puškin's *The Queen of Spades*. Significantly, all three — Segeliel', Saint Germain, and Petromixali — are creations of the year 1833.

In regard to plot outline, however, *The Portrait* has no more to do with *Melmoth the Wanderer* than with any of the other works proposed by the scholars previously mentioned. Rather, it comes from Hoffmann's novel *Die Elixiere des Teufels* (1816), and specifically from the story-inset which the hero, Medardus, reads in Part II, Section 2 (*Die Busse*) and which is the manuscript biography of his ancestor five generations removed, Franzesko the Painter, whose sin involved all his descendants in sin.

Franzesko, Medardus learned from the manuscript, had studied painting with holy dedication under Leonardo da Vinci until the revered.

Master's death. Then Franzesko fell into evil company. Pagan-minded painters, even sculptors, became his associates, whose sole concern was with the fleshly art of the ancients.[10] When wild living with these riotous companions had reduced him to poverty, he recalled an unfulfilled promise to paint a picture of Saint Rosalia in the chapel of a certain Capuchin monastery. Simultaneously the wicked idea enters his mind to flout the silly monks by painting the Saint nude and with the face of Venus. He actually begins to carry out his plan, when lo! a spirit of holy awe seizes his hand and makes him clothe the naked form and to place angelic features where he meant to depict unholy ones. His mind becomes troubled and he cannot complete the painting. His doubts turn to physical illness. Whereat his jolly companions come to him, one of them disguised as a doctor offering medicines, but the medicines are really the devil's elixirs which rouse in him a frantic sensual desire. He recommences his task of desecration, but the saintly face emerges even when he is most eager to paint the face of Venus. Suddenly the eyes of the painting come alive. Their glance strikes Franzesko like lightning to the ground. He rouses from unconsciousness to behold the countenance of Venus smiling down at him. With frenzied passion he seeks to force the whole body to come to life, and on the third day of his infatuation with the picture he hears his chamber door open and amid a rustling of garments sees the very original of the painting advance toward him.

The beautiful creature becomes his mistress directly. They live in sinful delight until their son is born. At that moment the beautiful creature is transformed into a blue-spotted monster that dies with a shriek and Franzesko realizes that he has contracted an alliance with a female devil (Teufelshexe). Taking the infant, he flees to the wilderness, abandons the child, and lives as a hermit. One evening, amid the sunset he beholds a vision of Saint Rosalia and hears her intercessory prayer. But a voice from the clouds cries out that he shall wander accursed as long as his race continues to live in sin. Endowed with ghost-like life he watches the sinning generations of his line until Medardus, the greatest sinner of them all, triumphs at last over evil and achieves sainthood.

---

[10] This passage, unusually partisan and doctrinaire for Hoffmann, reflects the aversion of the German Romantik to Hellas and to sculpture as an art medium. Painting, the art capable of nuances and moods and capable of representing distance, was commended far above sculpture, and the Middle Ages, not Greece, was to be its inspiration.

Hoffmann's own source, it may be added, was the Gothic romance *The Monk,* 1795, by the Englishman, Matthew Gregory Lewis, translated into German in 1797 as *Der Mönch.* In Lewis's novel, Matilda, whom Lucifer ultimately reveals to be one of his minions, first tempts the monk Ambrosio by means of a painting of herself as the Madonna. By supernatural devices she introduced the painting into his cell, and, contemplating it there, the un-genuine holiness of Ambrosio was turned to carnal lust, which led him in turn to compact with the Evil One. Thus the line of development passes from Gogol' by way of Hoffmann and Lewis back to the general area of the English Gothic romances, to which *Melmoth the Wanderer* was a belated addition in 1820 and which had as its point of origin Walpole's *The Castle of Otranto* in 1765.

In his double story Gogol' apportioned the Hoffmannian motifs equally to his two artists. To Čertkov he gave the temptation, fall, luxury, wealth, and catastrophe of Franzesko; to the artist who painted Petromixali he gave the sin of painting the blasphemous portrait, with resultant disasters to members of his family, but also Franzesko's repentance and expiation and the peace which both Franzesko and Medardus found in the holy enclosures of the monastery. Just as Franzesko once beheld the vision of Saint Rosalia in the sunset and later painted her picture in Medardus's home monastery, so Gogol's unnamed artist is vouchsafed a vision of the Virgin and ultimately achieves peace by completing the picture of her.

Further details that entered into the amalgam of Gogol's story may be traced to still other points of origin. Gorlin mentions [11] the interesting fact that there lived in Petersburg in the 1830's a money-lender named Modžeram-Motomalov who was thought to be the prototype of Petromixali. Something of the baleful Coppelius of *Der Sandmann,* Gorlin claims,[12] has entered the concept of Petromixali, together with some of the powerful magic — benevolent in the original — of Archivarius Lindhorst in *Der goldene Topf.* A final impulse came, Gorlin thinks,[13] from an episode of a picture-come-to-life in *Die Irrungen,* translated in 1829 as *The Magic Portfolio* (Očarovannyj Bumažnik).

All of these suggestions are valid, for the truth of the matter is that Gogol', like Puškin, had read a good deal of Hoffmann and a good deal

---

[11] Gorlin, *N. V. Gogol und E. T. A. Hoffmann, op. cit.,* p. 14. (Gorlin here draws on Karatygin's Memoirs.)
[12] *Ibid.,* p. 15.
[13] *Ibid.,* p. 11.

of Romantic literature in general by 1833 and was working within an
established repertory of motifs and symbols. Readers expected a re-
currence of themes, and writers could manipulate familiar patterns
at will. Puškin, as we have seen, penetrated to the substratum of the
Romantic area and built anew with consummate genius of originality.
Gogol' did not delve quite so far. He clung to the more familiar practice
of adapting and combining isolated episodes. Fundamentally, *The
Portrait* may be defined as a reworking of the Franzesko-inset from
Die Elixiere des Teufels with skillful overlay of additions from other
works, most notably from *Melmoth the Wanderer*.

His purpose, however, was unique. His story is a sermon in moral
contrasts. Čertkov was tempted and fell. His end was catastrophe. The
old painter of Part II, on the other hand, succumbed only partially
to evil. His painting of Petromixali was left incomplete. He suffered
from his association with Evil, but he repented, sought the ways of the
Good, and died blessed in a monastery after having executed a sacred
work of art. The religious naïveté of Gogol' is reflected in Čertkov's
sin, which was to have desired fame without work. It was an incontes-
table moral that he wished to convey and he conveyed it with convincing realism. With the more cosmic, mystical, and eerie intrusion
of Evil into the lives of people in Part II, he was less successful. The
old painter is portrayed vaguely, by comparison with Čertkov, and his
whole story carries appreciably less conviction. Gogol's religious didacticism is blurred by the profusion of motifs of the art-tale, just as his
attraction to *Die Elixiere des Teufels* was of an ambiguous kind. He
was drawn to the religiosity of that novel,[14] the grandiose saint's legend
with its convulsive struggle between the powers of Light and Darkness
fascinated him, yet its gorgeous colors and gaudy melodrama delighted
his Romanticist's heart. The Franzesko-inset in particular glorified

[14] There is irony in the fact that Gogol', a Russian Orthodox, should be so
attracted to the Roman Catholicizing *Elixiere des Teufels,* which was written by
Hoffmann, a nominal Lutheran. Boris de Schloezer's biography, *Gogol, op. cit.,*
pp. 149–153, discusses Gogol's ambiguous favoring of Roman Catholicism while
in Rome in 1837–1838. Whatever temporary influence may have been exerted
upon him at the time by the Polish mystics of Princess Volkonskaja's Roman
salon, he later turned most unpleasantly hateful toward the Roman church,
vilifying its rites and practices in contrast to those of Russian Orthodoxy. As
for Hoffmann's pro-Catholic feelings, Hewett-Thayer (*Hoffmann: Author of the
Tales,* pp. 123–128) is inclined to take them quite seriously, at least during the
Bamberg period. It was the puzzle of the Catholic world how Hoffmann and
Tieck, after such works as *Die Elixiere des Teufels* and *Genoveva,* should not
renounce their Protestant affiliations. The attraction for both men seems to have
lain in the external beauty of Catholic rituals rather than in the dogma.

painting, and Gogol' yearned to become a painter; it termed Art holy, and Gogol' was thirsting for holiness. The combination was irresistable. His own story of alternate outcomes was constructed on a much more modest scale but it was wholly consistent within its limits. It was with distress that he discovered that readers were taking it as a mere art-tale, missing the vital message he had sought to convey.[15]

2. *THE NEVSKIJ PROSPEKT*

Late in 1833, presumably right after completion of *The Portrait,* Gogol' began a second Hoffmannizing story which took its title, *The Nevskij Prospekt,* from the great boulevard of Petersburg. Like the former work, it was first published in *Arabesques* in 1835.

The opening section, which recalls Chapter I of *Eugene Onegin* (1823) and which anticipates Dostoevskij's *White Nights* (1848), is a brilliant prose poem, an evocation of the metropolis through a series of descriptions of its famous thoroughfare from the hour of dawn "when all Petersburg smells of hot, freshly-baked bread" to the mysterious time of evening dusk and the lighting of the street lamps. It is the latter time amid which Gogol' produces his two characters, the young artist Piskarev and his companion, a gay blade of a Lieutenant Pirogov, walking on the avenue. Almost simultaneously each espies a girl who excites his imagination, Piskarev a brunette, Pirogov a blond, and they separate (never to meet again), each in pursuit of his own ideal. The story, sharply divided like *The Portrait* into two parts, presents their separate adventures as a study in moral contrasts.

Piskarev's pursuit of the brunette, who seems not unaware that she is being followed, brings him to a tawdry fourth-storey brothel. The girl is beautiful, aged seventeen, and happy to have a customer; Piskarev, who has followed a vision of beauty, flees from her in horror.

Dejected and disillusioned, he sits alone in his room that night, when a footman in gorgeous livery knocks and brings him a message from his mistress, the same brunette of the evening's pursuit: she has sent her carriage to fetch Piskarev. The painter takes the carriage, arrives at a magnificent ball where the young lady is dancing with a distin-

---

[15]   Z. Serapionova, "Gofmanskie motivy v Peterburgskix povestjax Gogolja", an article in *Literaturnaja Učeba,* a monthly journal of Soviet writers, 1939, No. 8—9 (August-September), pp. 78—92, sees Čertkov's tragedy as the tragedy of the artist in the capitalistic city, a victim of capitalistic economics. Gogol', she opines, was prevented from knowing the real Hoffmann, whose works were distorted by the regime of Nicholas I.

guished personage. She is a gracious beauty, friend of important people, mistress of languages, and cynosure of all eyes. But the ball fades away. It has all been a vision seen in Piskarev's candle-flame.

The young man's life becomes an alternation of waking torment and blissful dreams. When sleep forsakes him he has recourse to opium, which he obtains from a wily Persian shawl-merchant in return for voluptuous pictures painted at the Persian's dictation. The opium-dreams become shorter and more frequent.

Suddenly it occurs to Piskarev that the girl may be an unfortunate victim of circumstances longing to be rescued. He hurries to her, pours out his offers of help, only to be laughed at for his pains. She wants no sewing and washing and domestic drudgery. He goes home, crushed. A week later, neighbors batter down his door and discover his corpse on the floor, the throat slit with a razor.

Lieutenant Pirogov's pursuit of his blond, meanwhile, has taken the form of a series of attempts on the virtue of a pretty and stupid wife of a German merchant named Schiller. The Lieutenant plans various stratagems to circumvent the drunken Schiller and his crony the drunken Hoffmann — not the famous Schiller and the famous Hoffmann, Gogol' explains, but merely two dull Germans of the same names and domesticated in Petersburg — and at last comes upon the frightened woman alone. At that moment Schiller, Hoffmann, and a third crony arrive unexpectedly and beat Pirogov soundly.

In fury, Pirogov sets out to report the humiliating affair to the authorities. But on his way he stops at a café, eats two jam puffs, reads a selection from *The Northern Bee,* and discovers that his wrath has subsided. By evening he is dancing at a ball, having dismissed the whole episode from his memory.

At this point the author emerges to close the story as he had begun it, with a description of the boulevard. He cautions his readers to beware of its deceptions:

It deceives at all hours, the Nesvkij Prospekt does, but most of all when night falls in masses of shadow on it, throwing into relief the white and dun-colored walls of the houses when all the town is transformed into noise and brilliance, when myriads of carriages roll over bridges, postillions shout and jolt up and down on their horses, and when the demon himself lights the street lamps to show everything in false colors.

All scholars have agreed that the story is Hoffmann-inspired but have disagreed as to the precise source. The Soviet critic, Z. Serapionova, properly looks first at the earliest known sketch of the work, which bore the tentative title of *The Terrible Hand* (Strašnaja Ruka) and which had as its hero, not an artist, but a Dorpat student. Wandering in the streets of the town by night, the student came to a window through which he glimpsed a beautiful woman and a hideous man. Miss Serapionova points out the parallel with the paragraph at the end of the "Zweites Abenteuer" of *Meister Floh,* where George Pepusch peers in at a window to behold the lovely Dörtje Elverdink with old Johannes Swammerdamm.[16] Slight as the passage is, it may well have served Gogol' as a point of departure — we recall how Polevoj had developed *The Felicity of Madness* out of a passage only slightly longer from that same "Zweites Abenteuer" — and it would then follow that Piskarev and Pirogov are transpositions of George Pepusch and Peregrinus Tyss. This would account for the otherwise unexplained friendship of the ill-assorted Russian pair, a friendship which is mentioned once and then lost sight of immediately, for Pepusch and Peregrinus Tyss were friends, and even rivals for Dörtje's love, in the German story. Piskarev's pursuit of the unnamed beauty would then be parallel to George's pursuit of Dörtje through the streets of Frankfurt. But Gogol's altered plan, Miss Serapionova says, substituted an artist for the Dorpat student, transferred the action to Petersburg, and imposed upon the hero that quest for beauty which brought the student Anselmus, the hero of *Der goldene Topf,* to the enchanted house of Archivarius Lindhorst and ultimately to "Atlantis", the land of Art. Thus Piskarev pursues Anselmus' vision but discovers it to be a Satanic delusion. Stender-Petersen makes the same claim for a Piskarev-Anselmus connection, but adds that it is "freilich unbeweisbar".[17]

Michael Gorlin, by all odds the most perspicacious and reliable investigator of the Hoffmann-Gogol' relationships, equates the *problem* of Anselmus with the *problem* of Piskarev and finds the resolution in both instances to be through dreams, in Hoffmann's case positive and optimistic, in Gogol's case negative and tragic. No story-elements are brought over from *Der goldene Topf,* however. For these Gorlin seeks elsewhere. Čudakov's proposal of a source in *Die Jesuiterkirche in G.* he rejects as completely wrong, which it is, but finds that Vinogradov has furnished "convincing proof" [18] that the brunette girl in *The Nevskij Prospekt* is a direct imitation of the trollope-heroine in the novel *L'Âne mort et la femme guillotinée* by the popular, though now forgotten, writer Jules Janin. This overgrown short story, published in Paris in 1829, is told in first person by the hero, a young man who has

[16]   *Ibid.,* p. 84.
[17]   Stender-Petersen, "Gogol und die deutsche Romantik", *op. cit.,* p. 645.
[18]   Gorlin, *N.V. Gogol und E. T. A. Hoffmann, op. cit.,* p. 32.

fallen in love with the pretty grisette Henriette. Much of his narrative
is occupied with his ultra-sentimental efforts to make an honest woman
of her, but, like her Russian successor, Henriette laughs at the very
thought of domestic chores and drab toil. Hers, however, is not a life
of mere pleasure. She is involved in crime, and a series of misdemeanors
leads eventually to her committing a murder, for which she is brought
to trial and executed.

Vinogradov also points out [10] that Janin's *La Confession* (1830),
another tale of disillusioned love, contains a discussion of opium as an
"invention of romancers". Anatole, the hero of *La Confession,* makes
a conventional mariage, only to discover that his wife's affections are
dissipated in fantastic dreams of wealth and social position. He strangles
her on their wedding night. Later, overcome with remorse, he confesses
his crime and becomes a priest! It is entirely plausible that Gogol' read
both books of Janin, as well as other authors whom Vinogradov lists
as being interested in opium and opium-dreams: Hugo, Sue, Dumas,
Michel Raymond, Balzac, Maturin. But he did not borrow from any of
them in making *The Nevskij Prospekt.*

Not the least popular or least significant of the books dealing with
the topic of opium was De Quincey's famous *Confessions of an English
Opium Eater,* published in Petersburg in 1834 with no mention of De
Quincey, as *Confession of an English Opium User, a work of Maturin,
the author of Melmoth* (!) (Ispoved' angličanina, upotrebljavšego opium,
soč. Matjurina, avtora Mel'mota). On the basis of its publication date,
August 21, 1834, an attempt was made to force the composition of
The Nevskij Prospekt forward to as late as October-November 1834,
whereas all evidence indicates the preceding winter as the time of its
writing. Yet there is indeed a connection between the two works, as
Vinogradov states,[20] not through the Russian translation of 1834, but
through the French translation, or more correctly the French adaptation by Alfred de Musset, which appeared in the *Bibliographie de la
France* in 1828. This version included an interpolation of considerable
length which corresponds to nothing in De Quincey's original, and it is
precisely this section added by Musset, a ball-room sequence, that has
bearing on Piskarev's hallucinatory vision.

But of all the investigators of Hoffmann-Gogol' relationships, Miss

---

[19] V. V. Vinogradov, *Evoljucija russkago naturalizma* (Leningrad, 1929), a
collection of six articles. Article 2, pp. 89—126, entitled "O literaturnoj
ciklizacii", discusses the opium-literature in Russia in the 1830's. See p. 91.
[20] *Ibid.,* p. 93.

Jeannette Eyre alone has seen the vital connection between *The Nevskij Prospekt* and Hoffmann's *Aus dem Leben dreier Freunde,* (translated 1831 in *The Moscow Telegraph*). She mentions the matter only casually [21] after reaffirming Gorlin's stand on the equation of the *problem* of Anselmus with the *problem* of Piskarev, but it is that story of Hoffmann's which opens with the simultaneous perceiving of a beautiful unknown girl by a trio of friends and which continues with their separate pursuits of her with different degrees of success. [22]

The story opens with three friends, Alexander, Marzell, and Severin, gathered after long separation on a fine afternoon in the Tiergarten of Berlin to tell their respective adventures. Alexander's adventure has consisted of his installation in a house which he inherited from a deceased maiden aunt and his subsequent encounters with her ghost. As he concludes his tale, a family group of four persons takes the adjoining table. The beautiful daughter catches the eye of all three, and when they leave, each decides to seek out the girl.

Two years later the three friends are again met at the same table in the Tiergarten to exchange information about their lives in the interim.

Marzell had sought the girl in vain for some time. One day when he delivered a letter to a certain Privy Councillor Asling from the latter's nephew, he was met at the door by the beauty herself. She was Pauline Asling, the Privy Councillor's daughter. He became a frequent visitor at her house, in time declared his love to her, but eventually came to the decision that she was a frivolous creature interested solely in fine clothes and amusements. He left her forever and has spent most of the two-year period in the Army.

Severin, a highly sensitive young man, admits that two years previously he had been in an unhealthy mental state. He was obsessed with dreams and fantasies. Like a Persian mage, he imagined that he understood the language of the birds. Certain odors produced hallucinations in him, particularly the odors of roses and carnations, which he associated with life and death respectively. His unwelcome suit to Pauline Asling had ended in a grotesque hoax perpetrated by her father when that elderly man had met him at the door in a ridiculous costume that included a cap decorated with carnations. In horror Severin had fled from the scene and has spent most of the intervening time, like Marzell, in the army. He has completely recovered from his former morbid notions.

---

[21] Eyre, *Gogol and German Romanticism, op. cit.,* (see footnote 2 above), p. 50.

[22] As originally scheduled for the third and fourth volumes of the *Fantasiestücke* in 1814, the work dealt with the lives of Marzell and Severin only, and was entitled *Szenen aus dem Leben zweier Freunde*. Temporarily abandoned, the story was revised in 1815 to include the third friend, Alexander, and *his* narrative. In augmented form it was included in Volume I of *Die Serapionsbrüder* (1819) with the title: *Ein Fragment aus dem Leben dreier Freunde.*

Alexander begins his tale about his courtship of a beautiful girl but is interrupted by the arrival of Pauline herself: she is his wife.

Aus dem Leben dreier Freunde is a variant of the classical "comedy of errors" but interspersed with Romantic lore about ghosts, hallucinatory dreams, flower symbolism, and the like. Its core is the farcical wooing by two inappropriate suitors and the successful wooing by a third. Gogol's transformation reduced the number of wooers from three to two — entirely unaware of the fact that Hoffmann's own first draft told the story of *two* friends under the original title of *Aus dem Leben zweier Freunde* —, and of these two, one he directed into stark tragedy, the other he reduced to a parody. Piskarev was made to combine Marzell's impassioned pursuit with Severin's morbid dreams. But he was not allowed to be consoled for his loss like the former, nor to be cured of his hallucinations like the latter, much less to rejoin his friend Pirogov at some later date to talk over cheerfully the outcome of their respective quests. The brunette he pursued was not the creature of varying moods that Pauline Asling was, but a common tart with the sordid views of Janin's *femme guillotinée*. In visions born of his lonely candle-flame he imagined her as a kind of Princess, but such Hoffmannesque visions of beauty sank back into the candle-flame from which they arose. He had recourse to De Quincey-Musset's consoler, opium, prostituting his art to purchase the drug, but in the last analysis he had to recognize that the pursuit of beauty was an illusion. Nothing remained for him but to slit his throat with his razor.

Gogol's reason for assigning his hero this tragic course is not immediately clear. That Piskarev is a painter at all seems explainable only in external terms, because Gogol' aspired to be a painter, because painters were fashionable as heroes in the early 1830's, and perhaps because he was allied in the author's mind with his close contemporary, Čertkov. Certainly very little is made of the fact that he paints. If he prostitutes his art as Čertkov did, he does so belatedly in order to purchase opium from the lubricious Persian, yet he perishes as miserably as his predecessor without having committed his predecessor's sin. In fact, it is the very dedication to beauty, which would have been Čertkov's salvation, that destroys him. We perceive that Gogol' is indicting the Anselmus-inherited aspiration to beauty which he had championed in *The Portrait*.

Anomalous too is Piskarev's friendship with the insensitive ladykiller, Lieutenant Pirogov. Their association is to be explained only by reference to *Aus dem Leben dreier Freunde,* which was based on

the device of contrasting narratives, and perhaps by reference to the
friendship and love-rivalry of George and Pepusch and Peregrinus Tyss
in *Meister Floh,* assuming that the earliest plan of the story did derive
from that source. The conscienceless officer reflects none of Hoffmann's
three friends. He exists because in the story-model there were different
friends with different fates. His adventure itself is Gogol's own invention, and as it complements the adventure of Piskarev, the author's
bitter intention is fully revealed. He means to say that the sensitive
perish and the insensitive survive. The conclusion is more darkly pessimistic than any yet considered, for Piskarev's fate becomes "the baleful
consequences of an unbridled imagination" while his sufferings have
about them nothing that could merit being called "the felicity of madness".

The whole of this sombre fable is enclosed in a vision of the metropolis,
where all things are contained. Awareness of the urban scene is a mark
of modernity amid Gogol's Romanticism, as it had been amid Hoffmann's Romanticism, and there is reason to believe that when Gogol'
abandoned Ukrainian settings, he chose to write Petersburg tales as
Hoffmann had written Berlin tales. Both Stender-Petersen [23] and after
him Serapionova [24] label Hoffmann "the poet of Berlin", with a slight
exaggeration, since Hoffmann's tales are laid in many and diverse
places. It was realistic setting for fantastic events that interested him,
rather than the glorification of Berlin or any other city.[25] It is noteworthy that upon Serapion-Brother Ottmar's conclusion of *Aus dem
Leben dreier Freunde,* Serapion-Brother Theodor — who most frequently speaks with the voice of Hoffmann himself — comments:

You had definite reason for transferring the setting of the piece to
Berlin and for citing streets and public squares. In general, it is, in my
opinion also, not bad at all to designate the locale exactly. Besides
the fact that the whole thing thereby gains an illusion of historical
actuality to aid a dull imagination, it also gains extraordinarily in

[23]   Stender-Petersen, "Gogol und die deutsche Romantik", op. cit., p. 641.
[24]   Serapionova, *Gofmanskie motivy v Peterburgskix povestjax Gogolja, op. cit.,*
p. 81.
[25]   Hoffmann was skillful in evoking illusions of local color even in the case of
cities where he had never been, e.g. Rome, in tales like *Prinzessin Brambilla*
and *Signor Formica.* Of his total production — over sixty stories — only about
ten have Berlin as their locale. It is interesting that precisely these stories
figure so prominently in Russian translations and adaptations: *Aus dem Leben
dreier Freunde, Das öde Haus, Die Brautwahl, Datura fastuosa* (where Berlin
was not specifically identified), *Die Irrungen, Die Abenteuer der Sylvesternacht,
Ritter Gluck.*

vividness and freshness, even for one not acquainted with the place designated as the scene of action.

Whether Gogol' read these added words or not, the list of his Petersburg tales coincides with the list of his tales of Hoffmannian inspiration.

Finally, *The Nevskij Prospekt* reveals Gogol's inability to cope with the interlocking worlds of Real and Ideal that regularly mark Hoffmann's writing, or even with the interlocking of characters' lives. Even *The Portrait* combined its two parts by a fragile link. In the present work almost all pretense at weaving the two sections together has been abandoned. Each stands independent within the framework of the urban poem. Gorlin's remark is apt: [26]

The Hoffmannian interpenetration [Ineinander] is here replaced, even more markedly than in *The Portrait,* by a parallelism [Nebeneinander].

3. *THE DIARY OF A MADMAN*

Only the title *Notes of a Mad Musician* (Zapiski sumasšedšego muzikanta), preserved among Gogol's notes, gives any hint of his original intentions for his third tale in the Hoffmannizing tradition. Inevitably the subject summons to mind Hoffmann's immortal Johannes Kreisler and *Kater Murr*. A bold departure from the more typical Romanticism is indicated by the suppression of all associations with music, or indeed with any of the arts, in the completed version of the story, which appeared together with its predecessors in *Arabesques* in 1835 under the title *Notes of a Madman* (Zapiski sumasšedšego), or more familiarly in English: *The Diary of a Madman*. The hero, Aksentij Ivanovič Popriščin, is a clerk in a government office, the first of the important line of such hero-clerks in Russian fiction, whose real-life counterparts only a decade before had been the idealistic poets of the "Archive Youth". He is aged forty-two, he is physically unprepossessing and socially a non-entity. His diary entries compose the tale.

The first of these, dated October 3, surveys his existence: menial work, contempt of his fellow-workers for him, fawning efforts to please per-

[26] In view of Gogol's original plan to work from *Meister Floh,* one can only wonder whether the Petersburg artisans, Schiller and Hoffmann, were conceived as ghostly figures like Leuwenhoek and Swammerdamm and later allowed to stand as realistic figures with "coincidental" names in the finished version for the purpose of parody.

sons he fears and despises, and a wistful adoration of his employer's daughter. Recently he has overheard a conversation between the young lady's dog Madgie and another canine named Fido and is much intrigued to hear more. The entries of October 4 and of November 6, 8, and 9 elaborate the daily humiliations he endures and the fantastic dreams he dreams.

On November 11 he records his unsuccessful interrogation of the dog Madgie in an effort to discover whether his beloved lady is to be married or not. On the following day he tries to interrogate Fido, who angrily attacks him, but he succeeds in snatching from the dog's bed a packet of letters which have been exchanged between Madgie and the other dog.

The long entry of November 13 reproduces the Madgie-Fido letters, which reflect the candid opinion of normal people about Popriščin and which contain the information that his beloved lady is about to marry a handsome kammer-junker.

December 3 shows him imagining himself with various exalted titles. December 5 finds him fascinated with a newspaper article about the vacancy of the Spanish throne, and on December 8 he is quite engrossed in problems of the Spanish succession.

The next entry, "2000 A.D., April 43", records how he terrified his housekeeper with the announcement of being the King of Spain. Under "Martober 86, between day and night" he tells of his appearance at the office in sorrowing incognito, and three entries later, under "Madrid, February thirtieth", he announces his arrival in the Spanish palace — the madhouse. The ceremonies, such as the shaving of his head, are preliminaries to being allowed to reign.

The final entry, dated "34 Февраля Yrae 349", is a cry of anguish for release, for cessation of the keepers' beatings, for a troika to whirl him through the air, over Italy and on to the huts of Russia, where in one of the huts his mother sits by a window ... The appeal breaks off with a sly remark of stark idiocy: "And do you know that the Bey of Algiers has a boil just under his nose?"

From almost continuous narration in *The Portrait* Gogol' has come almost to the point of discarding plot entirely, and in so doing has discovered a means of giving fullest play to his genius for elaboration of detail. He has also entered into the character of Popriščin in a way he had done with no preceding characters. The final product is an immensely moving lyric monodrama.

The extraordinary newness and power that mark the creation of Popriščin and his significance for the following two decades of Russian literature have set scholars to work with even more assiduity than before to seek out his prototypes. To this end, Gorlin says,[27] the in-

---

[27]   Gorlin, *N.V. Gogol und E.T.A. Hoffmann, op. cit.*, p. 42.

vestigator V. Gippius made a long list of stories about madmen. Gorlin himself mentions Prince Odoevskij's *House of Madmen,* adding that madness for Odoevskij was "the extreme form of an idea carried to the point of paradox". He mentions, as does Serapionova,[28] the news printed in *The Butterfly* (Babočka), "Pogorel'skij's" magazine, in 1829, about a French officer who fancied himself King of Spain and drew up a Spanish constitution. Nearer to the point, he mentions that Popriš-čin realizes that he is King of Spain somewhat as Hoffmann's Giulio Fava in *Prinzessin Brambilla* realized that he was really the Abyssinian Prince Chiapperi. To cite *Prinzessin Brambilla* was to go unnecessarily far afield, since more than one tale of Hoffmann includes the discovery of the latent true selves of the characters. That was the whole theme of *Meister Floh,* in which all the characters pre-existed in a better age, to an awareness of which they gradually come by means of the events in the story. In *Prinzessin Brambilla* the principle is applied, with much-debated success, to the theatre: Giulio Fava is an actor spoiled by bad drama and bad acting technique; the Abyssinian Prince Chiappari is his own better self, which he will discover progressively as true Art is revealed to him. Gorlin might well have mentioned the lucid madman who, in Hoffmann's first story, solemnly said: "I am the Chevalier Gluck." Yet, of all these instances, it can only be said that they belong to the general area of story-creation in which Gogol' was operating.

Gorlin is disinclined to accept the much more plausible suggestion of Stender-Petersen, that Popriščin is based on the madman Nettelmann in *Aus dem Leben dreier Freunde,* saying that the similarity consists solely in both men's fancying themselves to be kings. A connection is the more likely in view of Gogol's use of other aspects of that story when writing *The Nevskij Prospekt.*

The episode about Nettelmann is introduced by Marzell as a counterpart to the tale about the ghost of Alexander's aunt. Upon arriving in Berlin, Marzell relates, he had rented a room on the Friedrichstrasse and gone to bed early. He woke to find a spectral personage in a long white gown gazing at him where he slept and holding a double candlestick in one hand and a glass in the other. The strange man performed a kind of ritual with the two objects, then silently withdrew. Next morning the landlady explained that the nocturnal visitor was former Privy Secretary Nettelmann, a gentle madman who fears that new-

[28] Serapionova, *Gofmanskie motivy v Peterburgskix povestjax Gogolja, op. cit.,* p. 87.

comers in the house may prove to be enemies. By means of the glass and candles he divines the intentions of strangers. Marzell he pronounced to be good. Of late, however, he has fancied himself the King of Amboina .

There was no more than this to the anecdote when Marzell was speaking to his friends at the beginning of the story — (Did Gorlin read no further?) —, but at their reunion two years later there is a sequel to be added. On his way to the recruiting office after his disillusionment with Pauline Asling, Marzell had gone to his room on the Friedrichstrasse to pack his belongings. Just as he was leaving he witnessed poor Nettelmann's removal to an asylum. Nettelmann was now entirely persuaded that he was King of Amboina and in token thereof was wearing a gold-paper crown and carrying a sceptre of sorts, to which a gilded apple was fixed. With majestic gravity he observed to Marzell in passing: "Now that the Bulgars have been defeated by my general, the former Captain Tellheim, I am returning to my pacified states."

Gorlin is mistaken in rejecting altogether the Nettelmann-Popriščin connection. They have in common not only their madness and delusion of being kings, but also their harmlessness and pathos, and above all, their status of government officials of minor rank. There must have occurred in Gogol's mind, however, some process of coalescence by which Nettelmann was blended with a foregoing mad *musician,* and the presence in the story of the talking dogs can point only to *Kater Murr,* of which fragments had been printed in *The Moscow Telegraph* in 1831. Juxtaposed in that masterwork of Hoffmann's are to be found both talking animals and a mad musician.

In the early stages of his literary career Hoffmann had composed some thirteen prose sketches which were included, in two blocks, in his first collection of tales, the *Fantasiestücke* (1814—1815), under the general title of *Kreisleriana.* The name derived from the figure of Johannes Kreisler, the author's *alter ego,* who recurs in the various pieces. While preparing the second edition of the *Fantasiestücke* in 1818 — it was published in 1819 —, Hoffmann contemplated an addition to be called *Die lichten Stunden eines wahnsinnigen Musikers,* in which Kreisler was to appear as a madman. Half fictional, half autobiographical, this musician-hero developed through Hoffmann's career into a literary creation of great depth and understanding. As such, he emerges in the unfinished novel, *Kater Murr,* which is usually reckoned the masterpiece of its author. (Spengler puts the figure of Kreisler on a par with Faust and Don Juan as great symbolic expressions of Western European civilization.) Within that novel as we possess it, Kreisler is perfectly sane, though it is generally agreed that the unwritten third part would have found him mad, perhaps literally so, perhaps in some ironic sense of the term. The text represents fragments of the hero's biography, such pages being included as the Tom-cat Murr tore out of the complete biography and used for support of the sheets of his own autobiography and then left unsorted in his pile of manuscript. By this ingenious device Hoffmann was able both to manipulate the complex mysteries of his hero's story and to offer ironic parallels between Kreisler's life and the life of the incarnate-Philistine cat. Over against the fascinating cast of characters of the serious sections stands a whole society of felines and canines who surround the inimitable Tom-cat Murr. Nor are these the only talking animals in Hoffmann's works. The Tales abound in animals with human characteristics, though in only a few cases do they have names and particularized personalities. By far the most elaborate of all, however, are precisely these animals in *Kater Murr.*

Stender-Petersen says that Madgie and Fido in Gogol's story are imitated from the apes in *Kater Murr,* an error which Miss Eyre repeats.[29] For there *are* no apes in *Kater Murr.* In fact, Hoffmann's sole ape is Milo, the unsubtle caricature of a virtuoso pianist, in his early sketch, *Nachricht eines gebildeten jungen Mannes.* Madgie and Fido have a more illustrious ancestry, being derived, canines though they may be, from the admirable Murr himself and his remarkable friends. Their letters, as Gorlin says, are wholly in the spirit of Murr, that "Homme de Lettres très renommé", or at least in the spirit of his feminine counterpart. They are chatty, earthy, gossipy, Philistine, and they dwell on the themes of good food and physical comfort. Significantly, Gogol' never undercuts the Madgie-Fido episodes by stating that they are delusions of Popriščin's brain. Both author and hero accept them as demonstrable reality, as they are accepted in *Kater Murr.*

The talking dogs, excellent as they are, remain a subordinate motif in *The Diary of a Madman.* It would seem likely that they represent salvaged sections of Gogol's original plan. The madman figure, who began as Kreisler and who took on aspects of Nettelmann, developed finally into something very remote from Hoffmann's characters. Gogol's emancipation from his model was progressing rapidly in 1834. Once again to cite aptly with Gorlin:

---

[29]   Stender-Petersen, *op. cit.,* p. 642, and Eyre, *op. cit.,* p. 52.

In *The Portrait* he tried to travel Hoffmann's road; in *The Nevskij Prospekt* he realized the impossibility of this road; in *The Diary of a Madman* came the setting to rights [Auseinandersetzung].

4. *THE NOSE*

"N. Gogol' " appeared as signature for the first time upon the two volumes of *Arabesques* published in Petersburg in January, 1835. The three fine stories which have been discussed were embedded like gems in the trash of that grotesque miscellaney, which included articles of moderately interesting criticism, pretentious art reviews, impressionistic history, and shallow pedagogical theory. They were to be appropriately disengaged from their surrounding matter when Gogol' put together his four-volume collected works in 1842. The over-haste to achieve bulk was all the more unnecessary in view of the fact that his two-volume *Mirgorod* collection, containing his finest Ukrainian tales, was published only two months later. But in 1835 Gogol' still had hopes of being a savant. And he still wanted to be a moral teacher. He seems always to have undervalued the true and unique genius in him. Restless and dissatisfied with short story writing, he began in 1835 to look to the theatre as the proper forum for his didactic and moral purposes. With the impetus from Puškin, *The Inspector General* took shape during the winter 1835—1836, and April 19th witnessed its famous première. Its enormous success was all that any dramatist except Gogol' might want. He had meant it as a sermon, as a moral corrective, as an implement of spiritual reform, whereas his play was construed to fit every political and personal point of view but his own. Two months later he set out in precipitate flight to Germany and western Europe, just as he had fled after the failure of *Hans Küchelgarten*. This time he was to remain abroad for five years. He had already been gone several months when Puškin's newly-founded *The Contemporary* (Sovremennik), the most famous of nineteenth century Russian periodicals, published a story of his entitled *The Nose* (Nos) in the September 1836 issue.

There are indications that such a story had been considered as early as 1832 or 1833. It was written to be published in the spring of 1835, but the version in *The Contemporary* represents a revision from the early months of 1836. The public of the time found it puzzling, even when the allusions were topical. The modern public finds it still more puzzling, and without an understanding of its relationship to Hoffmann its *pointe* is bound to be missed.

The story is divided into three parts.

Part I. — Ivan Jakovlevič, a Petersburg barber, is dismayed one morning at breakfast to discover a human nose inside a hot and freshly baked loaf of bread which his wife has just removed from the oven. Terrified lest he be somehow involved in a crime, he wraps the nose in an old rag and sets out to dispose of it. Acquaintances and passers-by prevent his every attempt until at last he flings it down from St. Isaac's Bridge into the river. Just then a policeman begins to question him about his actions.

"Ivan Jakovlevič turned pale . . . but the incident is completely veiled in obscurity, and absolutely nothing is known of what happened next."

Part II. — Collegiate Assessor Kovalëv, a vain young man fond of being addressed as "Major", awakes one cold morning to consult his mirror about a pimple that had come on his nose the previous day and is aghast to discover that his nose is gone. A blank, white space occupies the middle of his face. On the way to the police to report the disappearance, he encounters the nose itself, uniformed as a Civil Councillor and wearing a very high collar. He addresses the nose, but the nose rebuffs him and moves rapidly away among the crowds. Kovalëv wishes to advertise in the "Lost" columns, but the newspaper clerk refuses such an item for fear it may compromise the newspaper. The police are all taking a siesta when Kovalëv arrives there. Gloomily, he goes home. He is meditating the possibility of his having been bewitched, when the policeman from St. Isaac's Bridge appears. He has the nose with him. To Kovalëv's inquiry about how it was recovered, the policeman replies:

"He was caught almost on the road. He had already taken his seat in the diligence and was intending to go to Riga, and had already taken a passport in the name of a government clerk. And the strange thing is that I myself took him for a gentleman at first, but fortunately I had my spectacles with me and I soon saw that it was a nose."

Kovalëv now has the nose, but neither he nor any surgeon can make it return to his face. He considers anew the chances of witchcraft. Meanwhile, rumors of noses fill the city.

". . . but here again the whole adventure is lost in fog, and what happened afterwards is absolutely unknown."

Part III. — One morning Kovalëv awoke to find that his nose was restored to its proper place, as though nothing had ever happened.

In a long final paragraph the author protests his own bafflement at the events he has chronicled. He concludes:

. . . But what is stranger, what is more incomprehensible than anything is that authors can choose such subjects. I confess that is quite beyond

my grasp, it really is . . . No, no! I cannot understand it at all. In the
first place, it is absolutely without profit to the fatherland; in the
second place . . . but in the second place, too, there is no profit. I
really do not know what to say of it . . . and yet, when you think it
over, there really is something in it. Whatever anyone may say, such
things do happen — not often, but they do happen.

Originally, the events up to Part III were to have occurred in a dream
and Kovalëv's awakening was to have restored normalcy. Perhaps
Gogol' had been deterred from so facile a solution by the criticisms
leveled by *The Northern Bee* in 1834 against the same device as
Puškin had used it in *The Undertaker*. It is more likely that the first
intention was a simple joke about Romantic "Doppelgängerei". By
1836 Gogol's feelings about Hoffmann had turned acrid enough to
produce this bitter parody, for the story is comprehensible only as a
reductio ad absurdum of the author whom he had once tried in all
seriousness to follow.

The nose is a "double". But it does none of the things that Hoffmannian doubles might do. It does not thwart, rival, displace, or confuse Kovalëv, nor has it unilaterally surrendered to the Evil One; it
merely wants to get away. When accosted by its owner in the street, it
replies haughtily:

You are mistaken, Sir, I am an independent individual. Moreover,
there can be no sort of close relations between us. I see, Sir, from the
buttons on your uniform, you must be serving in a different department.

That a nose might be mistaken for a person at all is dependent, of
course, on the male attire of the period, particularly the very high
winged collars which, making allowance for some bit of exaggeration,
could reduce some profiles to a nasal projection above white starched
cloth. Vinogradov, however, has listed [30] a number of other factors that
gave point to the conceit. A veritable "nose-ology" existed in Russia,
the beginnings of which may be placed as early as 1804—1807 when
the six-part translation of *Tristram Shandy* caught the popular fancy,
particularly with the lengthy discussion of the misfortune that befell
the nose of the hero at his birth. The extent of the book's appeal may
be judged by the success of Jakov Sanglen's native imitation, *The Life
and Opinions of the New Tristram* (Žizn' i mnenija novogo Tristrama),

[30]   Vinogradov, *Evoljucija russkago naturalizma, op. cit.* (see footnote 19 above),
Article I, "Naturalističeskij Grotesk, Sjužet i kompozicija povesti Gogolja 'Nos' ",
pp. 8—88.

1825. One example among others of the concern with the topic at a time near the inception of Gogol's story was *The Nose. A French Anecdote* (Nos. Francuzskij Anekdot), published in *Literary Contributions to "Russian Invalid"*, 1831. The journal *Gossip* (Molva), to which Gogol' subscribed, carried that same year a translation of Zschokke's *In Praise of the Nose* (Poxvala nosu). Its contention that the form of the nose was an index to a man's honor was echoed in 1832 in a translation of Karlhof's *Panygeric to the Nose* (Panegérik nosu) in *The Russian Invalid,* where it was submitted that many aspects of character could be inferred from the shape of the nose. An opera-vaudeville adapted from the French in 1825 and called *The Magic Nose, or Talismans and Dates* (Volšebnyj nos, ili Talismany i finiki) presented a pair of Oriental lovers eating dates and discovering that their noses were growing longer. A popularly quoted couplet by Béroalde de Verville gave a bawdy turn to the idea of the nose as index:

> Regarde au nez et tu verras combien
> Grand est cela qui aux femmes fait bien.

Popular interest veered to the pseudo-scientific with the account of a plastic surgery operation reported September 8, 1817 in *The Russian Invalid.* The twenty-seven-year-old woman patient vouched that "on the twelfth day after the operation the (artificial) nose took on natural warmth, feeling, and color". Similar operations were reported in *The Son of the Fatherland* in 1820 (No. 35) and again in 1822 (No. 3) as well as in *The Northern Bee* in 1829 (No. 30). Karl Friedrich Greff's *Rhinoplastik,* about the art of restoring lost noses, commanded widespread interest in translation. Kovalëv's broodings about possible surgical restoration of his own nose reflects an awareness of Greff's book. To all these factors may be added the fact that Gogol' himself had a rather long nose — which troubled his vanity — and the fact that he had something of an obsession about noses. A whimsical passage in a personal letter to E. G. Čertkova offers the idea of noses' meeting like human beings, taking a liking to one another, and striking up a friendship. Another letter to Miss Balabina praises the springtime and expresses the desire to consist of nothing but a huge nose, the better to appreciate the fragrance of roses. Nose-lengths are debated in *How the Two Ivans Quarrelled,* and the "Schiller" and the "Hoffmann" of *The Nevskij Prospekt* drunkenly debate noses and the cost of supporting them.

Finally, there deserves to be mentioned a story called *Another*

Nose (Eščë Nos) which appeared in 1839 over the signature "Ivan Vanen'ka". It opens with an argument about the significance of Gogol's story, *The Nose*. The defender of Gogol's comprehensibility then tells a story of his own to prove his point. The hero of *his* narrative has two noses, the tobacco-vendor who sells him snuff also has two noses, and so on. Clearly the point of *ne plus ultra* had been reached.

As for the literary provenience of Gogol's story, a wholly satisfactory source has been identified for Part I in James Morier's *The Adventures of Hadji-Baba of Ispahan,* the novel about daily life in contemporary Persia, published in London in 1824. The complete translation into Russian appeared in 1831, but the section pertinent to *The Nose,* an independent set of adventures subtitled *The Baked Head,* had been twice rendered separately, in *The Moscow Messenger* in 1827 and in *The Son of the Fatherland* in 1831. In this sequence a tailor who has been summoned to make a garment for the Sultan picks up, not the bundle of cloth assigned to him, but another bundle, which upon being opened is found to contain a severed human head. The terrified tailor attempts to dispose of the grisly object by hiding it in the grain which he will take to the baker for bread-making. The baker is horrified in turn and hits on a new device to get rid of it. Swathing it in towels and propping it on a wall bracket, he gives it the appearance of a customer in the shop of a blind barber across the street. The barber in time discovers the nature of his customer, passes the head on to a Greek restaurant-keeper, who passes it on to a Jew, and so on through more and more peregrinations.

For Part II, the long central portion of Gogol's story, Vinogradov quite properly proposes an origin in Hoffmann's *Die Abenteuer der Sylvesternacht,* more specifically in the quasi-independent fourth chapter of that work, *Die Geschichte vom verlorenen Spiegelbild,* which had served Puškin-Titov in part of the scenario of *The Lonely Cottage on Vasil'evskij Island.* This was the tale of Erasmus Spikher who, in a moment of passion, allowed his mirror-image to be taken from him by the female demon who inhabited Florence in the guise of the courtesan Giulietta. When Erasmus at last fled from Italy and rejoined his wife and little son in Germany, he discovered that the absence of his mirror-image was an immense disadvantage. His wife and child are horrified, and their horror drives poor Erasmus almost to the point of renewing his alliance with Giulietta and her demon-master, Dr. Dapertutto. Just at the crucial moment he rejects the infernal temptation and exorcises the demons. At the end of the story his domestic happiness has been restored, but he still has the task of seeking through the world for his lost mirror-image. It is during his travels in search of it that "The Traveling Enthusiast" — Hoffmann's whimsical name for himself — encounters him. The nose in Gogol's story is a double, just as the mirror-image is a double, and Kovalëv's fruitless search at police headquarters, at the newspaper office, and elsewhere is a parody of Erasmus Spikher's search. Kovalëv's recurrent suspicions that he has been bewitched at the instigation of Mme. Podtačina ("Mrs. Undermine"), who wants to win him for her daughter or else drive him away entirely, may be reminiscent of the snares of Giulietta. Vinagradov feels that a secondary influence may have from Chamisso's *Peter Schlemihl* [31] which was Hoffmann's own inspiration for the tale of Erasmus Spikher. Schlemihl's sale of his shadow to "the Man in Grey" is fundamentally identical with Spikher's surrender of his mirror-image, though in his case no sexual passion was involved, and hence the motifs cannot be disengaged sufficiently to determine Gogol's methods of dealing with them.

That Hoffmann and not Chamisso was the primary source, indeed the primary target, is substantiated by Gogol's history as a whole, but it is confirmed anew by the closing lines of Parts I and II of *The Nose*. These protestations of the author that everything dissolves at those points into fog and obscurity, that "absolutely nothing is known of what happened next", are rather well-taken criticism of the loose jointure of the four sections of *Das Abenteuer der Sylvesternacht*. There was, to be sure, a connecting thread, however tenuous, to bind the four episodes into a single story, but Gogol's series of non-sequiturs burlesques Hoffmann's tale as an incoherent jumble. No logic, rational or fanciful, ever reconciles Kovalëv's adventure with the adventure of the Petersburg barber of Part I, or the concept of the nose as capable of being embedded in the new-baked morning loaf with the concept of its independent existence as a stroller in the city streets. The narrative as a whole ends on an unresolved chord: Kovalëv went about *as though nothing had happened*. Gogol' intends that, quite literally, "nothing" *has* happened. Hoffmann's art itself is inane.

[31] *Peter Schlemihl* was not translated into Russian until 1841, but it was popular throughout Europe in the French version of 1822. This version was the combined work of Chamisso himself and his brother Hippolyte, with extensive modifications by their French publisher Charles Ladvocat. The definitive French version, done by Chamisso alone, did not appear until 1838. The original German version dates from 1814.

The final address to the reader, especially the last lines, is meant ironically:

... and yet, when you think it over, there really is something in it. Whatever anyone may say, such things do happen — not often, but they do happen.

At first glance these words seem to hint at a deep significance in *The Nose* for the perspicacious reader. Actually they are the speech of the master-puppeteer who concludes his jest with suppressed tears and says that art and life themselves are inane and void of all meaning. By 1836 Gogol' had already embarked upon those restless journeyings that were to take him back and forth across Europe until he died, and even on one long trip to the Holy Land. Again and again he was to lament his incapacity for feeling anything. Even in the Holy Places he was to cry bitterly: "I was wooden. I felt nothing!" The monstrous void was within him. Its despair presses to the fore in the sad mockery of this concluding paragraph. Yet the paragraph itself may be a transposition of the concluding lines of *Die Abenteuer der Sylvesternacht* itself, where the "Travelling Enthusiast" reports to the author that the events of the story *may* have been an illusion. The lines must have shifted meaning for Gogol' since the days when he composed the adventures of Čertkov and Petromixali:

... You see, my dear Theodor Amadäus Hoffmann, that only too often does a strange dark Power visibly intervene in my life, and, robbing my sleep of its best dreams, thrusts very curious figures into my path. Wholly filled with the apparitions of the Sylvester-Eve, I almost believe that the Councillor was really made of sugar-plum, that his tea really was a Christmas or a New Year's display, that the lovely Julie, however, was that seductive female figure of Rembrandt or Callot, who robbed the unfortunate Erasmus Spikher of his fine resembling mirror-image. Forgive me this!

5. *THE PORTRAIT* (second version)

Gogol's precipitate flight from Russia in June of 1836, without even the elementary courtesy of farewells, had carried him to Germany, then to Paris, and at last to Rome, a city which he came to love. There he established himself for a time, alternately fascinated with the Italian scene and devoured with homesickness. There he worked at Part I of his masterpiece *Dead Souls,* a text as alien to the blue Roman skies as the *Hexenküche* scene of *Faust* which Goethe had composed there half a century before. There, too, he meditated his past career and in particular his story *The Portrait*. The work irritated him. It was not Russian enough, it was not Orthodox enough, it was not realistic enough. It had too much Romantic Hoffmannism in it. He would, belatedly, remedy the fault. He would rewrite it as it should have been written in the first place. In 1837 he set about the revisions. In 1841 he made further changes before submitting it to *The Contemporary,* where it was printed in the June 1842 issue. De-Romanticized and de-Hoffmannized, the second version of *The Portrait* proved simply to be a less distinguished variant of the 1833 version. Gorlin's tabulation of the alterations [32] may be given here in slightly altered form to show how Gogol' was working and thinking:

1833—1835	1837—1842
After purchasing the portrait of the sinister old man, Čertkov leaves it at the dealer's, requesting that it be delivered to his room. Upon his arrival home he finds the portrait already hanging on his wall, though no one had been there.	Čertkov brings the picture home himself.
The lady and her daughter appear without any explanation.	Čertkov prepares the arrival of the ladies.
The old man comes to life out of the picture while Čertkov is in a state of half-dream, half-waking.	The old man appears in a regular dream.
Petromixali is either Anti-Christ or in league with Anti-Christ.	Petromixali is an "uncanny figure".
Petromixali tells in detail about his bond with the Evil One.	Petromixali refers only casually to a bond with the Evil One and the artist pays no attention to the remark.
The artist's attempted confession of his contacts with Petromixali results in the deaths of his wife and child.	(These episodes are deleted entirely.)
The artist once burned Petromixali's picture on the hearth. When he turned around the picture was hanging as before on the wall.	The portrait disappears at the auction, some one had stolen it.

[32] Gorlin, *N.V. Gogol und E. T. A. Hoffmann, op. cit.,* pp. 7—8.

The aging artist is described as "One of those modest, devout painters such as were common only in the religious Middle Ages."	These words are changed to: " . . . a painter . . . one of those wonders that only Russia, out of her inexhaustible spring, can produce."
The sacred painting is a Madonna. (The German Romantik had made a cult of the Sistine Madonna.)	The sacred painting is a Nativity.
Much is made of the gleaming, evil, piercing eyes of the portrait.	This characteristic is less prominent and there is no hint of a magnetic spell emanating from the eyes.

The changes are not only petty, they are artistically wrong. But the motivation for them was not merely a desire to spite Hoffmann or to relive Gogol's own artistic past. The latent Realist in him, as in other Russian Hoffmannists, was urging him to anticipate the era not yet born. With major energies absorbed by *Dead Souls,* which would take very long to complete, this work of revision was the utmost he could muster in the meantime to keep his name before the public.

6. *THE OVERCOAT*

Years passed. From time to time journeys carried Gogol' to various places, on one occasion, he claimed, to Spain, though rumor reported him in jail for debt. Always he came back to Rome. His mother and sisters urged him to come home, where family finances required attention. He had no money to give them, his own means being straitened in the extreme. He begged Žukovskij to obtain a pension for him, but the Tsar refused, sending instead a gift of 5,000 rubles. Reluctantly he agreed at last to return to Russia. Even after arrival in Moscow he continued to date his letters to his mother from Vienna, postponing the family meeting as long as possible. Matters ended by his mother's and sisters' coming themselves to Moscow, where the reunion took place beneath the roof of Gogol's friends the Aksakovs. Throughout the visit he was restless to be back in Rome, and at the earliest possible moment he began the return trip. Once in Rome again, he wished himself anywhere in the world but there. More restless travels, then a new visit to Russia in 1841. This time he brought with him the manuscript of *Dead Souls, Part I,* which was published in Moscow on May 21, 1842. Its powerful realism was immediately acclaimed as the first work of a new era in Russian literature.

During this visit he also prepared with meticulous care the definitive edition of his collected works in four volumes, which were then issued in Petersburg in 1842. These were his legacy. He sensed, as though clairvoyant, that he would never again write great literature. Volume I, as was expected, contained *Evenings on a Farm near Dikan'ka;* Volume II complemented it with the quartet of *Mirgorod* Ukrainian tales; Volume IV reprinted *The Inspector General* and other theatre pieces, several of them fragments. But Volume III contained surprises. It was composed entirely of short stories. The three Petersburg tales from *Arabesques* appeared there, wholly disengaged from the puerile essays that surrounded them in 1835; *The Nose* was reprinted, together with a fragmentary Ukrainian tale, *The Carriage* (Koljaska), which had appeared in *The Contemporary* for March, 1836; a new fragment entitled *Rome* (Rim) was included. But the story that fascinated all readers was a totally new item composed at an uncertain date since 1836, probably in 1840—1841, and called *The Overcoat* (Šinel'). Its significance for the next generation of Russian writers was to be even greater than that of *Dead Souls.* Of it, Turgenev was later to remark: "We are all descended from Gogol's *Overcoat.*"

The basis for this famous tale was a real-life anecdote furnished to Gogol' by friends. [33] A Petersburg functionary, he was told, had one interest in life: hunting. But he was too poor to afford a rifle. By the severest economies, pinching a kopek here and a kopek there, he finally acquired the coveted possession. On his very first expedition, the rifle, left poised on the edge of a small boat in the marshes, fell into the water and was lost. The clerk grieved himself almost to death for chagrin. Then his fellow clerks noted his plight, took up a collection among themselves, and bought him a new rifle.

The literary version modifies the anecdote considerably. The hero is still a Petersburg government clerk, now ridiculously rechristened Akakij Akakievič Bašmačkin and endowed with the insignificance and unattractiveness of Popriščin, the clerk-hero of *The Diary of a Madman,* without, however, Popriščin's madness or his aspirations to the love of his employer's daughter. His single intense desire is not for a rifle, but for an overcoat to replace the inadequate and pitiful rag that he has worn year after year through the winter's snows. Gogol'

[33] Schloezer, *Gogol, op. cit.,* p. 188.

recalled the thin top-coat of his own early winter in the capital. Akakij Akakievič, absurd, naive, pathetic, fumbling, well-intentioned, hard-working, forlorn, eventually scrimps and saves until he is able to buy the new coat. The collar is made of cat-fur, but "at a distance it might be taken for marten". His fellow clerks give a party to celebrate the acquisition of so noble a garment. But on the way home a pair of street thieves rob him of the coat, and next day he appears at the office in utter dejection. His companions take up a small collection but it does not begin to approach the cost of a new coat. He takes his complaint to a Person of Consequence, but the Person of Consequence, irked by the intrusion of an insignificant clerk, has a small fit of bad temper and shows him the door. Poorly clad as he is, Akakij Akakievič takes ill from exposure, develops a fever, and dies. They bury him as a pauper.

Up to this point the story has been conducted with the severest realism. Suddenly it takes a Romantic turn.

Rumor has it that in the neighborhood of the Kalinkin Bridge a dead man appears at night in the form of a clerk looking for a stolen overcoat. Regardless of grade or calling, he stops all passers-by and takes their overcoats from them by force. One cold and snowy night the Person of Consequence himself is driving in that vicinity, not home-bound to his wife and children, but to visit a lady in another part of the city. Suddenly a gust of wind strikes him with unnatural force. The ghost of Akakij Akakievič seizes him by the collar and strips his over-coat from him. The Person of Consequence arrives at his door-step pale and shaken. Next day he is more conscientious at his work and of meeker mien than before. Robberies of coats continue in Petersburg streets, but the robber is known to have great mustaches and not to resemble Akakij Akakievič in the least.

Critics have generally agreed that the ghost-episode, which alone raises the story from the level of a well written item among the "Neediest Cases", is Hoffmann-inspired, but all admit that a specific source is difficult to identify. Genuine ghost-scenes are rare with Hoffmann, and the few that there are have been mentioned before: the brief episode of Alexander's aunt in *Aus dem Leben dreier Freunde,* the isolated eerie anecdote *Eine Spukgeschichte,* and the impressive scenes with the conscience-harried ghost in *Das Majorat.* Miss Eyre alone ventures to cite the latter in relation to Gogol's story, and in so doing she is almost certainly right.[34] Not that there is any plot-con-

---

[34]   Eyre, *Gogol and German Romanticism, op. cit.,* p. 58.

nection between the two works at all, but from *Das Majorat* two impressions remain with the reader long after the details of the narrative have faded from his mind: the magnificent description of the snowy night and the apparition of the old serving man Daniel, who in life had murdered his master and then become stricken with remorse. For the rest of his life he had moved in a trance-like state, reenacting over and over again the events of the night of the murder. After death his spirit continues its mournful rounds, carrying out unceasingly the movements of that night. Events of the story finally give him peace. Snowy night and a restless ghost make up the essence of Gogol's concluding scene. The echo from Hoffmann is remote admittedly, and undemonstrable, but it is there. The influence of Hoffmann had pervaded Gogol's artistic mind more thoroughly than he knew.

At 1842 Gogol's career ended. His subsequent works distressed and embarrassed those who admired him. Sections of Part II of *Dead Souls* were yet to be forthcoming, but his genius foundered amid the work. Part I must stand as a magnificent fragment, already, it is said, part of the age of Realism. Yet even in *Dead Souls,* does not Čičikov appear out of nowhere and vanish again into nowhere like a daemonic character out of Hoffmann? [35]

---

[35] I am indebted for this observation to Professor V. Lednicki of the University of California, who made the remark in a lecture.

VII

AT THE EBB-TIDE OF ROMANTICISM

The remote, indistinctly Hoffmannian quality of the final pages of *The Overcoat* may be taken as a sign of the retreating tide of Russian Hoffmannists. After 1835 that tide had fallen rapidly, together with the waters of general Romanticism. It had floated major writers and critics to a high point, from which they now wished to proceed onward in a new direction, while lesser writers and critics, and much of the public, continued to drift with the receding flood. New translations appeared: *Die Serapionsbrüder* in 1836, *Kater Murr* in 1840, and the versions of *Meister Floh* and *Klein Zaches* from the hand of the future Slavophile M. N. Katkov. But these appeared as translations of established classics irrelevant to the new creative processes of the day. Hoffmann was now both respectable and safe, and thus, where lesser works had previously evoked imitation upon imitation, these masterpieces roused no echoes.

In discussing the declining phase of Russian Hoffmannism, the scholar Levit claims that indices of the decline are to be sought in letters and human documents rather than in creative works.[1] He cites a letter of Stankevič to Bakunin, dated November 8, 1835, in which the writer praises *Der goldene Topf* and the figure of Kreisler but says he prefers *Ritter Gluck*. And again, two letters of Granovskij to his sisters, written in January of 1840, in which he urges them to read Hoffmann's works twice each but with an interval in between: in this way their total strangeness will present less of an obstacle to understanding. After praising the remarkable originality of *Prinzessin Brambilla* and of *Kater Murr,* he recommends his sisters read *Don Juan* and "the musical things", and suggests they orient their critical opinion in accordance with that of Sir Walter Scott, whose admiration of Hoffmann, it will be recalled, was on the whole a somewhat grudging one. As for himself, Granovskij says he does not read Hoffmann any more;

---

[1] Tit Levit, Introductory article to *E. T. A. Gofman: Sobranie Sočinenij,* ed. Z. A. Veršinina, Vol. VI, p. 349. Further details have been drawn from Section II of Levit's essay, pp. 348–357.

he had been living in an unreal world, but has now "awakened from
the dream".

1. ALEXANDER HERZEN

A fair index to the Russian critical opinion of Hoffmann as of 1836
may quite properly be seen in the article entitled *Hoffmann,* which
the young Aleksandr Herzen published that year in *The Telescope.*
He wrote, in part:

At the beginning of the present century there appeared in German
literature a unique writer, Theodor Amadeus Hoffmann. Dominated
by unbridled fantasy, of powerful and profound spirit, *an artist in the
full meaning of the word,* he drew with his bold pen certain shadows,
certain phantoms, now terrifying, now laughable, but *always beautiful.*
And these imprecise, sketched shadows are his stories. The usual dull
order of things put too much constraint upon Hoffmann; he spurned
wretched, clear-cut verisimilitude. His fantasy knows no limits; he
writes in fever, pale with terror, trembling before his own inventions,
with his hair standing on end. From his pure heart he believes in them
all, even in the Sandman, and in witchcraft, and in apparitions, and
by this faith subdues the reader to his authority, strikes his imagination,
and leaves long-lasting effects. Three elements of human life serve as a
basis for the larger part of Hoffmann's works, and these elements
constitute the soul of the author: the inner life of the artist, marvelous
psychical appearances, and supernatural effects. All this is on the one
hand submerged in the black waves of mysticism, and on the other
resolved by lively, sharp, biting humor. Hoffmann's humor is very
different both from the terrible, devastating humor of Byron, which
is like the laughter of an angel cast down into the underworld, and
from the poisonous, hellish, serpent-like mockery of Voltaire, that
smile of self-satisfaction with pressed lips. His is the humor of the
artist suddenly fallen to earth from his El Dorado, of the artist who
amid dreams observes that his Galatea is a piece of stone, of the artist
of whom at the moment of ecstasy a woman begs money for her
children's shoes. With such humor Hoffmann strewed his works, and
he constantly switches from the most ardent pathos to the most
malicious irony. This humor is natural to Hoffmann, for he is above
all the genuine, the perfect artist.

Between the lines here, and despite the wholly sincere admiration
expressed, one perceives the misgivings of a sternly moral conscience
in the face of "the genuine, the perfect artist". To Herzen, as to more
than one Russian, Hoffmann's works were indeed *"always beautiful",*
but alas, *only* beautiful and never concerned with moral indignation
at human and social wrongs.

It was from Vjatka (where he had been exiled for singing irreverent songs at a student gathering) that Herzen mailed this very first article of his to Polevoj, in the hope that the latter would be able to place it with one magazine or another. Polevoj replied with fatherly concern for the young man's welfare and strongly advised that it would be "indispensible before censorship to cut out certain expressions". As for Herzen's estimate of Hoffmann, Polevoj felt that the fledgling critic had "judged him well and justly". Meanwhile, Herzen mailed a second copy of his manuscript to another literary friend (apparently N. X. Ketčer) without mentioning that he had submitted it to Polevoj as well. The piece appeared in *The Telescope* [2] under Herzen's nom de plume "Iskander", thereby offending Polevoj, who now added one more enemy to his list. [3]

But when Herzen came to compose stories of his own, moral indignation prevented his turning to Hoffmann for inspiration. Aggrieved sentiment and social protest mark the tale called *The Thieving Magpie* (Soroka-vorovka) of 1846, in which the famous actor Ščepkin is presented as the narrator of a "true incident". A certain Count Kamenskij of Orël province has brought Ščepkin to his estate in the hope of enlisting his services with his troupe of serf-performers. The visitor is struck by the deeply moving interpretation of the role of the serving-girl falsely accused of jewel-theft in the old drama, *The Thieving Magpie,* only to discover that the actress is held captive by her employer and subjected to the most grievous mistreatment for having refused to become his mistress. The supporting actors are frequently kept in jail and even have their roles sent to them in their cells for study. Schiller's *Kabale und Liebe,* specifically mentioned as a work which the Count refused to have performed, is patently the chief *literary* source.

A related theme is touched in *The Mental Patient* (Povreždënnyj) (1848), where a melancholic young nobleman is traveling with a companion on the Riviera to forget a love affair with a poor serving girl named Charlotte. Whether innocent or guilty — and the story is told both ways by alternate narrators —, the girl was implicated in a theft and the broken love unhinged the young man's wits. *On Taking a*

---

[2]   A. I. Herzen, "Gofman", *The Telescope,* 1836, No. 10, pp. 139—168.
[3]   The excerpt translated here from Herzen's article and an excerpt from Polevoj's letter of February 25, 1836 are given by Kozmin, *Očerki iz istorii Russkago Romantizma, op. cit.* (See footnote 4 of Chapter III), pp. 484—487. Polevoj's acid next letter to Herzen said that " . . . serious people do not give one and the same article to two magazines".

Glass of Grog (Tragedija za stakanom groka) (1863) deals with a poor waiter harried by haughty superiors. *From Boredom* (Skuki radi) (1867) relates the lynching of an Algerian native who did not know enough French to disclaim a murder charge before a vicious Colonel. *The Doctor, the Dying Man, and the Dead* (Doktor, umirajuščij i mërtvye) (1869) is a bitter anti-clerical anecdote from the Paris of 1848, in which family and servants conspire to make an aged republican of 1793 die reconciled to the Church.

All these tales are anecdotal in form and realistic in method, all are concerned with liberal protest, and no touch of Hoffmann is anywhere to be discerned. Their qualities are typical of the turn of mind common to a significant number of those young men who may be called "the last class" of the Muscovite Schellingians.

2.   COUNT SOLLOGUB

Parallel to the career of Herzen, in its initial enthusiasm for Hoffmann and subsequent far digressions from his manner, is the career of the minor literary figure Count Vladimir Aleksandrovič Sollogub (1814—1882). Unlike Herzen, Sollogub remained a writer of fiction all his life and became neither an exile nor a revolutionary. His initial story is a fair index to the shallow and popular Hoffmannism in the last stage of the Russian Romantic movement. Published in 1839, it bears the title of *A History of Two Galoshes* (Istorija dvux kaloš).

A Petersburg cobbler named Müller is about to deliver a new-made pair of galoshes to Court Councillor Thedorinck when he is disagreeably surprised to discover that his apprentice has botched the work. Since he urgently needs money for a party he has promised his wife, he determines to take the spoiled pair to a poor musician client named Schulz, who had ordered some made, and to take a good pair to the Court Councillor. Schulz is unable to pay even for the botched galoshes, but the cobbler agrees to accept his playing of the piano for his wife's guests as suitable return.

A lengthy flashback recounts the life of Karl Schulz from his unhappy childhood in Düsseldorf, through years of devotion to an aged organist who gave him lessons and still more years as a poor music teacher in Vienna. In the latter capacity he had fallen in love with his pupil Henriette, the ward of the haughty Russian Princess G., a self-styled patroness of music and the arts. At present he is living a garret existence in Petersburg waiting for the day when the peregrinating Princess will return to the Russian capital and bring Henriette with her.

At Müller's party Karl plays dance music listlessly until, forgetting himself for a moment, he wanders off into magnificent improvisations. The company stands in silent awe — they were mere burghers, but German, and therefore could sense musical genius. An old piano-tuner determines to see Karl famous, and, as a first step, he urges the young man to beg the Princess G. for the use of her salon in which to give a recital. Karl had not known of the Princess' return to Petersburg, but he hurries now to see her. Coldly and reluctantly she grants his request. Karl is too overawed by her to inquire whether Henriette is still a member of her household.

Without the inspiration of Henriette the all-important recital is a fiasco. Karl plays wretchedly. The guests indignantly leave. Suddenly, there among the few remaining listeners he perceives Henriette, and now he plays with glorious power. But too late. His reputation is ruined, and, what is worse, Henriette is married now, married to Court Councillor Thedorinck.

Tender but chaste interviews are now granted Karl whenever the pompous husband is absent. For his part, the husband is more than once puzzled by alternating sets of galoshes in his closet, now the excellent pair that cobbler Müller made for him, now a miserable pair of the same size. Ultimately he returns unexpectedly to surprise the lovers. He creates a frightful scene. Three days later Henriette dies. Karl directly falls into a brain fever and dies also. To his deathbed a repentant Müller brings a fine new pair of galoshes. But the dead musician has no use for them now.

It is readily apparent that this sentimental story, once very popular, is closely related to the tales of Polevoj and of Prince Odoevskij. Indeed, its structure and manner are borrowed from those authors, though the *Literaturnaja Ènciklopedija* is correct in noting an inspiration from the *Kreisleriana* of Hoffmann,[4] precisely those "musical things" which Granovskij was recommending to his sisters. The amusing little frame-tale involving the galoshes is itself faintly Hoffmannian, but it is the long musical biography of the hero which displays a sentimentalized version of the life and sufferings of the famous Johannes Kreisler.

In the preface-piece to the *Kreisleriana* proper Sollogub could have found the basic traits of the musical genius he wished to portray: the hours of ecstatic musical composition through the night, the sympathetic garret-neighbor who could be wakened to listen to the new work, the habit of improvisation. In *Kreislers musikalisch-poetischer Klub* he could have found the reaffirmation of the pianist's ability to improvise "symphonic fantasy" as well as the ironically presented

---

[4]   *Literaturnaja Ènciklopedija* (Moscow, 1929): article "Gofman", Vol. II, p. 679.

comments thereon by the club members, whose opinions run the gamut of criticism. And in *Johannes Kreislers musikalische Leiden* he could have found a superb model of an inspired muscan playing for an ungrateful audience of frivolous society people. Nothing about the sentimentally irresponsible Karl Schulz, however, resembles the rugged character and rugged musicianship of Kreisler, who, inveigled by a dilettantish guest to play from a volume marked "variations", did indeed play the *Goldberg Variations* of Bach and grimly watched the company melt distressfully away, variation by variation. In that same *Kreislerianum* appear both the host's "magnificent niece", who inspired Kreisler *by her singing,* and the poor youth Gottlieb who endured lackey-status by virtue of Kreisler's musicianship and kindly interest in him. Vaguely these figures have their parallels in Henriette and in the young poet who attends the dying Schulz. But Sollogub's hero is all compounded of forlorn love and bad luck and neither he nor the author seems to understand what music is. Actually, Karl is the stock figure of the hapless tutor, just as Henriette is the stock figure of the hapless ward, and music has been attributed to them by their creator without any true conviction. And without real musical conviction Sollogub's tale was bound to fall short of the *Kreisleriana* and be no more than the pale story that it is.

An interesting feature of the *History of Two Galoshes* is its attempt to deal sympathetically with members of the bourgeois class. Comparable works of Polevoj and Odoevskij had always represented their characters as aristocrats, though not necessarily of the higher ranks of the aristocracy. Sollogub, significantly, offers only German bourgeois, who somehow can be cobblers and piano-tuners and live in a Russian environment and yet retain their German instinct for music. But by 1839 it had become a mannerism of Russian literature to make Russianized Germans the central characters of stories derived from Hoffmann.

The Hoffmannian genre quickly revealed itself as unsympathetic to Sollogub. The very next year, 1840, his new tale *High Society* (Bol'šoj svet) addressed itself to satire of the Russian *haut monde,* while his best known work, *The Tarantas* of 1845, was to be a travel book that portrayed scenes of the Ukrainian countryside. Non-Hoffmannian social criticism mark both of these, while his comedy-vaudevilles were intended solely as diversions. Realism was the order of the new literary day and Hoffmann's Tales were losing favor even with the casual readers.

3. ALEKSEJ KONSTANTINOVIČ TOLSTOJ

The claim has sometimes been made that the roster of Russian Hoff-mannists should include the name of Count Aleksej Konstantinovič Tolstoj, the nephew of "Pogorel'skij" who won in his own time a literary fame far greater than his uncle's. Young Tolstoj, declared sole heir to "Pogorel'skij's" immense fortune upon the latter's death in 1836, and already depressed by his captivity in government offices, set out upon travels to Europe. In 1838 he came to Frankfurt-am-Main, where he made the acquaintance of Gogol', who at that point was the house-guest of Žukovskij. With Žukovskij the young Count went on to Italy to spend the winter with his mother. The summer of 1839 found him in Paris. Not until December of 1840 did he return to his governmental duties in Russia. He had only recently passed his twenty-third birthday.

Insulated thus from the rapid changes in literary fashion in his native land, Tolstoj entered upon his literary career in 1841 with a fine disregard for the new aesthetic and critical climate. He had, of course, read Hoffmann and admired him, but his own Romanticism was of a decidedly international kind and Hoffmann was only one author among many whom he admired. He admired Walter Scott, Charles Nodier, and even Horace Walpole. He was fond of any writer who dealt in the fiction of the supernatural. His special predeliction was for the lore about vampires. Thus it is not surprising that his name was concealed beneath the pseudonym "Krasnorogskij" which stood as signature to the prose tale entitled *The Vampire* (Upyr'), submitted to the censor A. V. Nikitenko on May 11, 1841.[5]

Though the story had been tested in an oral reading at the home of Count Sollogub, critical reaction, except for Belinskij's praise, was unfavorable. *The Northern Bee* called it a parody of *The Mysteries of Udolpho; The Son of the Fatherland* said the author must be an opium addict. For once, modern feelings tend to concur with the conservative opinions of that era, for this belated Gothic novel, over-burdened with plot and carrying little psychological conviction, has little to recommend it. In a rather amusing opening scene the hero, Aleksandr Andreevič Runevskij, is warned by one of his guests, a

[5] *Upyr'* (*Razskaz*), published in SPb, 1841, in a limited edition, signed: "Krasno-rogski". (Krasnyj Rog — "Red Horn" — was a second estate of "Pogorel'skij's" in the Ukraine, not far from Pogorelcy.) The text may be found in *Polnoe Sobranie Sočinenij gr. A. K. Tolstogo,* ed. S. A. Vengerov (SPb, 1907), Vol. III, pp. 12–80.

certain Mr. Rybarenko, that several vampires are present at this soirée. For example, the elderly lady, Mme Sugrobina, who is inviting her pale and lovely granddaughter Daša to come to her country estate for a visit. If Daša accepts that invitation, says Mr. Rybarenko, she will be dead within three days. Moreover, Mme Sugrobina is herself actually dead — Rybarenko attended her funeral —, and so is the elderly Mr. Teljaev with whom she is talking now. Runevskij disregards the warning, comes to know Daša better, falls in love with her, and accepts her grandmother's invitation to join the company at her country estate. Events at the manor house, including an unnerving encounter with a ghost, are sufficient to warrant Runevskij's demand for an explanation but he prefers to discount them. Back in Moscow to make preparations for his forthcoming marriage, he encounters Rybarenko in the course of a midnight stroll, and then it is that the story is diverted for almost half of its total length to include the mysterious adventures of that strange young man while on a visit to Como in Italy, three years before. When the narrative returns at last to Runevskij, we discover him involved in a comic dilemma. Daša's aunt misconstrued his visit to the country house as a sign that he was enamored of her own unattractive daughter. Her son, Captain Zorin, challenges Runevskij to a duel over the supposed slight to his sister. In the duel Runevskij is wounded and carried in an unconscious state to Mme Sugrobina's country house, which, by coincidence, was near the place of encounter. During convalescence Runevskij is beset by fever-hallucinations, but one sequence of these, in which he sees Daša, bound and unconscious, about to be slain in a kind of ritualistic murder, is apparently real and not a hallucination. Abruptly the story leaps to a quiet scene of marital happiness. Runevskij has married Daša. Mme Sugrobina has died. Daša's governess provides some sound rational explanations for a number of the mysteries, and Captain Zorin, who is Rybarenko's friend since childhood, makes it clear that Rybarenko's mind has been unsettled since their trip to Italy together. Just then news comes that Rybarenko has leaped to his death from the top of Ivan the Great's bell tower. The governess now feels free to reveal that the unfortunate young man was Mme Sugrobina's illegitimate son, and with this information the complex events both in Russia and in Italy take on a logical relationship. Everything seems to be satisfactorily accounted for. At this moment Runevskij notices a scar on his young wife's throat. She cannot explain it, but it dates from the night of her grandmother's death, and she recalls waking to find her pillow soaked in blood. In the breathless last-page reversal the hero suddenly sees that the vampire story was only too real and that the faithful governess rescued Daša in the ghastly ritual murder scene, presumably by murdering the grandmother in the girl's stead. Daša herself is wholly innocent, however, and all will henceforth be well.

Hoffmannian elements are surely included in the catch-all plot of this lurid tale, and the elements in question tend to cluster about *Die Elixiere des Teufels.* Both works depend upon complex family histories; Don Pietro d'Urgina seems, like Franzesko the painter, to have initiated a hereditary sin which distorts the lives of successive generations; the fever-hallucinations are at least parallel to the horrible dreams that plague Medardus during *his* convalescence; the geographical sequence: Russia-Italy-Russia resembles Medardus's travels from Germany to Italy and back again to Germany; the extreme complexities and mystifications themselves and the breakneck speed of their narration suggest that the author was imitating the manner of Hoffmann's novel. But the sixty-eight pages of the story manage to include almost every horror-tale motif from Horace Walpole to Eugène Sue: portraits-come-to-life, the sale of the soul to the Evil One, haunted houses, prophetic ballads, ancestral ghosts, doomed families, ritual murder, etc. etc., until specifically Hoffmannian components are submerged in a welter of popular and debased Romantic materials.

From approximately the same period as *The Vampire* comes Tolstoj's companion piece composed in French, with the title of *La Famille du Vourdalak,* which remained in manuscript through the author's life and was published in Russian translation in 1884, nine years after his death.[6] Cast in the form of a reminiscent account of events from the year 1769, the story is told by the chief personage in his old age to a group of ladies identified solely as "Mesdames". He is a nobleman named D'Urfé, and in that long ago was assigned to government duty in far-off Serbia. His beloved Duchesse de Gramont, lately so capricious, became sombre at his departure and hung about his neck a cross to protect him from evil in those exotic regions. Lodged with a native family, he was witness to the departure of the grandfather, Gorša, into the hills to fight the brigand-cur Alibek, and to his return as a "vurdalak", a Slavonic vampire. This particular breed of vampire,

[6]   The Russian translation of *La Famille du Vourdalak* was published with the title of *The Family of the Vurdalak. From the Reminiscences of an Unknown Man* (Sem'ja Vurdalaka. iz vospominanij neizvestnago), an unpublished tale of Count A. K. Tolstoj, with notes by the translator, B. M. Markevič, in *Russkij Vestnik* (The Russian Messenger) CLXIX (Jan. 1884), No. 1, pp. 5—31.

we are told, is concerned with molesting only members of his family and close friends. Gorša's family resisted his baleful influence yet continued to give him harborage as their venerable clan-head, but, one by one, beginning with the little grandsons, they were lured away from the house to return as evil and as bloodthirsty as Gorša himself. D'Urfé was persuaded to leave before the disaster was complete. The following spring he returned to his former hosts, only to find that the entire region had been deserted before the onslaughts of the "vurdalaki". He himself suffered a grievous temptation from the lovely girl Zdenka, but the cross given him by the Duchesse de Gramont saved him from her wiles. The story ends with D'Urfé's hairbreadth escape from pursuit by the whole vampire clan.

The tale bears no resemblance to Hoffmann's brief *Vampirismus* close to the very end of the *Serapionsbrüder* collection, except in a generic way, and no resemblance at all to any other work of Hoffmann's.

Themes more literarily conventional than vampires engaged Tolstoj when he came to his serious works, the historical novel *Prince Serebrjannyj* and his historical plays centering about Boris Godunov, but in 1873 he composed a charming poem in eighty-seven ottava rima stanzas, entitled *The Portrait* (Portret),[7] in which he returned to one aspect of his youthful works. After a leisurely description of an old house where childhood memories cluster, the poem's narrator recounts an episode of his boyhood. Each afternoon, once his dull tutorial sessions were ended, he used to dress up in his best clothes to go and pay court to his "Ideal", the painting of a lovely lady that hung in the hall. The lady was painted in high Rococo fashion with a bouquet of roses at her bosom and a silk apron caught up full of roses. One afternoon he interprets her meaningful glance to signify that he should return at three o'clock in the morning. He does so, and as he gazes at her in the ghostly moonlight, suddenly all the candles leap into flamelets, the lady descends from the portrait, and the roses spill from her apron to the floor. A minuet is heard. He bows. They dance. There is a pause, a kiss, and suddenly he knows no more. He awakes in the morning on the cold floor, a rose in his hand.

The poem, apart from an over-long beginning is an exquisite bit of composition, full of "la nostalgie du vieux siècle", as fragile as a lyric of Austin Dobson. What is interesting for Tolstoj's career is the fact

---

[7]   *The Portrait* (Portret) was written after June 1873 and published in January, 1874 in *The Messenger of Europe*.

that it distils and clarifies the subject matter of two whole scenes from *The Vampire* of 1841. The ghost that troubled Runevskij's first night at Mme Sugrobina's estate was the ghost of his hostess' sister, Praskovija Andreevna, who had died at the age of seventeen. She materialized apparently out of her painting, which closely resembles the painting in the poem, even to the bouquet of roses clasped to the young woman's bosom. In the Italian sequence of the same story another lovely lady, this time a guitarrist, seemed likewise to materialize from a painting. In both instances the ghost was mistaken for a living girl, in the first case Daša, in the second case the Italian maiden Pepina. *The Portrait* concentrates its entire attention on an isolated episode of a portrait-come-to-life, and though that motif occurs in Hoffmann's *Die Elixiere des Teufels,* in *Die Irrungen,* and even in *Doge und Dogaresse* and *Die Fermate* (in a modified form), it is common to many Romantic authors, Horace Walpole, Washington Irving, Charles Maturin, etc., so that no specific source is ascertainable.

4.   LERMONTOV: "THE ŠTOSS FRAGMENT"

The absence of the major Romantic writer Lermontov from the company of the Russian Hoffmannists is to be explained very simply as a matter of dates. Born in 1814, he was eight years old in 1822, the year of Hoffmann's death and the year when the first of the Tales appeared in Russian translation. The heyday of Russian Hoffmannism, 1829–1836, spans the period from his fifteenth to his twenty-second year, and though he was precociously writing during that period, he was primarily interested in lyric poetry and in drama, genres where Hoffmann could not serve his literary purposes. Precisely at the point when his attention was veering toward prose fiction, 1836, Hoffmann was going out of fashion. Moreover, his guiding star upon the seas of literature was Puškin, and Puškin's enthusiasms did not favor Hoffmann or the Germans in general.

Yet Lermontov was far from unaware of German writing. At age fifteen in 1829 he had begun the serious phase of his career with translations of no less than seven poems of Schiller. The first of his five plays, *The Spaniards* (Ispancy) (1830) testifies eloquently to the intense impression made upon him by the performance of *Die Räuber* which he had attended in Moscow in 1828. Lessing's *Nathan der Weise* also had some effect upon that initial drama, and motifs from

Schiller's "Jugenddramen" other than *Die Räuber* are added to its components. Similar motifs from the "Jugenddramen" conspicuously mark his second play, *Menschen und Leidenschaften,* whose German title echoes *Kabale und Liebe,* and are not absent from the remaining three. Among Lermontov's verse translations from the German must be listed Goethe's *Über allen Gipfeln,* two or three Heine lyrics, and an adaptation of Zeidlitz' *Geisterschiff.* These fall chiefly in the years 1840–1841, and thus the poet may be seen in the last two years of his life to be harking back to the German lyric canon established by Žukovskij; only the element of Heine is new.

Nevertheless the total of these German factors in Lermontov's work, especially in his lyric output, up to 1836 is small by comparison with the influence of Puškin and of authors, notably Byron, whom Puškin had admired. In the evolution of *A Hero of our Time,* from the nine-chapter fragment of *The Princess Ligovskaja* of 1836 to the completed novel of 1840, Puškin is everywhere the model and the inspiration. Immediately upon publication of the work Belinskij spoke of the connection between Pečorin and Onegin, and remarked that "the dissimilarity between them was vastly smaller than the distance between the (river) Onega and the (river) Pečora". And in the matter of the component parts of *A Hero of our Time* it is possible to say, with no disparagement of Lermontov's originality and skill, that the very notion of the story *Bèla* would not have occurred to the author without the preexistence of Puškin's *Journey to Arzrum,* nor the notion of the story *The Fatalist* without the preexistence of Puškin's *The Shot.*

One may then ask why Lermontov was never sufficiently attracted to *The Queen of Spades* to compose his counterpart to that famous work. Had he ruled out the Hoffmannian genre completely? The negative answer to that question may be found in a story-fragment of 1841, hence from the last six months of the author's life, and known by editors' titles as *Štoss* or as *Fragment of a Story Once Begun* (Otryvok iz načatoj povesti).[8]

---

[8] The text was first published in 1845 in the almanac *Yesterday and Today* (Včera i Segodnja), Vol. I, pp. 71–87. Text and notes are reprinted in *M. Ju. Lermontov: Polnoe Sobranie Sočinenij,* OGIZ (Moscow-Leningrad 1948), ed. B. M. Ejxenbaum, Vol. IV, pp. 165–180 and pp. 468–470 respectively. A slight discrepancy in the notes is to be observed in the version printed in *Polnoe Sobranie Sočinenij M. Ju. Lermontova* (SPb, 1911), ed. Prof. D. I. Abramovič, Vol. IV, pp. 386–389. Where Ejxenbaum declares the last three words of the second note to be indecipherable, Abramovič reads: " ... bank ... skoropostiž-naja ... " and mentions I. M. Boldakov's deduction that the last word is "smert' ".

The extant text of some fifteen pages or so shows three subdivisions which presumably were to be designated as chapters.

1.   At a neither dull nor sprightly musical soirée in the home of Count V... there is a varied assortment of guests: celebrities from the world of art, literature, and scholarship, dowagers, young belles, home-grown "wolves", and the like. A young lady identified solely as Minskaja — presumably the daughter rather than the wife of a man named Minskij — slips off to a side room to chat with the painter Lugin. They are good friends but not in love. Lugin, a physically unattractive and socially awkward fellow, has spent three years in Italy undergoing treatment for his melancholia, and during that time has developed a passion for painting. His works are marked with real genius, but he shyly withholds them from all but intimate friends. For the past two weeks he has been beset by the oddest of hallucinations. For one thing, everyone looks yellow to him, as if he were walking through a gallery of the Spanish school; people seem to have lemons for heads. But what is more distressing, he has for several days now distinctly heard a strong, clear voice addressing him out of thin air. On each occasion the voice repeats a specific address: "In Carpenters Lane, by the Kokuškin Bridge, the house of Titular Councillor Štoss, Apartment No. 27." All this he circumstantially relates to Minskaja, who advises him to seek out the address, satisfy his curiosity, and then go to bed and get some rest.

2.   Through falling snow of a wet November morning Lugin makes his way to the poor district of Petersburg. His cabby ignores his question as to the location of Carpenters Lane, but a boy directs him to that dirty alley. A shopkeeper knows no person named Štoss. Suddenly a brand-new name plaque indicates that he has come to the right house. The porter says Štoss rents out quarters here but does not live here himself. As for No. 27, it has been vacant since the departure of a Colonel of Engineers; he will show it to Lugin. It proves to be a four-room suite, papered with red parrots and gold lyres on a green background, and for the visitor "the rooms have a certain strange, non-contemporary" look. Dust and cobwebs are plentiful. Lugin decides to rent the apartment. No sooner has he made this decision than his eye catches sight of a painting on the wall. It represents a man of perhaps forty, clad in a Bokharian dressing gown, and with a face of astonishing vitality, simultaneously haughty, sad, evil, and friendly. Lugin sits down opposite the picture. He is still sitting in the same position when his servant comes that evening to bring his belongings. When darkness has fallen, Lugin takes a candle to inspect the picture more closely. Then his eye perceives the word "Wednesday" written beneath it. This is Monday ...

3.   Restless and brooding, Lugin spends all of Tuesday staring at the portrait until, around midnight, he becomes calm and undertakes a drawing. He draws the man of the portrait. The door creaks, a cold wind blows, and there enters the man in question, dressed in a striped

dressing gown and bed slippers. He sits down at a table opposite Lugin, produces two decks of cards, gives one to his host, retains the other, and smiles expectantly. To Lugin's questions he makes no answer but a sigh. And all the while his face keeps passing through a kaleidoscope of expressions. At last he says: "Would you like to have a game of štoss?" Lugin agrees to play but warns him he will not wager his soul in the game.

They play. The visitor wins, to Lugin's irritation, then calmly collects his winnings and leaves. His retreating footsteps can be heard passing from room to room. Lugin falls asleep in his chair.

All of Thursday Lugin waits with feverish impatience until midnight brings the stranger. This time a young woman comes with the visitor, though not until the card game is in progress does Lugin ask who the second party is. At that moment Štoss, fixing his eyes on Lugin's trembling hand as it draws a card, asks: "What is it?" (Čto-s?). Frightened, Lugin replies: "Is *this* štoss?" (Štoss — èto?). Simultaneously, amid aromatic fragrance, a feminine form appears over Lugin's shoulder "like the morning star against the misty east", and the young man is possessed with a frantic desire to win at cards. The game proceeds. The visitor wins as before.

Night after night the card games continue. Lugin is wasting away from almost total abstinence from food. He never wins. The beautiful lady evinces sorrow at his losses and her glance seems to say that she is waiting for the moment when she will be free of the strange man's yoke, and that when that moment comes, she will be Lugin's. Meanwhile the painter has pawned his last possessions to stake himself to these losing games. He is desperate. "It was necessary to come to some decision. He came to a decision."

(With these words the text breaks off.)

A few supplementary hints, particularly as to the identity of the lovely lady, are to be found in Lermontov's notebooks. In the album used by him in 1840—1841 (now in the Saltykov-Ščedrin Library) we read:

Subject: At a lady's: yellow faces. Address. House: an old man and his daughter propose gambling to him. The daughter is in despair when the old man wins. The card-sharp: old man wagered and lost his daughter so that ... Doctor: little window ...

And in a notebook which Prince Odoevskij had given him (now also in the Saltykov-Ščedrin Library), Lermontov jotted:

"Now who are you, for Heaven's sake?" — "What is it?" (Čto-s?), replied the little old man as he winked one eye. "Štoss!" repeated Lugin in horror.

The card-sharp has his wits in his fingers ...

Three additional words, barely legible, may include:

> . . . bank . . . sudden . . ."

I. M. Boldakov guessed from the feminine ending on the adjective "sudden" (skoropostižnaja) that the last word was "death" (smert'), and then went on to guess that the "sudden death" would have come about by Lugin's leaping from the "little window", perhaps at the office of the "Doctor" to whom he would have had recourse in his state of mental illness.

The deduction is both shrewd and plausible, and, if correct, would suggest that the story had reached approximately its three-quarter mark at the point where the text breaks off. In other words, it would have approximately matched the length of *The Queen of Spades,* and like that famous work of Puškin's, it exhibits a fundamentally realistic attitude toward Romantic matter, as well as tongue-in-check whimsy in such matters as the threefold or fourfold pun: "Štoss", the man's name; "štoss", the name of the game of chance and the word by which the winner claims his victory; and "čto-s?" meaning "What is it?". Like Hermann in *The Queen of Spades,* Lugin is surely intended as a young man in a morbid state of mind who will be the victim of his own delusion. The picture, in all likelihood, did not come to life as did the portrait of Petromixali in Gogol's *The Portrait* — with which critics have inevitably compared Lermontov's story —, but only seemed to do so. On this point Lermontov is as elusively non-committal as Puškin had been on the point of the Count of Saint Germain and his transmitting of the secret of the three cards to the Countess. The word "card-sharp" (šuler) in the author's notes suggests a real person, as do the audibly retreating footsteps, rather than any supernatural personage, and the reader infers that the apartment, the voice, the card games, and all the other factors of the mystification would have proved of that unsavory rascal's contriving. Lugin is almost certainly a deliberately selected dupe whose mental sickness would have brought him to madness and disastrous death.

Unlike *The Queen of Spades,* on the other hand, the "Štoss Fragment" is *specifically* Hoffmannian, and its source-work is *Der Artushof.* Hoffmann's hero, Traugott, was, like Lugin, a young painter who left realistic acquaintances and a down-to-earth fiancée, Christine Roos, in the heart of Danzig to seek out a mysterious father and daughter at the city's outskirts. In that case, the old man was a mad painter who demonstrated his sublime paintings from wholly blank canvases and who was obsessed with fear that his daughter's marriage would, according to a prophecy once made to him, result in his death. For that reason he dressed Felizitas in men's clothing and passed her off as his son and ferociously denied access to all possible suitors. But Traugott, admitted to proximity as a serious disciple of art, discovered the truth, made love to Felizitas, and was ejected with violence from the house. After pursuing the eccentric old man and the lovely girl to Sorrento in Italy, he learned that they had gone to "Sorrento", a villa in the near-by countryside. Returning later, he discovered further that old Berklinger had died of a stroke when he had chanced upon his daughter with a suitor, and that Felizitas, the Ideal Beloved of an artist, had, not too long after her father's death, married still another suitor, a "jurist from Marienwerder". (The American equivalent might be " a lawyer from Schenectady".) But Traugott, who had abandoned his Philistine employer, Mr. Roos, and the latter's Philistine daughter, Christine Roos, for the fantastic Berklingers, went back to Italy a second time to rejoin the lovely Dorina and *her* elderly father, and the story concluded without disclosing whether this third pair were to provide a third disillusionment or a satisfactory middle ground between excessive realism and excessive Romanticism.

Like other Russian Hoffmannists, Lermontov regarded only one episode from the entire tale, in this case the chief episode, freely adapted the trio of characters, and undoubtedly would have brought the story to a tragic end. The procedure would suggest recollection of *Der Artushof* after some interval rather than close adaptation after recent reading, and the presence of numerous Hoffmannian motifs from other works testifies to considerable familiarity with popular items from the Hoffmann canon: the mysterious house and daemonic guidance to it (*Das öde Haus,* and also *The Queen of Spades*); the strange non-contemporary appearance of the rooms (*Ritter Gluck*); the note to the effect that "the old man wagered and lost his daughter" (*Spielerglück*); Lugin's compulsive drawing of the old man in the portrait (the Franzesko inset from *Die Elixiere des Teufels*). It should be mentioned also that *Die Irrungen* offered a duplicate trio of characters to Traugott-Berklinger-Felizitas, though the beautiful Greek lady of that story was the ward, not the daughter, of old Schnüspelpold. At the same time, that self-parodying work of Hoffmann's surrounded the mysterious lady with an aura of Levantine perfumes and colors, and is more closely related in mood to the "Štoss Fragment" than is *Der Artushof*. Still other echoes from Gogol's *The Portrait* and from Puškin's *The*

Queen of Spades indicate that Lermontov was consciously working within an area of Romantic matter well established with the readers of 1841.

Within that area he created his own wry mixture of wit, suspenseful mood, and strong, though controlled, emotion. The characters are interestingly altered from their *Artushof* prototypes. Lugin, gifted, physically unattractive, socially unprepossessing, intense, prey to an *idée fixe,* is no longer the bland and dreamily naive Traugott. Štoss may be mad and harmless like old Berklinger, but more probably he would have proved in the end closer to the malicious Spalanzani of *Der Sandmann,* who used his "daughter" Olimpia as a decoy with which to lure the over-impressionable Nathanael to destruction. Only Lermontov's heroine remains unclear. Felizitas Berklinger had vacillated between her natural impulse to love Traugott and her devotion to her aged and mentally infirm father, but in the end had emerged from her fantastic life of old-German costumes, lute-playing, and mascarading as a youth, to marry in haste with the "jurist from Marienwerder". All we know of her Russian counterpart is that she *seems* to Lugin to be a vision of loveliness "like the morning star against the misty east". Traugott shrugged off *his* disillusionment with Felizitas and went back to Italy and Art and Dorina. It would seem that Lugin was destined for a bitterer and more characteristically Russian disillusionment from the card-sharp's daughter.[9]

In any event, the witty, skillfully written fragment must remain a tantalizing mystery, and Russian literature lost a jewel of Romantic fiction when this story was left unfinished.

5. TURGENEV

Still another underground root of Hoffmannian influence is said to crop up amid the works of Turgenev. The claim proves upon examination to have only small validity. No touch of Hoffmann is to be discerned in those stories of Turgenev which deal in supernatural elements. In *Phantoms* (Prizraki), that "Fantasy" of 1863 which Dostoevskij mercilessly and not wholly undeservedly parodied under the title of

---

[9]   Ejxenbaum (see previous note) considers the fragment anti-Romantic, opposed to Hoffmann's favoring of the dreamer type, and speculates as to a possible connection with Odoevskij's *Sil'fida*. No specific Hoffmannian source has heretofore been suggested.

"Merci" in the course of *The Possessed,* the ectoplasmic lady called "Ellis" is little more than a wish-bestower who transports the narrator about Europe and Russia in swift spiritflights in order to confront glories of the West with unglamorous realities of the home scene. Less alien to the spirit of Hoffmann, though still remote from him, is the phantom canine in the story entitled *The Dog* (Sobaka) of 1866, in which Porfirij Kapitonič acquires a real dog, Trezor, to combat the spectral one. Out of nowhere a rabid cur materializes to attack him while on a walk, and again while sleeping on a hot night in the barn. Trezor saves him on both occasions but dies from the wounds of the second encounter. The anecdotal narrative ends with a question: What is "sound judgment" to make of such events? The set of international thieves who rob the title character of *Lieutenant Ergunov* (1867) bear a superficial resemblance in their Balkan exoticism to certain exoticisms and mysterious encounters in Hoffmann's *Die Irrungen,* but they bear a closer resemblance to the smugglers in the *Taman'* episode of Lermontov's *A Hero of our Time.* In *Knock ... Knock ... Knock* (Stuk ... Stuk ... Stuk ...) (1870) Turgenev undercuts all the supernaturalisms of the story with sober and rather deliberately commonplace rational explanations. Turgenev's sense of the supernatural was of Daniel Donglas Home's and Mme Blavatsky's kind, not of Hoffmann's.

On the other hand, the *Literaturnaja Ènciklopedija* is not amiss in saying that the novel *Spring Freshets* (Vešnye Vody) of 1871 repeats motifs of *Die Irrungen.*[10] It is that bizarre work of Hoffmann which Gemma, the Italian heroine of the novel, recalls vividly — though, as the author remarks, incorrectly — in Chapter XII. She and Sanin, the book's hero, had caught the sound of a hand-organ playing *Durch die Felder, durch die Auen* from Weber's *Freischütz,* and "from Weber the conversation glided to poetry and romanticism, to Hoffmann, whom everyone was reading at the time ...". The time, significantly, was 1840.

It appeared that Gemma did not particularly favor Hoffmann and even found him ... tiresome! The fantastically-obscure, northern element in his tales was not very perceptible to her bright, southern nature. "They are all fairy tales, written for children!", she asserted, not without disdain. She also had a confused consciousness of the absence of poetry in Hoffmann. But there was one of his tales, whose title, however, she had forgotten, which pleased her greatly. Properly

---

[10] *Literaturnaja Ènciklopedija,* the article "Gofman", *op. cit.,* p. 679.

speaking, only the beginning of the tale pleased her: she had not read the end, or had forgotten it also. It was about a young man, who, somewhere or other, in a confectioner's shop, so far as she remembered, meets a young girl of striking beauty, a Greek; she is accompanied by a mysterious and queer old man. The young man falls in love with the girl at first glance; she gazes at him so pitifully, as though entreating him to set her free ... He withdraws for a moment — and on returning to the confectioner's shop, he no longer finds either the young girl or the old man; he rushes to seek her, is incessantly coming across perfectly fresh traces of them, and by no means, nowhere, never can he overtake them. The beauty vanishes from him forever and ever — and he is powerless to forget her beseeching look, and is tormented by the thought that, perchance, all the happiness of his life has slipped out of his hands.

Hoffmann hardly ends his tale in just that way; but so she had constructed it, and so it remained in Gemma's memory.

"It seems to me", she said, "that such meetings and such partings occur in the world more frequently than we think."

Gemma has indeed scrambled Hoffmann's story in her memory, and sentimentalized it too, beyond, it would seem, anyone's capacity to sentimentalize and misread that zany spoof of a work, *Die Irrungen*. To disentangle Gemma's recollections from the actual events would serve no purpose, for the motif of the ideal beloved glimpsed once and then lost forever, is introduced by Turgenev as foreshadowing the course of his own novel. Sanin had met Gemma in Frankfurt in "the Italian Confectionery Shop of Giovanni Roselli", had fallen in love with her, manoeuvred her dismissal of her wealthy suitor, Herr Klüber, fought a duel with an impudently admiring officer for her sake, and set their wedding day. In search of badly needed cash for his new life, he encountered an old acquaintance named Polozov, who referred him to his wife as a possible purchaser of Sanin's lands. But Mar'ja Nikolaevna — a less successfully portrayed Hedda Gabler — laid a bet with her husband that she could take Sanin away from his fiancée in three days' time. She succeeded. Years later, in 1870 in fact, the wretchedly lonely Sanin discovers Gemma's married name and her address. She is now Mrs. Jeremiah Slocum, resident at 501 Broadway, New York, U.S.A. The novel ends with Sanin's preparations for departure to New York.

6.   FROM 1835 TO 1845

What is most significant in *Spring Freshets* for present considerations is its wistful evocation of the era of 1840 and its revelation of Hoffmann as a popular author of the time who was not always correctly understood. Gemma's sentimental and erroneous recollection of *Die Irrungen* is, in essence, not very different from Count Sollogub's sentimentalized misreading of the *Kreisleriana* (1839); or from Konstantin Aksakov's vaguely Hoffmannizing story of 1836 called *Life in a Dream* (Žizn' v mečte), in which the artist-hero Walter Eisenach, inspired by Cecilia (Hoffmannian name!), painted a picture of three maidens who came to life, then painted his own picture beside theirs — and died. Such misreadings are perhaps no more grave than the misreadings by previous authors discussed here. But the by-products of the misreadings are curiously pale in the period beginning at 1835, whereas Polevoj's Hoffmannizing stories of a few years before, however false to the genius of Hoffmann, nevertheless derived a striking intensity of emotion from him. These late comers are weary and tame. Lermontov's fragment of 1841 comes as a grateful surprise, but it was unfortunately to remain a fragment. Gogol's *The Overcoat* (1842) serves to emphasize the transition from the Hoffmannizing genre into the new realism. Odoevskij's *Russian Nights* and the rest of his collected works of 1844 come as a belated anomaly and represent creations of the previous decade.

By 1845, it has been customary to say, Hoffmann had been abandoned entirely by creative writers in Russia. Critical opinion equally disclaimed him. Belinskij, once enthusiastically admiring, considered that the young generation had nothing further to learn from him. Hence his disgust with his protégé Dostoevskij, who, in *The Double* (1846), misused his gifts by reviving the dead letter of Hoffmann. Warned of his error by Belinskij, he stubbornly persisted in his wrong course by composing the still more Hoffmannesque story *The Landlady* (1847). Then, tradition claims, with his artistic reputation damaged, he saw the truth of Belinskij's warning and mended his ways by banishing the dead letter henceforth from his works. The truth of the matter is precisely the opposite, for in Dostoevskij may be seen the greatest of all the Russian Hoffmannists, and his works fulfill the promise of his predecessors by absorbing and transforming Hoffmann's matter and genius to create works that rival and ultimately transcend the originals.

VIII

DOSTOEVSKIJ: THE CULMINATION OF THE HOFFMANNIZING PROCESS

Intended originally as the concluding chapter of the present study was a body of matter pertaining to Dostoevskij's use of the Tales of Hoffmann which ultimately proved so voluminous that it was detached from the foregoing and published separately under the title of *Dostoevski the Adapter*.[1] The extensive demonstrations offered there need only to be succinctly summarized here. In the perspective of the foregoing chapters the Hoffmannizing process of Dostoevskij will more properly be seen as the culmination of a far broader process that involved a whole generation of Russian authors.

Tedious and aggravating delays preceded the publication of Dostoevskij's first work, the novelette *Poor Folk,* on January 15, 1846. More than a year had elapsed since completion of the manuscript in November of 1844. But the interim had not been devoid of either fame or work. The striking realism of the story corresponded precisely to the notion that Belinskij had formed of what the new literary age required, and the author was already widely acclaimed in critical circles as "the new Gogol' ". Meanwhile he had been eagerly preparing a second work, *The Double,* which followed its longer predecessor into print within two weeks, on February 1, 1846. The momentum of his reputation at first carried the new story forward in popularity, but a heartsick letter to the young writer's brother Michael, dated April 1, relates the sudden reversal of public and critical acclaim in the two months since publication.[2]

The first impression was blind enthusiasm, great sensation, and endless argument. The second was the really critical one. They all — that is, my friends and the whole public — declare with one voice that my 'Gol-

---

[1] Passage, *Dostoevski the Adapter. A Study in Dostoevski's Use of the Tales of Hoffmann* (University of North Carolina Press, 1954).

[2] *Letters of Fyodor Michailovitch Dostoevsky to his Family and Friends* translated (from the German versions of Alexander Eliasberg) by Ethel Colburn Mayne (London, 1914; also Macmillan Co, New York), pp. 34–35.

jadkin' is tedious and thin, and so drawn out as to be almost un-
readable. One of our lot is now going in for the perusal of one chapter
a day, so that he may not tire himself . . .

The letter proceeds to a distressful self-accusation for having written
too fast and for having "spoilt what might have been a really significant
piece of work". The reproach to his aesthetic conscience is partly
justified, for *The Double* is of uneven composition, but, if the concept
of the work was imperfectly executed, the concept itself was wholly
valid, original, and brilliant. Basically, that concept depended upon an
amalgamation of matter from Gogol' with matter from Hoffmann, the
whole to be treated in a way of the youthful author's own unique
invention.

1. *THE DOUBLE*

The thirteen chapters of *The Double* portray successive stages of the
oncoming of madness in Mr. Jakov Petrovič Goljadkin, and by that
token represent an extension and intensification of Gogol's story *The
Diary of a Madman*, much as *Poor Folk* represented an extension and
intensification of Gogol's *The Overcoat*. The process, however, by
which Goljadkin advances into madness is not the simple linear descent
of Popriščin, but a complex process by which the personality, under
intense strain, splits into two antithetical selves, one meek and for-
bearing, the other arrogant and intent upon destroying its concomitant.
This idea is borrowed from Hoffmann, most particularly, though not
solely, from *Die Elixiere des Teufels*. Motifs are freely borrowed from
other works of both Gogol' and Hoffmann, some merely verbal, others
elaborately adapted, until it is evident that Dostoevskij intended a kind
of super-story that would distil and outdo the madness tales and the
lore of *Doppelgängerei* of his combined predecessors. Beginning at
Chapter 4 the work offers parallels to the over-all pattern of Hoffmann's *Die Abenteuer der Sylvesternacht,* so that one inclines to
believe that Dostoevskij undertook the narrative proper as a deliberate
amalgamation of Gogol's *Diary of a Madman* with Hoffmann's *Sylvesternacht,* and then, as his own vivid imagination developed the
theme, loaded the interstices of his narrative with detail after detail
from other works by his two author-models.

The opening chapter, which presents Mr. Goljadkin's morning preparations for an undisclosed major event, is full of Gogolian echoes. The
hero is a poor clerk like Popriščin and Akakij Akakievič. His first action

upon rising is to consult his mirror to determine whether "some repulsive pimple had made its appearance" on his face, which was precisely what Major Kovalëv in *The Nose* had done. He is attended by a servant named Petruška, blood brother of the lackey of the same name who attended Čičikov in *Dead Souls*. Chapter 2, on the other hand, is wholly Dostoevskian, with its unexpected visit to the doctor during which the hero weeps from terror at the mental distress that he is unable to describe even when he most desperately desires to do so. The shopping tour of Chapter 3 reveals that Mr. Goljadkin is on his way to the name-day party of Klara Olsuf'evna, his employer's daughter, of whom he is enamored just as Popriščin was enamored of *his* employer's daughter. Wholly Dostoevskian, however, is the grinding humiliation of his rejection at the door in full view and hearing of the invited guests. Still more acutely painful is the succeeding chapter which begins with Mr. Goljadkin huddled in the dark and cold on the back stairs of his employer's house waiting for the courage to dart in and join the guests. The courage and the opportunity finally come, he makes his way in, flings his coat aside, and pretends that he has been there all the time. After some horrible moments he finds himself, first in the hands of some gentlemen, then hurtling through the air, then landed on the street with his coat flying down after him.

In the first chapter (Die Geliebte) of Hoffmann's four-chapter *Abenteuer der Sylvesternacht,* the hero, identified only as "the traveling enthusiast", attended a New Year's Eve party at which he encountered a former beloved, the evil siren Julie, who shows herself so heartless that he runs away from the party in despair. Goljadkin, after this party at Klara Olsuf'evna's, picks himself up and races madly through the stormy November streets of Petersburg. The author's enumeration of well known landmarks traces his flight. The "traveling enthusiast" raced wildly past the well known landmarks of Berlin on that last night of December. In the second chapter (Die Gesellschaft im Keller) of Hoffmann's story the "traveling enthusiast" dropped in at a beer-cellar where all mirrors were draped over with cloth out of deference to the client Erasmus Spikher who hated mirrors, having surrendered his own mirror-image to the evil Giulietta in Florence long ago — she appears in the operatic *Contes d'Hoffmann* as the *Venetian* courtesan Giulietta. Here the 'traveling enthusiast" met Spikher, the double who had surrendered his mirror-image, and also Peter Schlemihl (out of Chamisso's story), the double who had sold his shadow to the Man in Grey. In Chapter 5 of Dostoevskij's story Mr. Goljadkin meets a double — his own double. Hoffmann's third chapter (Erscheinungen) offered the bizarre dreams that assailed "the traveling enthusiast" that night. In the crescendo of the nightmare he beheld the figures of the previous day's encounter "multiplied by the hundreds and the thousands". In Chapter 10 of the Russian story Mr. Goljadkin is likewise beset by dreams that review the past, and the crescendo of the nightmare like- wise develops a multiplication of figures, multiplications this time of the evil double, that "other" Mr. Goljadkin. Both heroes awaken around midday, Mr. Goljadkin to go to his doom, "the traveling enthu- siast" to yield place in his story to the memoirs of Erasmus Spikher. These constitute the fourth and last chapter (Die Geschichte vom ver- lorenen Spiegelbilde), and though story parallels are absent here, there is present the principal motif of mirror-reflections, a motif of consider- able importance for Dostoevskij's story. For it is repeatedly implied by Dostoevskij that the double, "the second Mr. Goljadkin", appears as a mirror-reflection of the real Mr. Goljadkin. At a restaurant the hero catches sight of him in what he "had taken for a looking-glass"; at the office the two are seated opposite each other; in the final scene the double enters "through a door which our hero had taken for a looking- glass". Every shiny surface upsets Mr. Goljadkin, just as the shiny surface of a snuff box had distressed Spikher in the beer-cellar: the flashing star on His Excellency's coat dazzles Goljadkin, and when he averts his eyes to the floor he is fascinated anew by His Excellency's patent leather shoes. Dostoevskij's story takes on much more coherence and poetic validity when the reader understands that the double's entrances are the sudden perceptions of the hero's self in the eerie world "through the looking-glass". Indeed, the four-day time analysis of the story as a whole reveals the sequence: soirée-office of days 1 and 2 "mirror-reflected" in the sequence: office-soirée of days 3 and 4.

Meanwhile the powerful scene of the first appearance of the double (Chapter 5) is derived from another Hoffmannian source. The dis- traught Mr. Goljadkin has paused in his flight to lean over a bridge. The double approaches, it is true, on foot, but the passage recalls that scene in Hoffmann's novel *Kater Murr* (near the end of Part I, Section 2) where Kreisler leaned over the bridge and beheld his double in the mirror-like water. Rushing away in terror, Kreisler sought refuge with his friend Meister Abraham, but at the entrance to the latter's house was again terrified to behold his double anew. This time the illusion proved to be his own reflection in the concave mirror that the wise necromancer had in his vestibule. Mr. Goljadkin is no less terrified than Kreisler, and when the mysterious figure vanishes, he breaks into a run, arrives home breathless, and finds his double seated on his bed waiting for him. There the scene is left without explanation, much as Hoffmann sometimes left unexplained scenes, particularly in the *Sylvesternacht* and in *Die Irrungen,* which mannerism Gogol' had parodied in *The Nose.*

Chapter 6 of *The Double,* which takes Mr. Goljadkin to the office and confronts him with his counterpart working *opposite him,* returns to the manner of Gogol'. Chapter 7 brings the two of them to the real Mr. Goljadkin's home for the night, and the comedy of the sentimental pact of blood-brotherhood amid wine and the telling of each other's life histories strikingly recall "Pogorel'skij's" Antonij and the Mr. Double whom he invoked to while away the lonely Ukrainian evenings.

But Chapter 8 shows Mr. Goljadkin awakened the following morning alone and then takes him to the office to discover that his treacherous double has preceded him there and already undertaken a campaign of destruction against him. As the day proceeds, episode after episode reveals the mounting hostility of the adversary. The hostile selves now take on the aspect of struggle that Hoffmann had portrayed in the identical halfbrothers, the monk Medardus and Count Viktorin, in *Die Elixiere des Teufels.* No realistic explanation can possibly account for the interpenetration of lives of that pair, even to the point where the mad Viktorin returns to the monastery near the close of the novel and, in confession, accuses himself of Medardus's crimes. Dostoevskij, a generation nearer the modern age, has brought this mysterious conflict into a single body and presented it as a quasi-medical case of schizophrenia.

The mysterious and unexplained exchange of letters in Chapter 11 recalls the whimsical correspondence between the dogs Madgie and Fido which was seized and avidly read by Popriščin in *The Diary of a Madman,* but the final scene, when Goljadkin again penetrates the house of his employer, brings, the story back to Hoffmann. The loading of Mr. Goljadkin into the carriage bound for the madhouse and the mocking presence of the double beside the vehicle patently echo the passage in *Die Elixiere des Teufels* (Part I, end of Section 3) where Medardus stands by and watches the mad Viktorin transported in fetters and on a cart filled with straw to a lunatic asylum.

The majestic scene just prior to this is clearly more than realistic. The employer is seated in an arm-chair like a judge; his daughter is dressed in white like an angel; the multitudinous guests stand row on row, hushed; white light pervades the room; the doctor, like a grim angel, conducts the hero down the stairs into outer darkness. In short, Dostoevskij is at pains to parallel a scene of heavenly justice pronounced upon a sinner. Though not *like* the gorgeous ecclesiastical finale of *Die Elixiere des Teufels,* this other-earthly close is analogous to it.

2. *THE LANDLADY*

Dostoevskij's next major effort was the story entitled *The Landlady* (October 1847) which directs its attention to three principal characters, a sensitive young man, a mysterious old man, and a beautiful young woman. This trio of basic types is immediately recognizable as that which Hoffmann used in astonishing permutation in story after story. This young man, whose name is Ordynov, is, we are told, a scientist, "but with the soul of an artist". At vespers in a Petersburg suburb he beholds the grim old man "Il'ja Murin, artisan" escorting the lovely Katerina to the shrine of the Virgin, where she kneels and prays and weeps in profound affliction. Ordynov follows them to their lodging and ultimately presents himself as a morning caller in search of rooms. Murin would gruffly turn him away, but the beautiful "landlady" immediately accepts him. Once established in his new quarters, he is unable to ascertain any facts about them, not even their relationship to one another. Katerina may be Murin's wife, mistress, ward, or daughter. During an illness of the young man's she comes to his bedside with passionate kisses; at other times she treats her lodger as a brother and a potential rescuer from her evil bondage to the old man; at still other times she behaves to Murin as a fanatic disciple to an omniscient mage. Murin himself seems to be utterly inscrutable, now a reverent elderly man, now a demon, now a man mad from some ghastly disaster long ago when he was a barge owner on the Volga, now a villainous murderer, now a shabby charlatan and fortune-teller. The author has carried mystification to — perhaps beyond — the limits in this story, where external action is held to a minimum and where depiction of impressions is all-important. No decisive resolution is offered even at the end, after Ordynov has returned to his former lodgings with the Špis family and their daughter Tinxen (Tinchen).

In 1917 an article by Rodzevič pointed out [3] that Katerina's narrative to Ordynov, told between ecstasy and hysteria as she is lying in his

[3] S. Rodzevič, "K Istorii russkago romantizma", *Russkij Filologičeskij Vestnik,* LXXVII (1917), pp. 194–237; pp. 231–236.

arms, portrays Murin as a villain compounded of the two evil hypnotists, Alban in Hoffmann's *Der Magnetiseur* and Count S---i in *Der unheimliche Gast,* plus the consummately malignant Coppelius of Hoffmann's *Der Sandmann.* In 1931 an article by Gesemann showed [4] that the latter sections of that incoherent narrative were derived from Gogol's early Ukrainian tale, *A Terrible Vengeance.* It is also obvious that much of that narrative is couched in terms of the old folk ballads of Russia, both in the archaic diction and in the visualization of scenes, for example Katerina's flight with Murin on horseback with her head nestled in his bosom, and the farewell to her horse at the river's edge. But neither Rodzevič nor Gesemann explained how this conception of Murin was to be squared with his reverent prayers and his failure to perpetrate any evil deeds within the scope of the story. Katerina by statement or by implication attributes almost every crime in the calendar to him *in the remote past,* but the reader *sees* nothing of the sort.

Rodzevič in the same article pointed out that Ordynov's narrative to Katerina of his own childhood made him clearly the equivalent of the sensitive child Nathanael in *Der Sandmann,* while by the same token the evil old man that plagued him was derived from the baleful Coppelius. The inescapable conclusion, not pressed by Rodzevič, is that Ordynov and Katerina share, in some mysterious way, a single existence haunted by the same demon — Murin.

All these statements are correct! For Katerina is insane, as Ordynov comes to realize, and she sees Murin in terms of a series of Hoffmannian and Gogolian villains, Coppelius, Alban, Count S---i, and the evil necromancer of *A Terrible Vengeance,* all of them, be it noted, semi-supernatural. But Ordynov too is insane, or rather in the process of becoming so, and we understand that, at the close of the story, his prostrations for hours on end in prayer and anguish upon the church pavement represent the parallel of Katerina's condition at the story's beginning. As the counterpart of Hoffmann's Nathanael he was necessarily in precarious mental balance and destined to be driven mad by the events of the story. And finally, Murin too is insane, by evidence of his derivation from the mad painter Berklinger in Hoffmann's *Der Artushof!*

For the fact of the matter is — and it is an astonishing fact — that

---

[4] Gerhard Gesemann, "Der Träumer und der Andere. Ein Kapitel zur vergleichenden Dostoevskij-Forschung", in *Veröffentlichungen der Slavistischen Arbeitsgemeinschaft an der Universität Prag,* I. Reihe: Untersuchungen, Heft 8 (1931) (Dostoevskij-Studien); p. 7.

Dostoevskij has here retold the central section of *Der Artushof,* the tale of how the young artist Traugott went to study with the painter Berklinger, discovered that the latter's "son" was actually his daughter Felizitas in youth's clothing, made love to her, and was driven from the house at knife-point by the frenzied father, for the latter was convinced that his daughter's marriage would fulfill a curse laid upon his head and cause his death. Into this framework Dostoevskij has incapsulated two narratives, one by Katerina, who in her own madness saw her *father* as a fiend, one by Ordynov, who in his own madness saw in Murin the Giuseppe Coppola incarnation of his childhood Coppelius.

Once this concept is clear, of two narratives contained within a larger narrative, everything else becomes clear. Murin is a lucid madman but a kind father; his daughter is his whole life; the sensitive suitor must be driven from the house before Katerina is induced to love him and go away with him. All the contradictions result from the delusions of mad persons. At one point (end of Chapter 2) Murin fires a gun at Ordynov at close range — and misses him. This, like Berklinger's drawing of the knife, is his sole wrongdoing.

Dostoevskij has disregarded the art-problem aspects of the Hoffmann original, and the threefold adventure of Traugott — with Christine, with Felizitas, and with Dorina — has been reduced to the single middle adventure. Yet this "scientist" Ordynov has the soul of the artist Traugott. The Vespers scene bears a resemblance to the mysterious late afternoon scene in the Artushof when the Berklingers first materialize out of an ancient mural of that venerable building. The German Špis (Spiess) and his daughter Tinxen may properly be seen as residual figures from the Philistine Herr Elias Roos and his Philistine daughter Christine. "*Spiess*bürger" is the German word for "Philistine", and Tinxen (Tinchen) is the diminutive of "Christine". Finally, the ambiguous but probably happy close of the German story has been brought to the sombre gloom that forms a regular feature of the works of Russian Hoffmannists.[5]

---

[5] It is most interesting to compare the three Russian works that derive from *Der Artushof:* Polevoj's *The Painter,* Lermontov's "Štoss Fragment," and Dostoevskij's *The Landlady.* Hoffmann had confronted his hero with three father-daughter pairs in sequence, the excessively Philistine Roos's, the excessively artistic Berklingers, and finally the Italian Dorina and her father, who may prove to offer a tertium quid. Polevoj's hero was made to confront only the first of these, and his story was a simple conflict of art versus love. Lermontov and Dostoevskij both dwelt on the Berklinger episode, the former to convert it into something evil (apparently), the latter to convert it into a story of madness and illusion. A brief tabular arrangement will facilitate comparison:

3. *A NOVEL IN NINE LETTERS*

The long twenty-one month period between *The Double* and *The Landlady* had produced plans a-plenty in Dostoevskij's mind but very little in the way of realized works. *Mr. Proxarčin,* published in October of 1846, was a slight piece about a miser who fretted himself into a fever over the possibility that his fellow-roomers might discover his hidden money and who died insane. Its literary sources are generally said to be Puškin's *The Covetous Knight* and Balzac's *Eugénie Grandet.*

Early in 1847 Dostoevskij began ambitiously to compose a full-length novel with the title of *Netočka Nezvanova,* but financial need compelled him to turn to something shorter and more quickly saleable. Moreover, *The Landlady* was claiming his energy and imagination to the point where it crowded out the time-consuming novel.

Meanwhile, determined to get something into print, he brought out a comic tale that he had written in 1845, called *A Novel in Nine Letters.* The letters in question are exchanged over a ten-day period between a pair of cuckolded husbands identified only as Pëtr Ivanovič and Ivan Petrovič and deal with a series of *démarches* relative to a young gallant named Evgenij Nikolaič who is playing havoc with their wives' affections. Each letter seeks to outdo its predecessor in audacity. Mystification of the reader is a primary objective, and hilarity, not unmixed with *Schadenfreude,* forms the essence of the story.

At first glance, nothing, it would seem, could be further from Hoffmann's art than such heavy-handed badinage about cuckoldry. Yet the over-all notion of a miniature epistolary novel involving preposterous misunderstandings was derived from Hoffmann's *Haimatochare,* one of the late tales included in the posthumous collection of *Die letzten Erzählungen.* In that case fifteen letters were included, the bulk of them written by two scientists who had sailed from Australia to Hawaii

Hoffmann	Polevoj	Lermontov	Dostoevskij
Traugott	Arkadij	Lugin	Ordynov
Herr Elias Roos	Veren'ka and	(none)	Špis
Christine Roos	her father		Tinxen Špis
Berklinger		Štoss and	Murin
Felizitas Berklinger	(none)	his daughter	Katerina
Dorina and	(none)	(none)	(none)
her father			

All three Russian Hoffmannists ignored the third pair which might offer the possibility for compromise and ultimate happiness.

aboard the ship *Discovery,* Captain Bligh commanding. Once arrived in the islands they became engaged in a bitter rivalry over a beautiful "Insulanerin". The word presumably means "a native girl". Letters 6—12, which parallel Dostoevskij's story, traced the mounting hatred between the two men of learning until they met in a duel and simultaneously shot and killed each other. The "Insulanerin", christened "Haimatochare" — Greek for "Blood Beauty" — proved to be an insect first discovered by one of the men among the dorsal feathers of a pigeon that had been shot by the other.

Neither piece is more than a squib, but their relationship is a striking index of the degree to which Dostoevskij was immersed in Hoffmann's works. One begins to take literally the statement by the seventeen-year-old Dostoevskij that he had read "the whole of Hoffmann in Russian and German" previous to 1838.[6]

4. THE SHORT STORIES OF 1848

Denounced as a wrong-headed Romanticist by Belinskij and alienated from the friends of that powerful critic, Dostoevskij faced bleak prospects after publication of *The Landlady.* Financial pressures still required short pieces for early sale rather than the continuation of his novel *Netočka Nezvanova,* and through the year 1848 no less than six short stories were produced.

Another Man's Wife (January) and its sequel, *The Husband under the Bed* (December), were ultimately combined into a single work with cumbersome double title. Grotesque farce in rather bad taste characterize both parts of this freely invented pot-boiler.

Polzunkov, likewise of independent invention, is, on the other hand, a highly interesting piece of bitter comedy because it presents the first of Dostoevskij's self-lacerating buffoons. The title character is a fore-study of the future Karamazov senior.

A Faint Heart (February) reverts to the theme of the poor clerk of Gogolian tradition. Vasja Šumkov, an uncommonly loveable hero, seems to have everything that his young heart might desire. He has a suitable job, a benevolent employer, a loyal and stout-hearted roommate, a lovely fiancée, and future parents-in-law who already con-

---

[6]   In a letter to the author's brother Michael, dated August 9, 1838. See Mayne, *Letters of Dostoevsky,* cited in footnote 2 above, pp. 3—5.

sider him as their beloved son. Yet, after a happy New Year's gathering of these characters Vasja confesses to his roommate that he is terribly distressed over a quantity of office work which he has neglected these past few days from sheer exuberance of happiness. He sets to work by night, works frantically and feverishly. His roommate rouses in the middle of the night to see him still writing. The pen is moving very fast, line after line, but nothing is being written. With eyes that will not turn from the work Vasja says: "At last I have made the pen go faster." The next day he is committed to the madhouse. Up to this crucial scene the tale is Gogol'-derived, but the motif of the blank pages is a skillful adaptation of that passage in Hoffmann's *Ritter Gluck* where the lucid madman who fancied he was the composer Gluck played for his astounded visitor the score of Gluck's *Armida* out of a tome where all the pages contained nothing but empty staffs. Significantly, Hoffmann's hero lived contented with his harmless delusion and even had genius of his own, mysteriously affiliated with the genius of the dead master, while the Russian character passes to inconsolable, clinical madness.

An Honest Thief (April) chronicles the life of a friendless old drunkard named Emel'jan Ilič who lives upon the hospitality of a retired soldier. One day he steals a pair of riding breeches and sells them to buy drink. When taxed with the theft he denies his guilt, but further reproaches so humiliate him that he leaves his benefactor, wanders about the city for three days, and is then discovered dying of starvation. As he dies he expresses the hope that his old cloak may be sold for enough to reimburse his friend for the theft of the breeches. Nothing in the story as it stands suggests Hoffmann, but it is not impossible that this forlorn urban wanderer represents a residue of impressions from *Ritter Gluck*.[7]

A Christmas Tree and a Wedding (September) is hardly more than a sketch. It is concerned with a sinister man named Julian Mastakovič

---

[7] The mad musician of *Ritter Gluck* was a forlorn urban wanderer whose delusion of being "the Chevalier Gluck" sustained him. If he were stripped of his artist characteristics he would be *only* a forlorn urban wanderer; if, in place of his artist characteristics, "realistic" alcoholism were substituted, the end product would not be very far from Emel'jan Ilič. The acceptability of such an adaptation by deduction will depend on how deliberately one believes Dostoevskij "adapted" Hoffmann's works. Compare the division of substance of the same brief story by Prince Odoevskij, who created a parallel madman to "Gluck" in the poor fellow who thought he was the architect Piranesi (*Opere del Cavaliere Giambatista Piranesi*) and also imitated "Gluck's" monologue about musical inspiration and other details of the story in *Beethoven's Last Quartet*.

who, at a children's Christmas party, roughly drives away the governess's little boy from playing with a beautiful eleven-year-old girl and
then is overheard muttering his computations of that little girl's dowry.
Five years later she is seen as his pale and frightened bride. In view
of the grimly repeated theme of child-rape in Dostoevskij's fiction (and,
by unconfirmed rumor, in his life), this brief sketch takes on significance beyond its literary merit. Faint reminiscences from the Tales of
Hoffmann may or may not be involved in its composition. *Meister
Floh* opens with a Christmas party, and *Nussknacker und Mausekönig*
(the basis for Čajkovskij's *Nutcracker* ballet) contains Christmas scenes
with children. *Signor Formica* and more particularly *Die Brautwahl*
are centered upon the theme of inappropriate marriage between an
old man and a young girl — and the thwarting thereof. More plausible,
however, is a connection with the fourth chapter of *Datura fastuosa*
where the adolescent Gretchen reports the subtly obscene attempt made
by Fermino Valies in the botanical garden, not to seduce her, but to
suggest to her consciousness the first intimations of sexual passion and
sexual jealousy. The odd detail of an indoor ivy-arbor as the scene of
the principal episode at Dostoevskij's Christmas party seems to be one
of those many incidental residual points common to adaptation. In this
case it is the residual detail from the botanical garden which figured
prominently in the source work.

White Nights (December) is the longest of the 1848 series. Its fine
opening passage of evocation of Petersburg streets in summer elaborates
a theme already accorded masterful treatment by Puškin (*Eugene
Onegin,* I, 47–48) and by Gogol' in the first pages of *The Nevskij
Prospekt.* The sensitive young hero (unnamed) observes a pretty girl
weeping as she leans on a parapet overlooking the water; a few minutes
later he is able to rescue her from the molestations of a drunken man.
Her name is Nasten'ka, and directly the two exchange confidences.
At their second meeting she explains that her sweetheart had gone
away for a year in order to make enough money to permit him to
marry her. He had agreed to meet her at that parapet when the year
was up, and the previous evening was the time. She was weeping because he had not come. The hero, in a little scene that duplicates
Figaro's and Rosina's letter scene in *The Barber of Seville,* agrees to
take a letter to the young man. At their third meeting he announces he
has delivered the letter to the proper address, but that he is now in
love with Nasten'ka himself. At their fourth meeting Nasten'ka is on
the point of accepting the hero's offer of marriage when the missing

young man appears and claims her. The hero is left to his dreams and to the savoring of "a whole moment of happiness."

The story is a free variation on the theme of Gogol's *Nevskij Prospekt,* where two young men had set off simultaneously in pursuit of pretty girls glimpsed in the city street. Gogol's story was, in turn, derived from Hoffmann's *Aus dem Leben dreier Freunde* where *three* young men had simultaneously set out to pursue Pauline Asling, the pretty girl at the table next to theirs in the Tiergarten. In Dostoevskij's single-hero story there are little details, such as the parapet scene, to suggest that he had in mind both the Hoffmannian and the Gogolian predecessor works.

It is noteworthy that this sentimental story situation seems to have had a particularly strong appeal for Dostoevskij, since he repeats it with only slight variations in the persons of Alëša and Nataša in Chapter 8 of *The Insulted and Injured* of 1861 and also in a section of a little known work entitled *Petersburg Visions in Verse and Prose,* also of 1861.

By and large these short stories of 1848 give the impression that Dostoevskij was giving heed to Belinskij's caveat against Hoffmannism by reducing that element to a minimum in his writing. As the next section will show, the impression is erroneous. And as for the six stories themselves, two exhibit definite Hoffmannian traits, two are wholly lacking in such traits, and two (*An Honest Thief* and *A Christmas Tree and a Wedding*) are in doubt. It may be of significance that the two Hoffmann-affiliated works, *A Faint Heart* and *White Nights,* are the best of the lot.

5. *NETOČKA NEZVANOVA*

By 1849 Dostoevskij felt able to resume his full-length novel project, *Netočka Nezvanova.* The abrupt change of topic and method at the beginning of Chapter 4 makes it likely that the first three chapters belong to 1847 and were contemporaneous with *The Landlady,* while Chapters 4–7 belong to 1849. Two installments had appeared by the time of the author's arrest for seditious activities on April 23rd, and the completed third installment was published during his detention in the Peter and Paul Fortress. The fourth and concluding installment was never composed.

The entire text is narrated in first person by Netočka Nezvanova

("Nettie Nameless") herself, though we never learn her age or station at the time of writing. The first three chapters deal with events of her eleventh year, but it is the little girl's violinist step-father Efimov, rather than herself, who is the principal character. Mysterious circumstances surrounded the early years of this man. As a clarinetist in a provincial nobleman's orchestra he had most scurvily served his kindly employer, especially after striking up a friendship with a sinister Italian violinist. Reading between the lines of the ambiguous narrative, one deduces that the Italian was one of those Romantic figures who had bartered his soul to the Evil One in exchange, in this instance, for skill upon the violin and that he had died wretchedly upon expiration of the bargain. Efimov somehow inherited the instrument and straightway became possessed of the Italian's evil character, perhaps by assuming his Melmothian bargain with the Devil. After embarrassing his patron by posing before visitors as a great violinist spitefully forced to play the clarinet, Efimov went away. Disaster after disaster befell him. All he met despised him. Suddenly he announced his marriage to a widow, Netočka's mother, and once married, put aside the violin, declaring that his wife had made it impossible ever to fulfill his genius. He lived at her expense, treated her miserably, and meanwhile did not repulse the decidedly unchildlike passion expressed for him by his little step-daughter. Near the close of Chapter 3, stung to despair by hearing a genuine artist, the "violinist S.", play as only long training and practice make it possible to play, he murders his unhappy wife, starts to murder Netochka as well, but on second thought takes her with him as he flees from the house. Then in mid-flight through the wintry streets of Petersburg he abandons the child. Netočka has been told that he died two days later, a madman, but there is reason to suspect that she is misinformed.

This composition of 1847 creates the same atmosphere of nameless terror and dread that marked its contemporary work, *The Landlady*. It bristles with Romantic motifs: the artist-hero — Dostoevskij's only artist-hero — the suggestion of an inherited Devil's violin, the suggestion of a bargain with the Evil One, and so on. This clarinetist who hoped to be a great violinist by virtue of a magic instrument and who was devastated by the revelation of true genius is clearly a new version of Gogol's painter Čertkov from *The Portrait*. By his mistreatment of his wife on the grounds that she has destroyed the artist in him, he is equally clearly a new version of Hoffmann's Berthold from *Die Jesuiterkirche in G*. It is possible that there is involved an extra borrowing from

210 DOSTOEVSKIJ: THE CULMINATION

the little tale at the end of Volume III of *Die Serapionsbrüder* known by alternate editors' titles as *Der Baron von B.* or *Der Schüler Tartinis*. This amusing anecdote concerned a famous violin teacher and pupil of the celebrated Tartini who gave superb instruction and charged high fees, but could not play a single composition. An incidental detail or two may also be taken from Krespel, the eccentric violin-maker (who *could* play) in the story *Rat Krespel*. But there is reason to believe that Efimov, in the novel as a whole, was destined to figure as a "sinning ancestor," and by that token we are brought back to *Die Elixiere des Teufels,* and specifically to the story-inset about the sinning ancestor, Franzesko the Painter. The flight of Efimov with the little Netočka would then correspond to Franzesko's flight with his little son. The relationship with *Die Elixiere des Teufels* is confirmed by a curious detail. Into that novel Hoffmann introduced at one point a lengthy digression portraying an eccentric flutist, an Irishman named Ewson. While traveling, this individual came to a certain inn, sprained his ankle in an attempt to demonstrate how to dance a hornpipe, and remained ever afterward. For twenty-two years he stayed there, and for the last three never missed a day trying to master a certain flute solo which eluded him. Into the Efimov story Dostoevskij has introduced a buffoon of a dancer, with the German name of Meyer, who serves as the butt of Efimov's cruel wit. But Meyer's interminable attempts at dancing and his sorry employment as a theatre extra also serve as a comic double for Efimov's own fiasco at genius. And with the concept of a comic double we are once again brought to *Die Elixiere des Teufels*. There the comic barber with the double name of Pietro Belcampo and Peter Schönfeld parodies the actions and life of the runaway monk Medardus even to final salvation after their wanderings, for Medardus dies a saint and Schönfeld-Belcampo enters the monastery as lay-brother Peter.

Chapter 4 is the first section of the novel when the title character emerges as the central interest. She is now, for unexplained reasons, an adopted child in the home of kindly Prince X. There is a curious passage at the end of the chapter, when, confronted with "the violinist S.", she first thinks he *is* Efimov, but then cries out that he is Efimov's murderer. One concludes that either Efimov had a dual life and that this is he in his benign aspect, or that he had an actual double, as did Medardus, the hero of *Die Elixiere des Teufels*.

Chapter 5, with its extraordinary portrayal of a homosexual passion between Netočka and Katja, the little daughter of Prince X, has no parallels in either Hoffmann or Gogol', but the episode motivates the heroine's removal to a new home. The long Chapters 6 and 7 deal with events in this second wealthy household, that of the sinister Pëtr Aleksandrovič and his beautiful long-suffering wife Aleksandra Mixajlovna at the time when the heroine is thirteen years old and thereafter. Some base intrigue is there afoot, with the husband covetously pursuing Netočka and at the same time persecuting his wife by devious psychological means. Netočka is on the point of an important discovery when the text of the novel abruptly breaks off.

Considerable attention is given in Chapters 4—7 to the complex family relationships of the characters, most of whom are capriciously designated either by given names only or even by mere initials. A diagram of fourteen of these characters and their interconnections startlingly reveals that Dostoevskij has lifted all save a few peripheral personages from Hoffmann's unfinished masterpiece *Kater Murr,* retained all their mysterious and complicated interrelationships, and transplanted them to the Petersburg environment of his own initial novel. Since the mysteries of *Kater Murr* were left unresolved, it is impossible to deduce the answers to Dostoevskij's mysteries. He must, it goes without saying, have resolved them in his own mind before undertaking his own novel, and to the enthusiasts for that superb fragment of Hoffmann's it is a fascinating though tantalizing task to deduce what Dostoevskij had concluded about its puzzles.

The important fact is, however, that Dostoevskij had planned his first full-length novel as nothing less than a superimposition of *Die Elixiere des Teufels* upon *Kater Murr,* not to mention the addition of motifs from smaller works of Hoffmann and from Gogol'! Since, in the diagram of characters, Efimov stands in the position of Kreisler, and since the return of Kreisler is the important event looked forward to in the unwritten sections of *Kater Murr,* one gathers that Efimov did not die but that he will reenter the story to precipitate its climax, either as "sinning ancestor" making revelations, or as a double ("the violinist S."), or both.

6. *A LITTLE HERO*

During the months of prison confinement before sentence Dostoevskij was allowed to compose but not to publish the pleasing short story called *A Little Hero*. The title character and narrator is a precocious lad of eleven, hence a kind of companion character of Netočka, though vastly more likeable than that exasperating girl. This narrator, who never divulges his name, is a guest at a country manor and there becomes involved in the lives of adults. He is fond of the gentle Mme M. and abets her clandestine love affair with young Monsieur N., simultaneously thwarting the subtle malice of Monsieur M. toward his wife. He also finds himself exasperated by "the teasing lady", Mme M.'s close friend (or cousin), of whose sexual charms he is uncomfortably aware. When "the teasing lady" taunts him with his fear of riding the stallion Tancred he rushes to mount that vicious animal, and though the beast runs away with him, he manages to stay on its back until the gentlemen of the party rescue him.

Once again the cast of characters is astutely modified from Hoffmann's *Die Fermate*, which had as its hero a young musician, of adult years however, who traveled in Italy with a pair of sisters, the musicians Teresina and Lauretta, who correspond respectively to Mme M. and "the teasing lady". A striking episode in that story involved an unruly horse and Lauretta's mockery of the hero for his inability to manage it.

Of thirteen works, including his unfinished novel, which Dostoevskij composed before his Siberian exile, seven certainly, possibly nine, were derived in some degree from Hoffmann, almost always with an admixture of Gogol'. Elaborate contrivances like the incapsulation of two Hoffmann stories within the framework of a third in the case of *The Landlady,* and the transferral of a large and complex cast of characters intact in the case of *Netočka Nezvanova,* indicate that Dostoevskij was not working merely from a fund of general memories but rather that he was consciously and deliberately adapting works of Hoffmann. The adaptations are ingenious in the extreme, utterly removed from any sphere governed by the word plagiarism, and the creations of a genius who understood that a source work was only a point of departure and that all merit lay in the development of matter. The evidence forces the conclusion that he operated with awareness and astounding skill on the basis of a formula: Hoffmann-plus-Gogol'-plus-Dostoevskij, with shifting proportions but with a tendency to favor Hoffmann over Gogol'.

7.   *THE INSULTED AND INJURED*

The two short novels which Dostoevskij composed in Siberia between 1857 and 1859 show no trace of Hoffmann and almost nothing of

Gogol'. *A Friend of the Family* seems to have had Molière's *Tartuffe* as its starting point, while *Uncle's Dream,* of Balzacian flavor, may have been independently conceived. The provincial lady scheming to marry off her reluctant daughter to a wealthy and senile nobleman bears a faint resemblance to the scheming Rätin Benzon of *Kater Murr,* but the resemblance is most likely fortuitous.

Once returned to Petersburg after his ten-year ordeal, Dostoevskij patently explored public taste in literature by means of various compositions. His prison memoirs, *The House of the Dead* (1861), was almost straight reporting at the highest level of journalism and could have no source but autobiography. The anonymously published *Petersburg Visions in Verse and Prose* (1861) contained among its rambling anecdotes the story of the narrator and "Amalie" with its curious extension of the situation from *White Nights,* of ultimate derivation from *Aus dem Leben dreier Freunde.* The same situation, further modified, appears in Chapter 8 of *The Insulted and Injured* (1861).

This first completed full-length novel of Dostoevskij's departs from previous practices to combine elements from Schiller's *Kabale und Liebe* with elements from Dickens' *The Old Curiosity Shop.* These borrowed elements are merged with other matter of heterogeneous origins, Hoffmannian among others. The entire opening scene, for instance, which on first inspection appears to be so thoroughly Russian and Dostoevskian, is a point by point adaptation of a sequence that occurs early in *Das öde Haus* when Theodor visits a confectioner's shop Unter den Linden to make discreet inquiries about the mysterious house adjoining the store. Indeed the two passages in juxtaposition offer the most sharply clear example of Dostoevskij's meticulous methods of transposition. It is particularly striking to observe how, in one small detail after another, the Russian author has darkened the cheerful scene of the original so that the time, the place, the characters, and even the dog have taken on aspects of profound misery. The ingenious device in *The Insulted and Injured* whereby two parallel stories are progressively disclosed to the reader, one of them entirely in the past and the other currently in development, is at least reminiscent of Hoffmann's procedures in *Die Elixiere des Teufels,* where the ghostly ancestor and the hero commingle past and present time, and of a *roman à tiroirs* such as *Spielerglück,* with its narrations of three successive gamblers' lives, each going further into the past than the preceding. Finally there is the figure of the villainous Prince Pëtr Aleksandrovič Valkovskij, whose name recapitulates the villainous Pëtr Aleksandrovič of *Netočka Nezvanova* (Chapters 6 and 7), who in turn was demonstrably a transposition of Prince Hektor, the sinister villain of *Kater Murr*. Valkovskij, too, has about him several traits in common with Prince Hektor, particularly the physical beauty which both authors stress. They also share Satanic pride, unpunished murder, high aristocratic rank, mystery, and infinite capacity for intrigue. There is good reason to think that Valkovskij is fundamentally Hektor, seen now through the prism of Dostoevskij's prison experiences. The most startling fact about him is that he is Dostoevskij's first true villain, and if he is not wholly credible, the fault lies with the author's unfamiliarity with literary means of portraying such a character, not with his Hoffmannian origin. His boundless self-will will pass five years later to Svidrigajlov in *Crime and Punishment* while his mask-like beauty will still later pass to Stavrogin, the hero of *The Possessed*.

8. *AN UNPLEASANT PREDICAMENT*

With the short story *An Unpleasant Predicament* (1862) Dostoevskij returned once again to the poor Gogolian clerk as hero. The utterly hapless Mr. Pseldonimov is celebrating his wedding evening with his shrewish bride, his brutal father-in-law, and a quantity of raucous guests, when his employer, the vain Mr. Pralinskij, condescends to drop in on the party in order to collect a bit of homage and flattery from these underlings. He comes as Gogol's Very Important Personage might have come to Akakij Akakievič's "coat-warming" party. But once there, Pralinskij drinks both homage and alcohol until he buries his face in a plate of blanc mange, from which he cannot raise it again. He spends the night, desperately sick, in the bed that was to have served as nuptial couch. It is, however, the earlier part of the tale that betrays the pattern of Hoffmann's *Die Brautwahl,* Chapter 1 principally. In that wildest and most brilliant of Hoffmannian scherzi the elderly Privy Councillor Tusmann, his head full of his forthcoming marriage to young Albertine Vosswinkel, had somehow not reached home at the usual hour of eleven but by virtue of the magic of Berlin streets on that equinoctial night had accepted the invitation of a stranger to come into a wine shop on the Alexanderplatz. What happened to him there was grotesque enough, but the night was spent in phantasmagoria. Tusmann knew that he was the prey of supernatural powers and spirits; Albertine's father believed the spirits were of the bottled variety; but one way or the other, Tusmann woke at dawn to find himself nestled in the bronze arms of the Great Elector's equestrian statue. Like Tusmann, Pralinskij takes a walk through the moonlit streets of the capital, unexpectedly varies his course to join a drinking party, and awakes in a very odd place the following morning. In his case there is no doubt as to the nature of the spirits that brought him there.

The formula for *An Unpleasant Predicament* is once more: Hoffmann-plus-Gogol'-plus-Dostoevskij, and one might well expect that its use betokened a return to the pre-exile manner of writing. The proportions of the ingredients, however, betray a change in spirit. The Hoffmannian component is small, the Gogolian component still smaller, and the story as a whole can no longer be reckoned among the works which are extensions of the Gogol' tradition. With *Notes from Underground* (1863) the definitive break is made with the past and it is a new Dostoevskij that emerges to write *Crime and Punishment* three years later.

Before leaving the immediate post-exile period of Dostoevskij's life it is worth noting that he paid fulsome tribute in print to Hoffmann's genius. The occasion was a little foreword of 1861 to a translation of three tales of Poe. After making the inevitable comparison of the two writers, he assigns "immeasurable superiority" to Hoffmann "as a poet". He then goes on to single out particularly admired qualities and particularly admired works, above all *Kater Murr* which he justly saw as Hoffmann's "best work".

9. *THE CROCODILE*

Of the unpleasant story *The Crocodile* it may be said that it is rather pointless if it has no meaning beyond the surface meaning, and that it is in unforgivably bad taste if it is, as contemporaries claimed (and Dostoevskij denied), an allegory of the transportation of Černyševskij to Siberian imprisonment. Literarily, it uses the devices of a talking animal in combination with the projected voice of a concealed person. *Kater Murr* used talking animals in profusion and also the projected voice of Chiara, "the unseen maiden", the latter as a trick of the charlatan Severino.

10. *CRIME AND PUNISHMENT*

With *Crime and Punishment* (1866) Dostoevskij achieved world stature. The art of that novel was now uniquely his, and though sources may be adduced for various of its component parts, these were now fused, as it were, in the fierce heat of his genius so that they were wholly transmuted. Only with the preceding discussions in mind is it possible to detect the traces of Hoffmann in the new alloy. Raskol'nikov, as extension of Hermann in Puškin's *Queen of Spades,* has something of Hoffmann at second remove. Slightly less remote from Hoffmann is Svidrigajlov, who continues the line of villains that began with Prince Hektor of *Kater Murr* and continued by way of the Pëtr Aleksandrovič of *Netočka Nezvanova* and Prince Pëtr Aleksandrovič Valkovskij of *The Insulted and Injured.* It is possible that Porfirij Petrovič and the explosive Lieutenant Zametov owe some part of their creation to the grim police official La Régnie and his energetic subordinate Desgrais in Hoffmann's *Das Fräulein von Scudery,* though Victor Hugo's Gervais in *Les Misérables* and Poe's C. Auguste Dupin must also be counted in the reckoning. The memorable dream sequences of Raskol'nikov and of Svidrigajlov could not have been written without the precession of the dream phantasmagorias of *Die Elixiere des Teufels,* and the dream-like terror of Svidrigajlov's first appearance before Raskol'nikov owes something to the same source. But these are details. The real debt of *Crime and Punishment* to Hoffmann is the over-all conception of its three major figures, the double Raskol'nikov between the extremes of Good and Evil, Sonja and Svidrigajlov respectively. For these loom up as altered versions of Medardus, the double in *Die Elixiere des Teufels,* and his flanking figures, the all-good Aurelie and the evil Count Viktorin.

11. *THE ETERNAL HUSBAND*

After *Crime and Punishment* the Hoffmannian element in Dostoevskij's fiction all but vanishes for about a decade (1866—1876). The most striking point to be made about *The Gambler* (1866) is that it has nothing whatever in common with Hoffmann's *Spielerglück.* The Idiot (1868) is equally devoid of Hoffmann's influence, as are *The Possessed* (1870—1872) and the late short stories. *The Eternal Husband* (1869), however, may well have had as its starting point the final pages (but not the long middle section) of *Der Zusammenhang der Dinge*. The domestic comedy is there resolved happily by Hoffmann, while Dostoevskij seems to have proceeded from the question: What if Euchar *had* been the lover of his friend Ludwig's wife after all? All the rest of *The Eternal Husband* is the development of such an alternate hypothesis. It is the epilogues of the two works, both after a two-year interval, that most clearly show their interconnection.

12. THE LIFE OF A GREAT SINNER

Traceable from December 1868 in Dostoevskij's letters and notebooks is the plan for a great super-novel in five volumes to which the author refers repeatedly with awe and excitement. Its title was to be *The Life of a Great Sinner* and its general plan was to trace from childhood to death the career of a Russian who in youth gave the appearance of being a saint but who was in actuality devoured with Satanic pride. He was to undergo temptation, fall, descend to a wandering life of monstrous crimes, and to emerge from some tremendous experience of purification a true saint. The plan, in so far as it can be reconstructed from notes and letters, is surely identical in outline with the plan of *Die Elixiere des Teufels,* where the runaway monk Medardus lived precisely such a life. The super-novel was never written. Under financial stress Dostoevskij drew upon the ideas accumulated for the Sinner's early years to make, first, some parts of the life of Stavrogin in *The Possessed,* and then even more to make considerable portions of the life of Dolgorukij in *A Raw Youth*. But the portion of the plan to which Dostoevskij referred with greatest enthusiasm was the monastery sequence which was to have occupied the second and perhaps the third volume of the five. In a sense, this portion was eventually realized, though with necessary modification, under the title of *The Brothers Karamazov*.

13. THE BROTHERS KARAMAZOV

The awesome achievement of *The Brothers Karamazov* was the crown of Dostoevskij's career. Ostensibly it deals more or less equally with the lives of three brothers at the time of their father's murder. The story of the eldest brother Dmitrij has been discovered to have its origin in the actual events in the life of a man whom Dostoevskij had known in Siberia as a fellow prisoner and who had been condemned to ten years of hard labor for the murder of his father. After serving much of the sentence it was proven that he was innocent of the crime. The lives of Alëša and Ivan, on the other hand, have a literary origin, and that origin is once again *Die Elixiere des Teufels*.

Alëša Karamazov, it has long been recognized by scholars, is a modified version of the Great Sinner. Once this fact is appreciated, the reader will quickly see that Alëša's story is only begun when the book closes. *The Brothers Karamazov* is, in short, a fragment. Or rather, the independent or nearly independent volume of a sequence of novels such as the *Great Sinner* plan called for but which was left without continuation by virtue of the fact that the author died two months after publication of the final installment. Explained herewith is the twice mentioned phrase in reference to Alëša: "my chief, though future, hero". In so far as Alëša *is* the Great Sinner he derives from Hoffmann's Medardus. Like the latter, he was mysteriously, even mystically, consecrated to holiness from childhood, Medardus by receiving the imprint of the Abbess's diamond cross upon his throat, Alëša by being placed under the protection of the Virgin by his half crazy but inspired mother. Both youths enter the monastic life early and attain early the reputation for saintliness. In both cases the saintliness is specious. Medardus undergoes a figurative temptation by drinking the devil's elixirs from the reliquary crypt of the monastery. Alëša's temptation is infinitely more impressive. He is tempted in his intellectual mind by the philosophical arguments of his brother Ivan, and at a certain moment accedes to the crucial objection against God's creation; he is tempted in his soul by doubt when the corpse of Father Zosima, far from working miracles, stinks; he is tempted in his body by the courtesan Grušen'ka. Multiple temptations surround this basic three-fold temptation — from his sensual father, from the disbeliever Rakitin, from grotesque fellow monks like Father Ferapont, and so on. And on all counts he fails. He falls. But we never see the results of his fall. He is ripe now for the life of crime, having yielded the major premises of evil, but the actual crimes must necessarily lie beyond that point when he leaves Skotoprigonevsk and goes forth into the world. In other words, beyond the last pages of *The Brothers Karamazov*. What was to have befallen him thereafter must be deduced from the notes for *The Life of a Great Sinner* — and from Hoffmann's *Die Elixiere des Teufels*.

But if Alëša Karamazov, in so far as he is the Great Sinner, re-capitulates the life of Medardus as false saint, criminal, and finally as true saint, Ivan Karamazov derives much of his essence from Medardus the double. In a previous adaptation as Mr. Goljadkin in *The Double,* Medardus's double nature had been subdivided into the real Mr. Gol-jadkin, who was meek and good, and the hallucinatory "other" Mr. Goljadkin, who was arrogant and evil. Dostoevskij has now gone vastly further and equated these halves or selves with the irreconcilable antitheses of nineteenth century Russia: Slavophile and Westernizer. It is the godless, anarchical European half of Ivan that holds that "all things are lawful", even to parricide; it is the Slavophile half of him that is purged and redeemed at the end. Medardus's evil half was his half-brother, Count Viktorin; Ivan's evil half is projected incarnate into *his* half-brother, Smerdjakov, the bastard and lackey. It is the evil pro-jection, Smerdjakov, who actually strikes down the father in murder, and then, like Judas Iscariot, hangs himself. But Medardus had also a second double, the whimsical, half unreal barber, Peter Schönfeld, alias Pietro Belcampo. So, too, Ivan has a second, non-corporeal double, the Devil, who comes as a hallucinatory projection of his corrupt mind. The fantastical appearances as to dress and speech of Ivan's Devil and of Belcampo-Schönfeld are points emphasized by both authors. Both serve as bitter mirrors for their respective heroes.

Finally, both *The Brothers Karamazov* and *Die Elixiere des Teufels* disregard specific geography in order to gain a quality of universality, much as mediaeval morality plays took place in "the world". Against a rarely broken chain of "Petersburg Tales" in Dostoevskij's career, the exception for this novel is striking. A cosmic purpose motivated both authors, Hoffmann who wished to write the modern equivalent of a saint's legend, and Dostoevskij who wished to encompass the whole of life as he saw it, and ultimately to establish his own modern saint amid the contemporary milieu. The Russian work is unquestionably the greater of the two: it stands on the shoulders of the former to acquire its breadth of scope and vision.

IX

RUSSIAN HOFFMANNISM IN RETROSPECT

The foregoing chapters have examined the connections, actual or supposed, between some seventy Tales of Hoffmann and some fifty Russian prose narratives, with a goodly hillock of sand-grains accumulated beneath the sieve of examination. A more succinct statement of the findings is now in order.

1. HISTORY

German artisans and German tradesmen had played an important role in Russian economic life since at least the reign of the first Romanov Tsar (1613–1645), but literary influence from Germany did not begin until the very late eighteenth century. The explanation of this fact lies primarily in the poverty of German letters until at least the 1760's and only secondarily in the preemptive supremacy of French culture of the same period. As soon as geographically closer Germany began producing works of merit, those works found Russian readers in spite of obstacles of language, censorship, and French canons of taste. The focus of such Russian interest in German books was the University of Moscow (founded 1755) and its important preparatory school, the Noble Pension, and the significant first propagator was Professor Johann Georg Schwarz, who in the 1780's urged his students to translations and amateur performances of plays by Lessing, Schiller, and Goethe. His protégés, representing the following generation, founded the little ten-member "Literary Society of Friends" in 1801, with interest centered upon *Werther* but directed also toward other German authors such as Wieland, Kotzebue, and minor lyricists. In their naiveté and tentativeness as well as in their anticipation of future developments, these ten youths, we have suggested, were parallel to the earnest little group of German youths who published *Die Bremer Beiträge* from 1745 to 1748. Russian literature was in the making now as German literature had been in the making fifty years earlier. After the disbanding of the

"Literary Society of Friends" there followed a period during which no tangible results of their efforts seemed to be forthcoming, but in 1815 their most important member, Žukovskij, assumed leadership of a new amateur club called the Arzamas, dedicated to the establishment of Romantic principles in literature. In the 1820's a younger generation of students at the University of Moscow developed a fresh interest in German books, concerning themselves this time with "philosophy", especially the new Romantic philosophy of Schelling and such works of fiction as they deemed in keeping with Schelling's doctrines, particularly Goethe's *Faust* and *Wilhelm Meister*. The dismal events of December 14, 1825 forced the discontinuation of their significant five-member discussion group known as the "Lovers of Wisdom" and the abandonment of their publication *Mnemosyne*, while natural end-of-school separations scattered their unorganized members. Within a decade many of these "philosophically" oriented "Archive Youth" were to be found in mutually hostile camps of *political* philosophies and known as either "Westernizers" or "Slavophiles". From 1827 to 1830 *The Moscow Messenger*, edited by Pogodin and Ševyrëv after the untimely death of Dmitrij Venevitinov, its poet-founder, served the interests of the scattered members and their increasing followers by publishing works and translations of works in "the German taste", notably four stories of Hoffmann.

Four stages of evolution may be here discerned, to identify which we arbitrarily assign the successive titles: *Die Räuber, Werther, Wilhelm Meister,* and the *Tales of Hoffmann*. By these captions we observe that Russian Germanophiles were recapitulating the evolution of literary tastes in Germany itself, though not precisely in the German order and though within a somewhat shorter span of time and always with a timelag of about one literary generation, so that Hoffmann whose career began essentially about 1813 and stretched to 1822, became a writer of special interest to Russians between 1825 and 1830.

In none of these stages and in no individual case did there prevail anything like the concept of German literature categories such as are now taught by literary historians. These Russians disregarded, if indeed they ever heard of, such classifications as "pre-classical", "Storm and Stress", "classical", and "early and later Romantik". To them, all German works were Romantic, Klopstock as well as Tieck, Lessing as well as Hoffmann; there were only differences in degree of Romanticism. Taste was similarly unselective, as in the case of Žukovskij's lumping Kotzebue together with Goethe. The unifying principle in all

German writers was, for them, a speculative and imaginative quality alien to anything they knew in French, or even in recent English, literature. They seem always to have worked from individual books, never on the basis of an author's total production. They took what appealed to them and let the rest be. As a result, their interpretations were subjective. Eclectic readings in Goethe, for example, gave rise to notions of that writer as partially true and as mutually contradictory as the reports of the seven blind men in the Hindu fable who described the elephant in terms of what portions of that animal's body their hands had touched. Russian scholarship did not strike the proper balance in Goethe-interpretation before mid-century, and by that time Goethe's works were "history" and no longer touchstones of the inventive imagination.

So also with Hoffmann. The Tales were German works among other German works, more recently composed than others, to be sure, more "German" than many, which is to say more speculative, more imaginative than many, even more vivid than many, but still parts of a wide category, without dates, known as "German". "Pogorel'skij" set Hoffmannizing tales in a framework dealing with the whole gamut of the occult sciences and side by side with the shallow popular Romanticism that sentimentalized about a boy's love for an orang-utan foster-mother amid the gaudy local color of a jungle setting in Borneo. Polevoj indiscriminately scrambled Hoffmann together with Klopstock and with Schiller's *Kabale und Liebe* in his stories. Prince Odoevskij, with a wider and more sober view of books, praised the uniqueness of Hoffmann's genius by juxtaposing it with the genius of Cervantes and Sterne, which comment indicates at the very least a conception of Hoffmann remote from our own. At no time before mid-century was the conception of Hoffmann scholarly-objective; at no time was he accurately placed within the evolving history of German literature itself; at no time was discrimination exercised within the range of his own productions.

The sequence of translations illustrates this latter statement. First came *Das Fräulein von Scudery* in 1822, the year of the author's death in Berlin, and we have suggested that its choice was dictated by its setting in Louis XIV's Paris, which might interest the French-classical-oriented reading public. Relatively minor pieces followed it, including the inferior companion-mystery-tale of *Die Marquise de la Pivardière*. No first-rate work of Hoffmann was translated until 1830, and then we find the distinguished *Das Majorat* in the same list with the poor tale

Das Sanctus. Excessive attention was given to the middle-flight tale *Der Sandmann,* which was accorded two separate translations in 1830 and 1831. The latter year saw the publication of fragments of *Kater Murr,* with limited magazine space doubtless as the explanation for the small sampling, but not until 1840 did the complete *Kater Murr* appear in Russian translation, or such masterworks as *Meister Floh* and *Klein Zaches.* A "complete Hoffmann" in Russian came only at the end of the century, long after the author had become "history".

The translations, like the imitations, cluster in the 1830's, in Russian Romanticism's own heyday. The time-stages are significant. Seven translations and most of "Pogorel'skij's" imitations were produced between 1822 and 1828, a total which is in itself striking, but all the more striking because the interest in Hoffmann necessarily came, not through French channels with the imprimatur of French taste, but directly from Germany by way of the Moscow Germanophiles. All of these items appeared in Muscovite publications, none of them in Petersburg publications. Russian literary life already had two rival capitals, Moscow where German things were favored, and Petersburg where French and English models were preferred. The largest number of translations and the lesser half of the imitations fall within the four-year period 1829–1833, which was precisely the time-span of the "complete Hoffmann" in the French translation of Loève-Veimars. Three more years, 1833–1836, include the great imitations: *The Queen of Spades,* four stories of Gogol', and the writing, though only the partial publication, of several of Prince Odoevskij's Hoffmannizing pieces. Chapter VII of our text describes the rapid decline of Hoffmann's prestige *as a model for creative writers* but with no loss of esteem for him as a writer of a previous epoch, and the descent of his works as sources of inspiration to ever feebler Russian authors during the decade ending at 1845. The astonishing fact in the years after 1845 was the new kind of Hoffmannizing practiced by Dostoevskij, which, for all that it was denounced by Belinskij as outmoded Romanticism, nevertheless fecundated, indeed made possible, a major literary career stretching to 1881.

2. HOFFMANNIZING METHODS AND PRACTICES

Two noteworthy generalizations are to be made at the outset concerning the Russian practice of Hoffmannization: first, that a process of "darkening" is only slightly less than universal in such Russian stories, and second, that every Hoffmannizing author sooner or later extricated himself from Hoffmann's influence.

The over-all impression left from reading the Tales *in extenso* is one of optimistic achievement of happiness in spite of obstacles. Not that Hoffmann is facilely cheery. The obstacles are usually grave and over-coming them requires effort, but in the long run they are normally over-come. Tales ending in bleak and unmitigated misery, such as *Der Magnetiseur* or *Der Sandmann,* are the exception with Hoffmann. Precisely the reverse is true with his Russian imitators. *Their* heroes come to calamity with distressful regularity and one has to look care-fully and among the lesser pieces to find a case where obstacles are overcome and happiness achieved.

Russian authors might begin careers under the influence of Hoff-mann, as "Pogorel'skij" did, or they might discover him after their careers were launched, as Gogol' did, but whether their Hoffmannizing was profound or shallow, protracted or brief, they invariably abandoned him. The process of abandonment was normally gradual, rarely abrupt, and the line of direction taken was invariably toward realism. After "Pogorel'skij's" *The Double,* a Hoffmannizing frame-tale with Hoff-mannizing insets, and after his Hoffmannizing fairytale for children, a Hoffmannizing novel called *The Hypnotist* was abandoned in favor of a novel — his final work — about rural Ukrainian life in which there is no trace of Hoffmann. The case is especially noteworthy since that realistic novel, with the date of 1830—1832, coincided, not with a general turn toward realism, but with the flood-tide of Russian Roman-ticism and Russian Hoffmannism. Likewise noteworthy is the case of Gogol' whose progression away from Hoffmann seems to have involved pique and dissatisfaction with his model. *The Portrait,* first of a series of Hoffmannizing tales, was strongly under Hoffmann's influence; *The Nevskij Prospekt* was less so; the plan of *The Diary of a Mad Musician* was scrapped in favor of a more realistic *Diary of a Madman* in which the hero is not a musician but a poor clerk, though an episode with talking dogs still betrays an origin in *Kater Murr* where there were both a musician hero (probably to go mad) and talking animals; *The Nose* was out-and-out parody of Hoffmann; almost, as it were, against the author's will.

The degree of Hoffmannian content in any given work may register at any point of the scale from wholesale adaptation of plot and cha-racters to insignificant details which could not be identified as Hoffmannian in origin if they were not seen in the perspective of the present study.

Typical procedures may be listed as follows:

1. *Near-plagiarism.* — "Pogorel'skij's" lugubrious story *The Baleful Consequences of an Unbridled Imagination,* far from being a real-life incident as the narrator claims, is a retelling of the entire central section of *Der Sandmann* with the characters renamed and the locale shifted from the University of Heidelberg (which Hoffmann had not specifically named) to the University of Leipzig. This extreme case of near-plagiarism is unique among Russian Hoffmannizing stories.

2. *Plot-conversion.* — More justifiable and more ingenious is the procedure followed by Puškin and "Kosmokratov" in *The Lonely Cottage on Vasil'evskij Island,* where the five principal characters of Hoffmann's *Datura fastuosa* (translated three years previously) and much of the plot outline embodying them compose the bulk of the story. So thoroughgoing an adaptation cannot have been, as claimed, a spur-of-the-moment improvisation of Puškin at Mme Karamzina's soirée, for the plot-conversion process involved a meticulous transformation of characters and events according to a consistent plan. All botanical features were eliminated from the original "botanical novel;" the vaguely indicated Berlin setting was made into a specific Petersburg setting; the characters acquired Russian names, lower middle class status, shallower motivations, and draber personalities; the supernatural elements were all brought into line with popular Orthodox conceptions. But the story in starkest résumé is still the story of *Datura fastuosa.* Moreover, where "Pogorel'skij" had left his *Sandmann* characters in Germany, in Leipzig if not in Heidelberg, Puškin had asked himself the more searching question: Why would the events of *Datura fastuosa* have to unfold differently here at home in Petersburg?

This procedure, together with its searching question, remained unparalleled until Dostoevskij's *The Landlady* (1847).

3. *Expansion of episode.* — More commonly Russian Hoffmannists were intrigued with the possibilities of one or more episodes in the *Tales* and sometimes worked on the basis of an episode inflated to full story scenario. Thus Polevoj's *The Felicity of Madness* made an 88-page narrative, published in two magazine installments, out of a passage of only four or five pages in the "Second Adventure" (chapter) of *Meister Floh.* Even those four or five pages described antecedent action, so that it was as though Polevoj had gone back to the German story's beginning and started the characters out on a new line of development

to rival the course set for them by Hoffmann. That the new course ran
in the opposite direction from Hoffmann's excellence was a fact due
primarily to Polevoj's lack of genuine creative talent, for the same
device worked successfully in Gogol's *The Portrait,* to mention only
one of several such instances.

4.   *"Contaminatio" of episodes and characters.* — Readers of Hoffmann cannot fail to notice how the Tales are made up of multiple
variations on certain basic motifs, characters, and situations. Astounding ingenuity, analogous to musical invention in, say, Beethoven's
Diabelli Variations, keeps these elements fresh and uncorrupted by
monotony. The Russian Hoffmannists must have observed the same
phenomenon. Perhaps they sought to imitate it, or perhaps they thought
any Hoffmannian element would go well with any other in any story.
However this may be, cross-blending of Hoffmannian motifs is discer-
nible in many Russian works. In *The Felicity of Madness* Polevoj eked
out the meager contents of those four or five pages from *Meister Floh*
with character delineations from *Der Sandmann.* Thus George Pepusch,
having been borrowed from the *Meister Floh situation* and rechristened
Antiox, acquired the hypersensitivity and the fate of Nathanael, hero
of *Der Sandmann,* just as Flea Tamer Leuwenhoek, rechristened
Ludovik von Schreckenfeld, acquired characteristics of Professor Spalanzani, while the new heroine, Adelheid, occupied the position common to both Hoffmann works between an evil guardian of a mage and
a sensitive beloved youth but had a personality compounded, one
might say, of everything under the sun except the qualities of *Meister
Floh's* heroine Dörtje Elverdink. Polevoj seems to have been imper-
vious to the fact that *Meister Floh* stood at the brightest and most
joyous end of the Hoffmann spectrum whereas *Der Sandmann* stood
at the blackest and gloomiest end of that spectrum, thus making a
jointure of their elements impossible. He made the jointure anyway,
with the result that his story is impossible. Again, the fault lay with
Polevoj's judgment, for Puškin and "Kosmokratov" were far more
successful in the use of the same device when they intruded an episode
from *Die Abenteuer der Sylvesternacht* into the scenario adapted from
Datura fastuosa. In fact, they went even further, to blend the intrusive
episode itself with elements from Žukovskij's ballads of Romantic but
non-Hoffmannian origin, thereby creating the most effective sequence
of their narrative, that of Paul's ride in the cab of the death's-head.

5.   *Isolated motifs and "echoes".* — Stories composed in the waning
stages of Hoffmann's influence on any given author exhibit little touches

of Hoffmannism amid surrounding matter quite alien to Hoffmann. Such stories viewed outside of the context of the present study would doubtless be declared void of any Hoffmannian influence, but within the present context they assume an interesting quality as evidence of how gradually the author's Hoffmannism wore off and of how deeply embedded were the Hoffmannian impressions in his consciousness. Little suggestions of the court satire of *Kater Murr,* for instance, linger in Polevoj's *Abbadonna,* which has nothing to do with *Kater Murr.* (It was the *Literary Gazette* reviewer of 1835 who claimed the resemblances.) Still more interestingly, a ghost beheld on a snowy night of bitter cold is the motif common to Gogol's *The Overcoat* and Hoffmann's *Das Majorat,* and though a connection between the two stories is impossible to prove, it is nevertheless felt, and felt, precisely, in terms of a dying echo of Hoffmannism in the writing of an author who had once been profoundly under Hoffmann's influence but who had rejected that influence and was now in full flight away from it.

6. *Special procedures.* — At least three instances may be cited of procedures unique in themselves and not classifiable under any of the five types listed above.

a) *Odoevskij.* When Prince Odoevskij wished to write stories with plot, action, and characters, he could well do so. *Princess Mimi* and the other pieces included under the heading of *Household Conversations* (Domašnye Razgovory) bear adequate witness to the fact. On the other hand, most of the works dependent upon Hoffmannian inspiration are curiously static in quality and give the effect of a meditation upon a certain set of circumstances. In the longest of these, *The Improvisor,* the mage Segeliel' and his poet-client Cipriano are most certainly Hoffmannian types, but the action is so slight that it is hard to decide even the point of what Tale of Hoffmann furnished the models, whether Prosper Alpanus and the student Balthasar from *Klein Zaches,* or Archivarius Lindhorst and the student Anselmus from *Der goldene Topf,* or even Leuwenhoek and Peregrinus Tyss from *Meister Floh.* Since all of these are happy tales and since *The Improvisor* is anything but happy, it is inevitable that whatever mage-poet pair from Hoffmann was used must be blended with an evil counterpart, almost certainly Coppelius and Nathanael from *Der Sandman.* The role of the heroine offers no clue because she is known to us only by indirect report in a single paragraph. The author was here concerned with speculation upon the idea of a human being's having omniscience conferred upon him. Appalling misery and ultimate madness were the results of such a gift, he concluded, and having made this point, Odoevskij had said all that he intended to say; there is no "story". Thus *The Improvisor,* first published in 1832 (then, as part of *Russian Nights,* in 1844) offers evidence of the conception of Hoffmann-as-philosopher, the prevailing conception of him among the "lovers of Wisdom" group in 1824–1825. (Odoevskij was leader of that group and meetings of the society were held at his house.) It also gives a clue as to what those Muscovite youths meant by the term "philosophy". Unlike all other Hoffmannists, Odoevskij selected a Hoffmannian situation and – contemplated its moral significance. He practiced neither expansion nor diminution of material, neither "contaminatio" of episodes nor plot-conversion.

b) *The Queen of Spades.* Unique and uniquely fine, Puškin's *The Queen of Spades* defies categorization. We have suggested that Puškin's uncanny genius, having abandoned *The Lonely Cottage on Vasil'evskij Island* together with its "recipe" of plot-conversion as artistically unsatisfactory, ranged widely in Hoffmann's works – Puškin had "the complete Hoffmann" in his library – melted down, so to speak, some of the formed metals of Hoffmann's art, compounded his own new alloy, and poured that alloy into a mold of his own designing. The finished product is thoroughly Russian; it displays one of the "darkest" of "darkenings" in Russian Hoffmannism; it strikes the reader as distinctly Hoffmannian; and yet no work of Hoffmann, nor any works of Hoffmann in combination, stood as its model. Puškin penetrated to the core of Hoffmann's spirit and in this story wrote as Hoffmann himself would have written if he had been a Russian.

c) *Dostoevskij.* Discussion of the complex Hoffmannizing procedures will be reserved until the end of the present chapter.

3. USE OF HOFFMANN'S MOTIFS

It has been mentioned that the Tales ring the changes upon a certain list of motifs and that a mutation analogous to musical variations keeps these motifs fresh and interesting. Russian Hoffmannists necessarily dealt with these motifs and it is of concern here to note what use they made of the most conspicuous of them.

1. *The artist-hero.* – Hoffmann was himself primarily a creative writer, though he thought of himself through most of his life as primarily a musician. Not only did he earn his living as an orchestra conductor for many years and by giving music lessons, but his musical com-

positions almost equal his literary compositions in total bulk. He was also a gifted amateur painter and caricaturist with a wide knowledge of the plastic arts. It is not surprising therefore to find that his heroes are very frequently artists — painters, musicians, poets — or near-artists — "students" or, in *Die Elixiere des Teufels,* a monk with a painter-ancestor. Moreover, Hoffmann wrote in an era when the aristocratic Prince-as-hero no longer interested the predominantly bourgeois reading public but when the common-man-as-hero was not yet admissible. These artist-heroes of his are bourgeois, but they are extraordinary men, and into them Hoffmann poured his own genuine and experienced awareness of artistic values.

Not one of the Russian Hoffmannists was himself an artist in any field except the literary one, not even Gogol', who for a time wished to become a painter but who had no pictorial talent. The artist-as-hero was, accordingly, an embarrassment and a stumbling-block to them. "Pogorel'skij" attempted none such. The others gave their protagonists artistic sensibility but only occasionally made them artists. Painter-heroes occur in Polevoj's *The Painter,* with the unhappy result of betraying the author's woeful taste in art, and in Gogol's *The Portrait* and *The Nevskij Prospekt,* with not wholly convincing artistic quality. Musician-heroes were even less convincing as musicians. Odoevskij's Beethoven and Bach could never have composed the works composed by their real-life counterparts; Count Sollogub's Karl in *The History of Two Galoshes* is a non-musician's sentimental notion of what a real pianist is like; Dostoevskij's violinist-character Efimov in *Netočka Nezvanova* is not only arbitrarily converted from a Hoffmannian painter, but the author has no knowledge of music to bestow upon him. The description of his violin-playing suggests that author and character alike conceived of music as Hungarian gypsy tunes wrung with sobs from the tortured instrument. Odoevskij's "Piranesi" as an architect is again an arbitrary substitution for a Hoffmannian musician in *Ritter Gluck* and his architectural knowledge is merely bizarre. Specifically poet-heroes do not occur. More successful were the heroes who merely appreciated art, and better still were those whose authors assigned them no artist-role at all, as with Gogol's poor clerks and Puškin's engineer in *The Queen of Spades.* Dostoevskij wisely avoided artist-heroes after Efimov, and the motif dies out with Ordynov, the hero of *The Landlady* (1847), who was a scientist "but with the soul of an artist".

2. *The Philistine.* — If there is no artist-hero, it follows that there

can be no Philistine-villain. Polevoj, working in *The Painter* on the basis of an art-problem-tale, *Der Artushof,* and seeking to create an art-problem-tale of his own, attempted to set Philistine opponents against his artist-hero, but since Arkadij's own taste seems so bad, we can hold no serious grudge against Veren'ka and her father for not sharing it. This was perhaps the one head-on effort by a Russian Hoffmannist to pit artist against Philistines. Gogol's moral-mindedness, rather than art-mindedness, is apparent in *The Portrait* precisely because Čertkov's opponent is a demon and not a Philistine; in the second part of that story the demon is baffled by a painting which is sacred in subject and *therefore* "good". The juxtaposition of the artist Piskarev with the brainless Lieutenant Pirogov in *The Nevskij Prospekt,* however, comes closer to the Hoffmann-type dichotomy, closer, in fact, than any other opponent-pair in Russian Hoffmannizing fiction. True Philistines in Hoffmann's sense never materialized in the Russian stories.

3. *Beauty.* — If Russian artist-heroes are relatively scarce and not very convincing as artists, and if Philistines are scarcer still, the reason is that the Russian writers were concerned by and large with moral values rather than artistic values. Beauty was to them a tenuous matter, morally ambiguous, and all too readily reduced (Philistine-wise) to the pursuit of a beautiful woman, as in *The Nevskij Prospekt.* In such reduction it all too readily proved not only vain but morally vicious: the object of Piskarev's adoration is a heartless prostitute. Except for Gogol's lipservice to Beauty and except for Polevoj's misunderstanding of it, the Russian Hoffmannists rejected Hoffmann's antithesis of Beauty versus Philistinism and substituted for it a decidedly Christian antithesis of Good versus Evil.

4. *Two worlds.* — With Hoffmann, Beauty casts its enchantments and wonders everywhere about us, but only the worthy can see them. Philistines see all things as crassly ordinary and dull. In *Klein Zaches* the students Fabian and Balthasar simultaneously behold a pair of quadrupeds grazing on Prosper Alpanus' lawn: Fabian says they are ponies with artificial horns bizarrely attached by human means to their muzzles; Balthasar knows they are unicorns. The greatest wonder of all is the living universe itself, Nature, in the exalted Pantheistic sense of Schelling and of Novalis' *Hymns to the Night:* ". . . the restless stars . . . the glittering, everlastingly reposeful stone . . . the sensuous, suckling plant . . . the wild, ardent, multiform beast . . ."

For all their interest in Schelling and Romantic philosophy in general, the Russian Hoffmannists put no Pantheistic notions of the universe into their writings, and as for the interpenetration of real and ideal worlds, they used the notion only in radically modified form. When the world of Beauty was in question, they allowed it to interpenetrate not at all; Beauty itself was Christian "Good" and its place was beyond this world in a position analogous to heaven. Mystical Powers of Evil, on the other hand, did "invade" the real world in the sense that Milton's Satan invaded it. Gogol's Petromixali was Antichrist and got into the world via a painting; the Evil One himself lights the street lamps of Petersburg to give everything a false and pernicious glamor in the splendid prose poem that concludes *The Nevskij Prospekt*. Odoevskij's Segeliel' owns a mansion full of wondrous things, but they are all dedicated to purposes as baleful as the witch's equipment in "Pogorel'skij's" elementary first tale of the poppy-seed-cake woman and her human cat-attendant. To the Russians, devils were fabulously ingenious and active while the "Good" remained painfully abstract and remote. Interpenetration of two worlds in Hoffmann's sense is a motif unused by them and all approximations to it were made on the analogy of Orthodox demonology.

5.   *Madness.* — The sensitive Russian heroes of these tales, whether artists or mere appreciators of art or wholly non-artistic meek clerks, embody the Good and for so doing suffer amid a Vale of Tears. (Puškin's guilty heroes are an exception.) Or, at the very least, they know the Good and sinfully reject it, as Gogol's Čertkov does, to ally themselves with Evil. Their sufferings all but invariably end in madness, the actual clinical madness of lunatic asylums. In Hoffmann's Tales, on the other hand, such clinical madness is the exception, as in *Der Sandmann,* and the "madness" incurred by his heroes is an ironic term for a state of higher happiness which seems mad only to Philistines too dull to understand it. Such "madness' was not even attempted by Russian Hoffmannists except for Polevoj in, precisely, *The Felicity of Madness*. By taking that key word "madness" literally, the Russians automatically transferred their stories to an area of sombre realism, and "breaking under strain" became automatically the emotional focus of their works. Dostoevskij's agonizing portrayals of such breakdowns constitute a motif not invented by him but rather one long under experiment before his career was begun.

6.   *Possession.* — In *Die Elixiere des Teufels* the monk Medardus is guided by a will which is not *his* will, first to Rome where he was determined not to go, and then back to his native monastery where he was determined never to return. That mysterious "other" will brought

him by many detours and in spite of himself to ultimate sainthood. Hermann in *The Queen of Spades* is similarly guided to the old Countess's house, there to begin his course of doom. Puškin allowed Hermann's guidance to appear like mere coincidence, and no Russian Hoffmannist subscribed to the notion of "possession" in precisely the Romantic and mystical sense used by Hoffmann, though quasi-realistic modifications of the notion were common enough among them, particularly the modified form which might better be termed obsession rather than possession. In Dostoevskij's *The Double,* for example, an obsessive "will" guides Mr. Goljadkin to his employer's house party, where excruciating humiliation and the beginning of his destruction await him; rejected at the door the first time, Mr. Goljadkin drives out the semicircular driveway and right back in again. Gogol's Piskarev has a fixed obsession on "Beauty", Puškin's Hermann on the secret of the cards, Vasja Šumkov in Dostoevskij's *A Faint Heart* on finishing his office work, and so on. But with the Russians that "other" will is always a malignant agent of doom, never an agent of benevolence as it is with Medardus.

7. *Ghosts.* — Contrary to popular report, ghosts, at least in the normal sense of the term, are exceedingly rare in Hoffmann's Tales. How Leuwenhoek in *Meister Floh* can have been buried in Delft in 1725 and yet be very much alive in Berlin in 1820 is never explained, but it is certain that there is nothing spectral about him. Real ghosts are only three in number in Hoffmann's works: a truly terrifying one in the tiny story which editors call *Der schwebende Teller,* a mild one wholly incidental to Alexander's narrative in *Aus dem Leben dreier Freunde,* and a memorable one impelled by his tormented conscience in *Das Majorat.* Only this last one has a Russian counterpart, namely in the ghost of Akakij Akakievič at the end of *The Overcoat.* The ghost of the old Countess beheld by Hermann in *The Queen of Spades* is almost certainly his illusion; its function in the story is to externalize a stage of Hermann's progressing madness and it has nothing to do with any Hoffmann work.

8. *Hallucinatory dreams.* — German Romantic philosophy saw in dreams the mysterious operation of the inner or sidereal self and devoted much speculation to the subject, though not yet in Freud's terms. Hoffmann gave literary form to their speculations, so that his works abound in descriptions of dream-content and more particularly of waking dream-content. In *Die Elixiere des Teufels* the hallucinatory dreams of Medardus, especially at the point of his repentance in the

Italian monastery, form highly impressive passages of imaginative writing. These and similar passages elsewhere in Hoffmann went unexploited by the first three Russian Hoffmannists, but Puškin seems to have taken up the motif in a striking paragraph of *The Queen of Spades* which we have quoted in Note 16 to Chapter V. One can only wonder whether the striking dream-sequence of Tat'jana's in *Eugene Onegin* (Chapter V, composed 1826) may not also have had a Hoffmannian origin, though the date is early and though Hoffmann had no monopoly on the theme even if he exploited it with uncommon power. Hallucinatory dreams are also skillfully used by Gogol', both in *The Portrait* and in *The Nevskij Prospekt* and by Lermontov in the "Štoss fragment", but Dostoevskij was to give such dreams their fullest literary development. The two dreams of Raskol'nikov and of Svidrigajlov, one more appalling than the other, in *Crime and Punishment* outdo Hoffmann in his furthest flights of fancy.

9. *Automata.* — The eerie horror which Hoffmann felt at the sight of mechanical devices in human effigy accounts for a very small fraction of his writing. Its one important application was the mechanical doll of *Der Sandmann,* where it served as a double satire against heartless debutantes and heartless sopranos. "Pogorel'skij" retold that story almost in toto with only part of the doll's significance retained, and Odoevskij used the motif once as an allegory of Europeanizing Russian girls. Both were minor treatments of a minor theme, and nothing further came of the matter.

10. *Doubles.* — The related theme of the Double or alternate self, however, was borrowed by Hoffmann from the fund of Romantic themes and developed in many forms, most elaborately in *Die Elixiere des Teufels.* "Pogorel'skij" first turned this theme to use in Russian and was obliged to coin a native word, "dvojnik", to translate the German "Doppelgänger". His adaptation is simple and pleasing, involving no more than the touching whimsy of confronting two aspects of himself, one skeptical and one credulous, as separate persons who entertain each other with tales through quiet rural evenings on a Ukrainian estate. The two halves of Gogol's *The Portrait* narrate merely two separate "invasions" of the world by Petromixali-Antichrist, while the two halves of *The Nevskij Prospekt* present merely two alternatives of the pursuit of Beauty, i.e. of beautiful women, one grotesquely tragic, one sardonic. Both cases relate as much to the theme of "two worlds" as to the theme of the dual selves, being equidistant from both. Dostoevskij, however, developed the theme with great insight and power. Already

in *The Double* (1846) he took the important step, in anticipation of modern concepts of schizophrenia, of containing the antithetical personalities of Mr. Goljadkin within a single body, with Mr. Goljadkin Junior a projection of the mind of Mr. Goljadkin Senior. At the opposite end of his career, in *The Brothers Karamazov,* Smerdjakov, though portrayed realistically as a separate person, is made the physical half-brother of Ivan Karamazov and the embodiment of Ivan's evil side. That evil half-self must die before Ivan can attain peace. There the concept comes much closer to the prototype of the half-brothers Medardus and Viktorin in *Die Elixiere des Teufels.* Hoffmann's theme, especially as treated in the novel about Medardus, interested Dostoevskij enormously precisely because Dostoevskij was himself "a man divided", and the elaborate permutations of the motif in Dostoevskij's works must be regarded as autobiographical matter in reenforcement of literary matter drived from Hoffmann.

11. *The "Faust theme".* — What we term reluctantly the "Faust theme", the motif of the sale of one's soul to the Devil (for whatever purpose), was widely current in folklore and in literary usage before Hoffmann and he himself made but very scant application of it in his Tales. It is often implied in his evil mages but rarely made specific, hence its occasional presence in the Russian tales may be called para-Hoffmannian, as with Gogol's Čertkov. Puškin merely toys whimsically with the idea in his report of the Count de Saint Germain in *The Queen of Spades.* Both instances have more to do with Charles Maturin's *Melmoth the Wanderer* than with Hoffmann.

12. *Hypnotism* (Mesmerism, magnetism). — Many ideas related to the phenomenon of hypnotism found multiple variations throughout Hoffmann's works, and in addition to these Hoffmann three times told the story of the evil hypnotist, in *Der Magnetiseur,* in *Der unheimliche Gast,* and in *Der Elementargeist.* The disproportionate influence of at least the first of these upon Russian authors has been noted. The scenario underlying all three was adapted by "Pogorel'skij" in his fragmentary novel *The Hypnotist,* details from it were used in Puškin's and "Kosmokratov's" *The Lonely Cottage on Vasil'evskij Island,* and a strikingly original adaptation of the subject formed a major block of Dostoevskij's *The Landlady.*

13. *Talking animals.* — A long list of animals with human qualities culminates in Hoffmann's works in the arch-Philistine cat Murr of *Kater Murr* and his feline and canine acquaintances. Of all the Russian Hoffmannists, only Gogol' made use of the device in the talking dogs

of *The Diary of a Madman*. Even there, the dogs are intended as ironic hallucinations of Popriščin's deranged mind. An echo of the motif may be detected in Dostoevskij's *The Crocodile* even though the talking is done by a human inside the crocodile's belly.

14. *Fairytale for children.* — Only two of Hoffmann's fairytales are specifically for children, *Nussknacker und Mausekönig* and *Das fremde Kind*. Of the second, itself a poor performance, nothing is heard in Russian works, and of the first only details were borrowed in "Pogorel'skij's" *The Black Chicken,* the true model of the latter being Tieck's *Die Elfen*.

15. *Character types.* — Three character types occur with marked frequency in Hoffmann's Tales: the youthful artist-hero, the youthful heroine, and the mage. Of these, the first has been discussed under Point 1 above, but the remaining two merit mention also.

Women past twenty years of age and with fates decided by matrimony rarely figure in Hoffmann's writing. The venerable widow Helms of *Datura fastuosa* is an exception comparable to the venerable Mlle de Scudery, while the fascinating Rätin Benzon, the spinner of court intrigues in *Kater Murr,* makes another exception but of a different kind. The numerous youthful group subdivides into two categories, those whose youth and virginal beauty are accompanied by gentle modesty or by sensitivity appropriate to the artist-heroes whom they marry, and those whose heartlessness and Philistine insensitivity represent dangerous lures for the artist-heroes. Skill at music, especially beautiful singing voices, characterize many of them. Most of them are vivacious and plucky, even spunky, none are languid or cloying. In all their list there is not one Klopstockian angel nor any impossible creature of "vapors" and incapacity for facing life. On the other hand, there are none among them who could embarrass a nineteenth century family reading-circle. Love by them and for them is their reason for being, they never challenge the hero's primacy in the story, and they receive definition in terms of the conflict between the hero and his opponents.

Sometimes a heroine — Candida in *Klein Zaches* is a good example — can be so deftly suggested by a few pen strokes that the reader hardly notices that she is a wholly marginal character, a mere excuse for the hero's actions. But nothing of the kind can be said of the mages; *they* not infrequently are of more vital concern to both author and reader than the nominal hero himself. In the prime of manhood or even past the prime but never aged, fatherly but never grandfatherly, these men are profoundly concerned with the youthful hero's fate. The benevolent ones are pedagogues who furnish advice, example, and aid; usually they are master artists engaged in skillful direction of youthful talents. The malicious ones are bent on using their extraordinary knowledge and great abilities for the hero's ruin and for the wanton destruction of beautiful things, including beautiful young heroines.

If the Russian Hoffmannists ever took any specific heroine from the Tales as model, the resulting character is not recognizable as so derived. They substituted rather their own heroines, not one of whom would fit into the framework of any Hoffmann story. "Pogorel'skij's" maidens are sweetly pale, Polevoj's preposterously sentimentalized. With Odoev- skij their roles are reduced to mere "postulated" heroines, as in *The Improvisor,* or eliminated altogether to permit that author's philo- sophical analysis. Puškin's and "Kosmokratov's" Vera is a non-entity, in sharp contrast to the fine portrayal of Lizaveta Ivanovna in *The Queen of Spades,* who is wholly Russian. Neither the vulgar prostitute nor the virtuous bourgeoise of Gogol's *The Nevskij Prospekt* owes anything, beyond the principle of contrast, to Hoffmann. More striking still is the fact that the remaining four Hoffmannizing tales of Gogol', as well as several early stories of Dostoevskij, manage to do entirely or nearly entirely without women characters at all, *The Overcoat* having none, while the merest suggestion of Klara Olsuf'evna suffices for the purposes of *The Double.*

The mages, on the other hand, are all recognizable as Hoffmann derivatives: "Pogorel'skij's" Andronij and Venturino, Polevoj's Ludovik von Schreckenfeld, Odoevskij's Segeliel', Gogol's Petromixali, Ler- montov's Štoss, and Dostoevskij's Murin. All are evil except for Murin who merely seems evil, though his merely seeming is more arresting than the actuality of some of the others. Andronij, Schreckenfeld, and Murin relate to the evil Professor Spalanzani of *Der Sandmann* and to the still more evil Coppelius of the same story, though Schreckenfeld should by rights be the equivalent of Leuwenhoek in *Meister Floh.* The minor figure of Venturino, we have suggested, is probably derived from the half-supernatural devil Fermino Valies in *Datura fastuosa.* The others all have their origins in benevolent mages. Murin, who only seems malignant to the demented Katerina, owes his true nature to the crazy but harmless painter Berklinger of *Der Artushof,* who is also the prototype of Lermontov's Štoss. Segeliel' reverses the benevolence of the great mages Prosper Alpanus and Archivarius Lindhorst relative to their poet-clients. Petromixali's ultimate origin lay with the stern but benevolent Franzesko the Painter of *Die Elixiere des Teufels*. Some touch of the evil hypnotist has been given to all these characters, while Segeliel' and Petromixali are ultimately identified with actual demons, the former with Satan (in the finale of *Russian Nights*) and the latter with Antichrist. Association with art, a prime factor with Hoffmann's benevolent mages, has been eliminated in every Russian case, and the evil substitutions are strikingly made in terms of Orthodox Christian conceptions of Evil.

16. *Involved and neglected areas of Hoffmann's works.* — Working at random among the Tales as the Russian Hoffmannists did, and on the basis of personal preferences, a very broad area of the seventy-odd stories was nevertheless canvassed. If major motifs and the major character-category of the benevolent mages were either rejected or completely reversed, it was not because the Tales embodying them were unknown. It remains to point out what works received primary attention and what works were, apparently, ignored.

The two novels, *Die Elixiere des Teufels* and *Kater Murr,* provided extensive inspiration to Russian writers. Of the three long, independent Märchen, *Meister Floh* was moderately influential, *Klein Zaches* only slightly so, while *Prinzessin Brambilla* (which Hoffmann readers from the outset have rated either very high or very low) exerted almost no influence at all. Significantly, the novels are predominantly sombre, the Märchen predominantly joyous.

Selection among the Tales proper was invariably made without regard to the four large collections as such, though the frame-tale of *Die Serapionsbrüder* created its own separate impression on Russian readers. Disproportionate interest was directed toward the two excessively gloomy stories *Der Magnetiseur* and *Der Sandmann*. Next in order of interest came the fine story of *Der goldene Topf* and the less distinguished *Die Abenteuer der Sylvesternacht,* which in turn are followed, oddly enough, by the two companion pieces, *Der Artushof* and *Die Jesuiterkirche in G.,* which debate the theme of whether the artist can marry and still remain an artist. Two posthumous works, *Die Irrungen* and *Datura fastuosa,* claimed more attention than one would have expected. Tales about music suffered the most radical alterations of any. *Ritter Gluck,* a story about music, impressed Odoevskij and Dostoevskij considerably, though not for music's sake, while *Don Juan,* sometimes placed as a companion work to the former, went wholly neglected. The musical sketches of the *Kreisleriana* were used only by Sollogub, the least gifted of the Russian Hoffmannists, and the influence of the famous musical tale *Rat Krespel* was of the slightest. The works which occasionally contributed motifs to Russian writers may be seen from Appendix III at the end of the present study. By and large, the works which were accorded Russian translation, however belatedly, were the works of significance for creative writers in Russia.

An understandable cluster of omissions involves four works representing one half of the contents of the *Nachtstücke* collection: *Das Sanctus*, which *was* translated, *Das Gelübde, Das steinerne Herz,* and *Ignaz Denner*, though one might have expected this last to be attractive to Russians. More surprising is the omission of *Die Bergwerke zu Falun,* which German readers have found so appealing, and of *Doge and Dogaresse,* likewise much admired in Germany at least during the nineteenth century. All mediaevalizing tales were ignored: *Der Kampf der Sänger* (important for Wagner's *Tannhäuser*), *Meister Martin der Küfner, Meister Johannes Wacht,* and *Der Feind* (all related to Wagner's *Meistersinger*). Dostoevskij once singled out *Meister Martin* for special praise, along with the excellent comic "Italian" tale *Signor Formica* ("Salvator Rosa"), but neither he nor any other Russian sought to imitate either one of them.

All things considered, the omissions were not serious. Relative to Hoffmann's total production they form a strikingly small percentage of the whole, and by comparison with the markedly partial nature of Russian interest in Goethe, or even in Schiller, Hoffmann may be said to have been eaten whole. Of all German writers he was the most thoroughly known in Russia and exerted the most extensive influence there.

4. DOSTOEVSKIJ'S UNIQUE POSITION

Everything about Dostoevskij's Hoffmannizing work is extraordinary. It is extraordinary that he should have begun a career under Hoffmann's influence around 1844 when almost everyone else in Russia had abandoned that model. It is extraordinary that he should have persisted in that genre of writing when by so doing he forfeited the influential backing of Belinskij at a moment when, in his poverty and obscurity, he needed all the assistance he could get. It is extraordinary that after gradually working his way out from under Hoffmann's influence, like all the other Russian Hoffmannists, he should revert thereto at a later date and continue therein until his death in 1881.

But most extraordinary of all was his Hoffmannizing method, the description of which reads like a grand synthesis of all the points made in this chapter.

Except for *Der goldene Topf,* he used the same Tales for source materials as had been used by all his predecessors collectively, though he also reached out for such unexploited items as *Die Fermate, Die Brautwahl,* and the obscure *Haimatochare.* Of the varieties of Hoffmannizing practice listed in Section 2 of the present chapter, all are to be found in his work, and with brilliant originality, except, of course, the first, near-plagiarism; his ebullient genius had no need for such a crass method. Plot-conversion transformed the scenario of *Der Artushof* into the over-all scenario of *The Landlady;* a striking but small episode from *Die Elixiere des Teufels,* the one wherein the guilty Medardus watches his double being transportd away under guard to the madhouse, was expanded to make the powerful closing scene of *The Double;* the isolated motif of the blank pages of music in *Ritter Gluck* was used with telling effect as the blank pages of Vasja Šumkov's office papers in *A Faint Heart;* and even the dying echoes of Hoffmannian motifs may be discerned in *Crime and Punishment.* And with what an amazing difference in quality in every instance.

But besides recapitulating the procedures of his predecessors Dostoevskij hit upon the startling notion of putting two or more Tales of Hoffmann together into a single scenario upon which to work. *Der Artushof* does indeed provide the over-all plan for *The Landlady,* but where the German story had one mad character Dostoevskij has three; *Der Sandmann* was used to construct the hallucinations that Ordynov has of Murin and *Der Magnetiseur* furnished the substance of Katerina's hallucinations about Murin, and in this way the entire story became a crazy set of mirrors reflecting and half-reflecting each other's fantastic images until the reader himself is plunged into the very medium of delirium. Still more flabbergasting was the conception of the unfinished novel *Netočka Nezvanova,* which superimposed the complex *Die Elixiere des Teufels* upon the complex *Kater Murr,* with elements from other Hoffmannian works thrown in for good measure. And if *The Landlady* and *Netočka Nezvanova* must be placed among the less successful of Dostoevskij's creations, the fault lay not so much with his daring conceptions as with his powers of execution. In maturer years he was to master projects still more gigantic than these.

But compounding Hoffmann with Hoffmann, whole Tales together, was not his normal procedure. Rather, he had developed a formula for compounding whole stories of Gogol' with large quantities of Hoff-mannian substance and effecting their alchemical fusion over the intense fire of his own genius. The results of this process as seen in his second published story, *The Double,* would have astonished Proteus and all the alchemists, and by skillful altering of the proportions of his ingredients he was to continue in a whole series of productions which, while not always equally successful, were always equally new and different.

By means of this formula of Hoffmann-plus-Gogol'-plus his own genius, Dostoevskij produced seven works unquestionably, nine works probably, out of a total of thirteen in the approximately five-year interval ending with his deportation to Siberia in 1849. And the five pieces created without Hoffmannian components were perceptibly the lesser ones. Ten years and two cautiously inoffensive stories later he was back in Petersburg, a free man and a frantically busy one. New works in the early 1860's show him experimenting with new formulae. His prison memoirs, *The House of the Dead* (1861), needed no models beyond the realities of the living hell on the banks of the River Irtyš. The anonymously published *Petersburg Visions,* however, harkened nostalgically back to moods and themes of his pre-exile days. A first completed novel, *The Insulted and Injured* (1861), merged materials from Schiller's *Kabale und Liebe* with materials from Dickens' *The Old Curiosity Shop,* but there were also an opening chapter straight out of Hoffmann's *Das öde Haus,* a poignant scene deriving ultimately from *Aus dem Leben dreier Freunde,* and a master-villain based upon Prince Hektor in *Kater Murr.* No Gogolian components seem to be present in this amalgam. A short story called *An Unpleasant Predicament* (1862) reverted to the original Hoffmann-Gogol'-Dostoevskij formula, but with proportions again so varied as to make the work seem quite new. The brief sketch entitled *The Crocodile* (1865) reduced the Hoffmannian component to the vanishing point, while *Crime and Punishment* (1866) contained just such dying echoes of Hoffmann as marked, in previous Russian Hoffmannizers, the end of the practice which we have been examining.

With the Hoffmannizing works now, as of 1866, at a total of either twelve or fourteen, we may summarize Dostoevskij's treatment of the Hoffmannian motifs listed in the preceding section of this chapter.

(1) Of *artist-heroes* there is only Efimov the violinist in *Netočka Nezvonova,* though all of Dostoevskij's heroes have uncommon sensitivity, for which they suffer profoundly. By profession, they are

(Gogolian) poor clerks or "students" in most cases; Ordynov is an engineer "but with the soul of an artist".

(2) *Philistines* as such are non-existent, but a new dichotomy of character-types was developed early in Dostoevskij's writing which is neither Hoffmann's artist-Philistine dichotomy nor yet quite identical with the Orthodox Good-Evil dichotomy of Dostoevskij's predecessors, but rather an opposition of sensitive people to insensitive people. The spontaneity of feeling on the part of the former is curiously closer to Hoffmann's artistic impulse than is the Christian "Good" of former Hoffmannizers, while the wooden apathy of non-feeling persons, their simple non-comprehension of suffering, is much closer to the art-blindness of Hoffmannian Philistines than were the purposes of such "invaders" of the world from outer space as Segeliel' and Petromixali. Mr. Goljadkin, for instance, encounters a whole series of such "Philistines-of-feeling" — his doctor, his employer, his office colleagues, even Klara Olsuf'evna, but none of these persons is evil in any positive way. The evil, significantly enough, lies within Mr. Goljadkin himself. Positively villainous villains entered Dostoevskij's fiction through the medium of Prince Hektor of *Kater Murr,* and by the time that personage had become converted into Prince Valkovskij of *The Insulted and Injured* the author termed all feeling persons "Schillers" and their opposites "wolves". (V-lk is the stem of the Russian word for "wolf".) The latter stalk and devour the former, not from hunger but for the lust of the chase and of the kill. In terms of psychological verity, this transition from evil as an inner thing to evil as a mechanical and external persecution of the innocent by the depraved was not an improvement, but *Crime and Punishment* brought the author back from the wrong turning he had taken in *The Insulted and Injured.*

(3) *Beauty,* as the entity pursued by artists, vanished from Dostoevskij's work along with the artists, and only the Vespers scene at the opening of *The Landlady* and perhaps the concluding garden-scene of *A Little Hero* make any pretense to Romantic loveliness. The mysterious twilight of the former is a very deliberate "Russian" substitute for the description of mysterious late afternoon in the old Artus-hof of Danzig, just as the point-by-point transformation of Hoffmann's tale also left, in the place of the Philistine Elias Roos and his daughter, a residual *German* family named Špis, with whom Ordynov comes to live, German "*Spiess*bürger" being a synonym for "Philistine".

(4) For the interpenetration of *two worlds* in Hoffmann's sense Dostoevskij substituted two interlocking worlds of interior and exterior

consciousness, for which two things the dual self or Double became both the symbol and the actual cause and agent. In other words, he merged this motif with the motif of the Double (Point No. 10), making all duality a subjective and psychological matter.

(5) *Madness,* in the usual literal sense of the Russian Hoffmannizers, became with Dostoevskij so frequent a conclusion for his heroes' "breaking under strain" that his writing was approaching the verge of a self-defeating mannerism. The works of 1861 to 1866 explore alternate outcomes without sacrifice of emotional intensity, and for a long time Dostoevskij avoided this favorite topic of his early works. It is the fever delirium of Ivan Karamazov, among other things, that indicates a return to Hoffmannian inspiration in the last and greatest of the novels.

(6) German Romantic *possession,* in the semi-realistic and more subjective sense of "obsession", became a commonly used function of the divided self.

Neither *ghosts* (7), nor *automata* (9), nor the sinister qualities of *hypnotism* (12) (except tangentially in the case of Murin), nor the "Faust theme" (11) appear anywhere in Dostoevskij's works in their original forms, though techniques used in dealing with them are merged with the motif of *hallucinatory dreams* (8). How ghost-*like,* or, for that matter, how *like* an evil hypnotic trance is the appearance of Nelly in the quarters of the hero of *The Insulted and Injured,* or again, the appearance of Svidrigajlov at the bedside of Raskol'nikov.

(13) The motif of *talking animals* occurs only once in Dostoevskij's works, in *The Crocodile,* and then as a mere echo, and (14) there is no example among them of a *fairytale for children.*

(15) As for the most common Hoffmannian triangle of characters: youthful artist-hero, youthful heroine, and mage of mature years, only *The Landlady,* properly speaking, offers an example of it, all three figures being individually and thoroughly transformed there. Until *The Insulted and Injured* of 1861 female characters in general were accorded only very minor roles, and when full-length portraits of women finally came to be made in Dostoevskij's fiction they were remote from their Hoffmannian counterparts. Mages, after Murin, disappeared altogether, though Bishop Tixon in *The Possessed* and Father Zosima in *The Brothers Karamazov,* themselves special cases, owe some debt to Prior Leonardus of *Die Elixiere des Teufels,* who was a unique variant of the mage type in Hoffmann.

Observing all these Hoffmannian motifs in their aggregate, it becomes clear that Dostoevskij disregarded such specific items as ghosts, automata, talking animals, and the like because they committed him to external and mechanical story-themes when his concern was with the devious heart of man. On the other hand, everything in Hoffmann that could serve this latter end was taken over and blended together without regard to separate motifs. Dostoevskij was not concerned with developing themes like "Philistine" or "Madness" individually, for their own sakes. Once the sensitive and suffering man was substituted for the sensitive and suffering artist, all the pertinent motifs grouped themselves around that center and all received their transformation together *en bloc.*

5. THE RETURN TO HOFFMANN

By the end of 1866 and the end of *Crime and Punishment* Dostoevskij had worked his way out from under Hoffmann's influence. *The Gambler, The Possessed, A Raw Youth,* and various short pieces of the 1870's pursued other lines of thought. In 1869, however, while in Dresden as one of his many stopping-places during the four years of his self-imposed "exile" in western Europe, he seems to have taken notice once again of the author whom he had so profoundly admired in his youth and so skillfully exploited in former writings. It is possible and, under the circumstances, likely that while in Dresden he had come upon a set of Hoffmann's Tales in their original language and that he browsed among them for old times' sake. Perhaps in his financial distress he actually sought them out, hoping to discover a topic that could be quickly turned into a money-making story. At any rate, the concluding section, and only the concluding section, of the not very distinguished *Der Zusammenhang der Dinge,* hardly a tale to linger in the memory from readings long ago, seems to have suggested the basic situation of *The Eternal Husband,* the work which grew out of the mere pot-boiler he had intended to write. At about the same time there were written the private letters in which Dostoevskij first broached his mighty new plan for a five-volume novel-sequence to be called *The Life of a Great Sinner.* Making all due allowances for transformation and substitution of matter, the plan strikingly coincides with the overall scenario of *Die Elixiere des Teufels.*

The Brothers Karamazov, in turn, in so far as it was a partial realization of *The Great Sinner,* also represents the final adaptation by Dostoevskij of a work of Hoffmann, and in a two-fold way: first, with Alëša Karamazov as false saint, sinner, and future true saint and as sent forth upon his worldly career by the wise, mage-like monk whom Hoffmann had named Prior Leonardus and whom Dostoevskij called Father Zosima; and secondly, with Ivan Karamazov and Smerdjakov as half-brothers and doubles, the salvation of the one being dependent upon the final elimination of the other, just as Medardus' salvation depended upon the final elimination of Count Viktorin.

The process employed was therefore one of plot conversion but in a curious dual form, one of the novel as a whole with its hero who sinned his way to sainthood, the other more properly described as a conversion of characters in isolation from their novel as a whole, namely the indivisible pair of doubles, Medardus and Viktorin. Just as *Die Elixiere des Teufels,* taken at that point as a story about a sinning ancestor, had once been piled upon the complex *Kater Murr* to make the single scenario of *Netočka Nezvanova,* so now these alternate conversions of *Die Elixiere des Teufels* were joined with each other and with still other matter to make the truly gigantic plan of *The Brothers Karamazov.* If Alëša-as-Medardus is evident only in the light of the *Great Sinner* project, it is because the author did not live to bestow upon that "chief though future hero" his full complement of story. But the case of Ivan-as-Medardus speaks for itself. Ivan is hyper-sensitive, he is divided between two worlds (in this case "Europe" and Russian nationalism), he has an evil half-brother who embodies his own worst side, he has hallucinatory dreams of a ghost-like Devil, he is possessed and obsessed by that Devil who is the lurid projection of his "spirit" (Geist), he "breaks under strain", and he lapses into "brain fever", which is surely the equivalent of Mr. Goljadkin's "madness". By every right he may be described as the final synthesis of the Russian Hoffmannizing process. In him and in his book a major nineteenth century Russian idea attained its culmination.

APPENDIX I

THE WORKS OF ERNST THEODOR AMADEUS HOFFMANN
(JANUARY 24, 1776 — JUNE 25, 1822)

(Dates of publication of individual stories previous to their inclusion in the collections are given in parentheses; if no date is given, the story first appeared in the collection where it is listed.)

A. Novels:
  Die Elixiere des Teufels — 1816
  Kater Murr
      Part I   — July 1819
      Part II   — December 1821
      Part III — (scheduled for Easter 1822; unwritten)

B. Independent Märchen:
  Klein Zaches — January 1819
  Prinzessin Brambilla — November 1820
  Meister Floh — April 1822

C. The Collections of Tales:
  1. *Fantasiestücke in Callots Manier*
     Volumes I and II — Easter 1814
     Volume III — autumn 1814
     Volume IV — Easter 1815
     (republished in two volumes, 1819)

     Volume I: *Jacques Callot*
                Ritter Gluck (1809)
                6 Kreisleriana (1810–1813)
                Don Juan (1813)

     Volume II: *Nachrichten von den neuesten Schicksalen des Hundes*
                     Berganza
                Der Magnetiseur

     Volume III: *Der goldene Topf*

     Volume IV: *Die Abenteuer der Sylvesternacht*
                7 Kreisleriana

  2. *Die Nachtstücke*
     Volume I: — spring 1817
     Volume II: — autumn 1817

     Volume I: *Der Sandmann*
                Ignaz Denner
                Die Jesuiterkirche in G.
                Das Sanctus

     Volume II: *Das öde Haus*
                Das Majorat
                Das Gelübde
                Das steinerne Herz

3. *Die Serapionsbrüder*

Volume I: — spring 1819
Volume II: — autumn 1819
Volume III: — autumn 1820
Volume IV: — spring 1821

Volume I: (frame tale)
             Der Graf von P. * (or *Der Einsiedler Serapion* *)
             Rat Krespel * (1817)
             Die Fermate (1815)
             Der Dichter und der Komponist (1813)
             Fragment aus dem Leben dreier Freunde (1818)
             Der Artushof (1816)
             Die Bergwerke zu Falun
             Nussknacker und Mausekönig (1816)

Volume II: *Die Automate* (1814)
             Alte und neue Kirchenmusik (1814)
             Der Kampf der Sänger (1818)
             Doge und Dogaresse (1818)
             Meister Martin der Küfner und seine Gesellen (1818)
             Das fremde Kind (1817)
             Eine Spukgeschichte * (or *Der schwebende Teller* *)

Volume III: *Nachricht aus dem Leben eines unbekannten Mannes* (or
                  Der Teufel in Berlin *) (1819)
             Die Brautwahl (1819)
             Der unheimliche Gast (1819)
             Das Fräulein von Scudery (1819)
             Spielerglück (1819)
             Der Baron von B. * (or *Der Schüler Tartinis* *) (1819)

Volume IV   *Erscheinungen* (1817)
             Signor Formica (1819) (sometimes referred to as "Salvator
                  Rosa")
             Der Zusammenhang der Dinge (1820)
             Die Königsbraut
             Zacharias Werner
             Vampirismus * (or *Eine Vampyrgeschichte* *)

4. *Die Letzten Erzählungen*
   2 volumes — 1825

Volume I   *Haimatochare*
             Die Marquise de la Pivardière
             Die Irrungen
             Die Geheimnisse
             Der Elementargeist
             Die Räuber

Volume II: *Die Doppeltgänger*
             Datura fastuosa
             Meister Johannes Wacht
             Des Vetters Eckfenster
             Die Genesung

* = Editor's title.

D. Miscellaneous:

Neueste Schicksale eines abenteuerlichen Mannes
Der Feind
Die Vision auf dem Schlachtfelde bei Dresden (1813)
Der Dey von Elba in Paris (1815)
Prinzessin Blandina (1814) (fragment of a play)

(numerous articles of musical criticism)

APPENDIX II

CHRONOLOGY OF HOFFMANNIANA IN RUSSIA

1822 (June 25) Hoffmann died in Berlin

Tr *Das Fräulein von Scudery* (Devica Skjuderi) — *Son of the Fatherland* (SPb) (Syn Otečestva) Supplement, Part III

Tr *Doge und Dogaresse* (Dož i dogaressa) — ibid., Part XII

1823 Tr *Spielerglück* (Sčast'e igrokov) — *Messenger of Europe* (Moscow) (Vestnik Evropy)

1825 Tr *Die Marquise de la Pivardière* (Markiza de la Pivard'er) — *Moscow Telegraph* (Moscow) (Moskovskij Telegraf)

Tr *Der schwebende Teller* (or: *Eine Spukgeschichte*) as *The White Apparition* (Beloe Prividenie) — ibid., Supplement for 1825

"Pogorel'skij": *The Poppy-seed-cake Woman of the Lafërtov Quarter* (Lafërtovskaja Makovnica) — *News of Literature* (Moscow) (Novosti Literatury) March

1826 Tr *Datura fastuosa* as *The Botanist* (Botanik) — *Moscow Telegraph*, VIII

1827 Tr *Der Magnetiseur* under its original title of *Träume sind Schäume*, as *As Foam in Water, so (are) Dreams in the Head* (Čto pena v vode, To sny v golove) (Venevitinov partial translator) — *Moscow Messenger*, III (Moscow) (Moskovskij Vestnik)

1828 "Pogorel'skij": *The Double, or My Evenings in Little Russia* (Dvojnik, ili moi večera v Malorossii) — book form

1829 Tr *Die Irrungen* as *The Enchanted Portfolio* (Očarovannyj bumažnik) — *Moscow Messenger*, XXV (Moscow)

Tr *Signor Formica* (Sen'or Formika)	*Son of the Fatherland* (SPb) and *Northern Archive,* 13 (Severnyj Arxiv)
Puškin-"Kosmokratov" (Titov): *The Lonely Cottage on Vasil'- evskij Island* (Uedinennyj domik na Vasil'- evskom)	*Northern Flowers: Almanac for 1829* (SPb) (Severnye Cvety)
"Pogorel'skij: *The Black Chicken, or The Subterranean Dwellers* (Čërnaja Kurica, ili Podzemnye žiteli)	*The Butterfly* (Moscow) (Babočka) (Pogorel'skij" editor)
Tr Walter Scott's article: *Novels of Ernest Theodore Hoffmann* (1827) as: *On the Supernatural in Fictitious composition*	*Son of the Fatherland* (SPb)
1830 Tr *Das Majorat* (Majorat)	*Moscow Telegraph,* XXXV (Moscow)
Tr *Der Sandmann* (Domovoj Pesočnik)	ibid., XXXVI
Tr *Zacharias Werner* (Zaxarij Verner)	*Moscow Messenger,* III (Moscow)
Tr *Die Jesuiterkirche in G.* (Iezuitskaja cerkov')	ibid., VI
Tr *Rat Krespel* as *The Cremo- na Violin* (Kreminskaja skripka)	*Messenger of Europe* (Moscow)
Tr *Das Sanctus* (Sanctus)	ibid.
"Pogorel'skij: *The Hypnotist* (Magnetizër)	*Literary Gazette,* 1 and 2 (SPb) (Literaturnaja Gazeta)
Tr articles from the French 1. *The Last Days of Hoff- mann's Life and Death* (O poslednix dnjax žizni i smerti Gofmana) 2. *Hoffmann's Fantastic Tales* (O fantastičeskix povestjax Gofmana)	*Messenger of Europe* (Moscow)
1831 Tr *Der goldene Topf* (Zolotoj goršok)	*Moscow Telegraph,* XL (Moscow)
Tr Fragments from *Kater Murr* as *Traits from the Life of Tom-cat Murr* (Čerty iz žizni Kota Mura)	ibid., XLI

Tr *Fragment aus dem Leben dreier Freunde* (Žizn' trëx druzej)	ibid.
Tr *Der Sandmann* (Pesočnyj čelovek)	*The Telescope*, XXII-XXIII (Dec) (Teleskop) (Moscow)
Tr *Die Brautwahl* (Vybor nevesty; skazka)	*Son of the Fatherland* (SPb)
Tr *Der unheimliche Gast* (Tainstvennyj gost')	*Northern Archive*, 50 (SPb)
Tr *Das öde Haus* (Pustoj dom)	*Literary Gazette* (SPb)
Odoevskij: *Beethoven's Last Quartet* (Poslednij kvartet Betxovena)	*Northern Flowers for 1831* (SPb) (almanac)

1832 Odoevskij: *Opere del Cavaliere Giambatista Piranesi* — *Northern Flowers for 1832* (SPb)

1833 Odoevskij: *The Improvisor* (Improvizator) — *Halcyon for 1833* (SPb) (Al'tsiona na 1833-ij god)

Odoevskij: *Variegated Tales* (Pëstrye skazki) — book form, SPb

Polevoj: *The Felicity of Madness* (Blaženstvo Bezumija) — *Moscow Telegraph*, 1 and 2 (Moscow)

Polevoj: *The Painter* (Živopisec) — ibid., 9, 10, 11, and 12

Tr article from the French: *Gofman*, by Xavier Marmier — *The Telescope*, 13 (Oct.) (Moscow)

1834 Puškin: *The Queen of Spades* (Pikovaja Dama)

Polevoj: *Emma* — *Moscow Telegraph*, 1, 2, 3, and 4 (Moscow)

Polevoj: *Abbadonna* — book form (Moscow)

1835 Gogol: *Arabesques* (Arabeski) containing: — book form (Jan.) (SPb)

　　The Portrait (written 1833-34) (Portret)

　　The Nevskij Prospekt (1833-34) (Nevskij Prospekt)

　　The Diary of a Madman (1834) (Zapiski sumašsedšego) — *Moscow Observer*, II (May) (Moscow) (Moskovskij Nabljudatel')

Odoevskij: *Sebastian Bach*

1836 Gogol': *The Nose* (Nos) — *The Contemporary*, Sept. (SPb) (Sovremennik) (initial issue)

Konstantin Aksakov: *Life in a Dream* (Žizn' v mečte) — *The Telescope* (Moscow)

Herzen: article: *Gofman*   ibid., 10
(signed "Iskander")

1837 Odoevskij: *Sylphida*   *The Contemporary* (SPb)
(Sil'fida)

1839 Tr *Der goldene Topf*   *Moscow Observer* (Moscow)
(Zolotoj goršok)

Sollogub: *A History of Two
Galoshes*
(Istorija dvux kaloš)

1840 Tr *Meister Floh*
(Mejster Flo) (translated by
M. N. Katkov)

Tr *Klein Zaches*
(Malen'kij Caxes (translated
by M. N. Katkov)

Tr *Kater Murr*
(Kot Mur)

Tr *Ritter Gluck*

Tr *Don Juan*

Tr *Kreisleriana*

1841 Lermontov: the "Štoss Frag-   (not published until 1845)
ment"

A. K. Tolstoj: *The Vampire*   book form (limited edition) SPb
(Upyr') (signed: "Krasnorog-
skij")

A. K. Tolstoj: *La Famille du*   (published posthumously, 1884)
Vourdalak

1842 Gogol': *The Overcoat*   (published in *Collected Works*)
(Šinel')

1844 Tr *Prinzessin Brambilla*
(Princessa Brambilla)

Odoevskij: *Russian Nights*   as Vol. I of his *Collected Works*
(Russkie Noči)

1845 Lermontov: the "Štoss Frag-   *Yesterday and Today,* Vol. I
ment" (written 1841)   (Včera i Segodnja)

1846 Dostoevskij: *The Double*   *National Notes* (Feb. 1) (SPb)
(Dvojnik)   (Otečestvennye Zapiski)

1847 Dostoevskij: *A Novel in Nine* *The Contemporary* (Jan.) (SPb)
Letters
(Roman v devjati pis'max)

Dostoevskij: *The Landlady*   *National Notes* (Oct.) (SPb)
(Xozjajka)

1848 Dostoevskij: *A Faint Heart*   ibid. (Feb.)
(Slaboe serce)

Dostoevskij: *An Honest Thief*   ibid. (April)
(Čestnyj vor)

Dostoevskij: *A Christmas Tree and a Wedding)* (Ëlka i svad'ba)	ibid. (Sept.)
Dostoevskij: *White Nights* (Belye Noči)	ibid. (Dec.)
1849 Dostoevskij: *Netočka Nezvanova* (written 1847; 1849)	ibid. (Jan., Feb., May) (unfinished)
Dostoevskij: *A Little Hero* (Malen'kij geroj) (signed: "M-----i"	ibid. (August)
1861 Dostoevskij: *The Insulted and Injured* (Unižënnye i oskorblënnye)	*Time* (Jan.-July) (SPb) (Vremja) (Dostoevskij editor)
1862 Dostoevskij: *An Unpleasant Predicament* (Skvernyj anekdot)	ibid. (Nov.)
1865 Dostoevskij: *The Crocodile* (Krokodil)	*The Epoch* (Feb.) (Epoxa)
1866 Dostoevskij: *Crime and Punishment* (Prestuplenie i nakazanie)	*The Russian Messenger* (serially) (SPb) (Russkij Vestnik)
1869 Dostoevskij: *The Eternal Husband* (Večnyj muž)	*Dawn* (Jan.-Feb.) (SPb) (Zarja)
1871 Turgenev: *Spring Freshets* (Vešnye Vody)	
1874 A. K. Tolstoj: *The Portrait* (Portret)	*The Messenger of Europe* (Jan.) (Moscow)
1880 Dostoevskij: *The Brothers Karamazov* (Brat'ja Karamazovy)	*The Russian Messenger* (serially) (SPb)
1897-1899 Tr of the Complete Works of Hoffmann, ed. by Panteleev	

APPENDIX III

THE WORKS OF HOFFMANN IN RELATION TO
THE WORKS OF THE RUSSIAN HOFFMANNISTS

NOVELS:

1. *Die Elixiere des Teufels*
   the inset about Franzesko the Painter

   Gogol': *The Portrait*
   Čertkov and the old painter of Part II, each as variants of Franzesko but with alternate destinies

   the artist in league with the Evil One

   Čertkov in league with Petromixali; the old painter of Part II in league with Petromixali

   Dostoevskij: *Netočka Nezvanova*
   Chapters 1, 2, and 3
   Efimov in league with the Evil One

   Franzesko as sinning ancestor

   A. K. Tolstoj: *The Vampire* (?)
   Don Pietro d'Urgina as sinning ancestor

   geographical pattern: Germany-Italy-Germany

   geographical pattern: Russia-Italy-Russia

   phantasmagorias of the convalescent Medardus

   phantasmagorias of the convalescent Runevskij

   plot complexities and consistent rapidity of narration

   plot complexities and consistent rapidity of narration

   Part I, end of Section 3 and end of Section 4

   Dostoevskij: *The Double*
   the final scene

   inset about Ewing, the eccentric flutist

   Dostoevskij: *Netočka Nezvanova*
   inset about Meyer, the eccentric dancer (Chapter 2)

   Viktorin-Medardus-Aurelie, the hero as double between extremes of good and evil

   Dostoevskij: *Crime and Punishment*
   Svidrigajlov-Raskol'nikov-Sonja

   over-all plan
   false saint tempted, falls, sins his way to true sainthood

   Dostoevskij: *The Life of a Great Sinner* and Alëša Karamazov in *The Brothers Karamazov*, in so far as Alëša is the Great Sinner

   Medardus-Viktorin-Belcampo the hero with *two* Doubles

   Dostoevskij: *The Brothers Karamazov*
   Ivan Karamazov-Smerdjakov-the Devil

2. *Kater Murr*
   satire on court life

   Polevoj: *Abbadonna* (?)
   satire on court life

   ironic animal autobiography

   Odoevskij: *Variegated Tales*, No. 3
   autobiography of the spider

	Odoevskij: *Letters to my Very Dear Uncle, Mr. Kater von Murr, from his Dutiful Nephew Kotovas'ki*
the talking animals	Gogol': *The Diary of a Madman* the talking dogs
the talking animals; the "unseen maiden"	Dostoevskij: *The Crocodile* (?)
Part I, Section 2 ("8th Makulaturblatt")	Dostoevskij: *The Double* Chapter 5
over-all plan of the Kreisler story	Dostoevskij: *Netočka Nezvanova* Chapters 4, 5, 6, and 7 over-all plan; transference of elaborate cast of characters with all their complex relationships retained intact
Prince Hektor as villain type	Dostoevskij: *Netočka Nezvanova* Pëtr Aleksandrovič
	Dostoevskij: *The Insulted and Injured* Prince Pëtr Aleksandrovič Valkovskij
	Dostoevskij: *Crime and Punishment* Svidrigajlov, in so far as he is an extension of Valkovskij

THE INDEPENDENT MÄRCHEN:

1. *Klein Zaches* Zaches, by virtue of his magic powers, gets credit for the accomplishments of others	Dostoevskij: *The Double* (?) The Double gets credit for Mr. Goljadkin's work at the office
Prosper Alpanus as mage with the student Balthasar as poet-client	Odoevskij: *The Improvisor* (?) the mage Segeliel' and Cipriano as his poet-client
2. *Prinzessin Brambilla*	Dostoevskij: *The Double* (?) (influence claimed by Rodzevič)
3. *Meister Floh* vision of the anatomy of the brain by means of the magic lens	Odoevskij: *The Improvisor* (?) vision of the fine anatomy of the body by means of microscopic vision
George Pepusch-Dörtje Elverdink-Leuwenhoek anterior life im Famagusta end of *Zweites Abenteuer*	Polevoj: *The Felicity of Madness* Antiox-Adelheid-Schreckenfeld anterior life in Italy Gogol': *The Terrible Hand* (first draft of *The Nevskij Prospekt*) (?)
the Christmas party for children	Dostoevskij: *A Christmas Tree and a Wedding* (?) the Christmas party for children

the later discovery of the hero's bride in the same household	Julian Mastakovič's discovery of his future bride
the visionary land of Famagusta	Dostoevskij: the vision of "Acis and Galatea" in *The Possessed* in *A Raw Youth* and in *The Dream of a Ridiculous Man* } (?)

THE FIRST COLLECTION OF TALES:
FANTASIESTÜCKE IN CALLOTS MANIER
(AS OF THE 4-VOL. EDITION OF 1814)

1. *Kreisleriana* Preface; No. 1 (Volume I); No. 3 (Volume IV)	Sollogub: *A History of Two Galoshes* biography of the musician hero
2. *Ritter Gluck* (Volume I) madman who fancies himself to be Gluck	Odoevskij: *Opere del Cavaliere Giambatista Piranesi* madman who fancies himself to be Piranesi
over-all story pattern; monologue of a visionary	Odoevskij: *Beethoven's Last Quartet* over-all story pattern; Beethoven's visionary monologue
the blank pages of music	Dostoevskij: *A Faint Heart* the blank pages of manuscript
the figure of the urban wanderer	Dostoevskij: *An Honest Thief* (?) the figure of Emel'jan Ilič
3. *Der Magnetiseur* (Volume II) general plan; the sinister hypnotist	"Pogorel'skij": *The Hypnotist* general plan (?); the sinister hypnotist
hypnotist villain	Puškin-Titov: *The Lonely Cottage on Vasil'evskij Island* hypnotist characteristics of Varfolomej
annihilation of a family	annihilation of Vera's family
Alban as sinister hypnotist	Dostoevskij: *The Landlady* Murin *apparently* a sinister hypnotist
4. *Der goldene Topf* (Volume III) Vigils 5, 7, and 10	"Pogorel'skij": *The Poppy-seed-cake Woman of the Lafërtov Quarter*
Veronika — the witch — the Tom-cat suitor	Maša — the witch — the Tom-cat suitor
Vigil 5: details given by the clairvoyante about the absent suitor	"Pogorel'skij": *Izidor and Anjuta* (?) details about Izidor's return from the war
Vigil 10: Anselmus and others as prisoners in glass bottles	Odoevskij: *The Retort (Variegated Tales,* No. 1) the narrator and a whole household inside the retort

Archivarius Lindhorst as mage
with Anselmus as poet-client

Odoevskij: *The Improvisor*
the mage Segeliel' and Cipriano as
his poet-client (?)

the hero with allegiance divided
between the real world and
the world of Beauty

Odoevskij: *Sylphida*
the hero with allegiance to the real
world and the hallucinatory
world of the Sylph

Anselmus-Veronika-Konrektor
Paulmann-Serpentina

Mixail Platonovič-Katen'ka-
Reženskij- the Sylph

Lindhorst as Salamander-Prince;
vengeance by fire

Odoevskij: *Salamandra* (?)
Elza as a salamander; her vengeance by fire

the artist as "madman"

Odoevskij: *Who are Madmen*? (in
Russian Nights)
the genius as madman

5. *Die Abenteuer der Sylvesternacht* (Volume IV)

Puškin-Titov: *The Lonely Cottage on
Vasil'evskij Island*

Giulietta's entourage of sinners
and devils (Chap. 4)

the Countess I.'s salon of devils

Erasmus Spikher's ride in the
cab with Dapertutto (Chap. 4)

Paul's ride in the cab with the
death's-head

Erasmus Spikher's surrender of
his mirror-image (Chap. 4)

Gogol': *The Nose*
Kovalëv's loss of his nose (Part II)

the search for the lost mirror-
image

Kovalëv's search for the lost nose
(Part II)

"discontinuity" of the four
chapters

non-sequitur of the three parts of
the story

the story-plan as a whole
a) Chapter 1 (*Die Geliebte*)

Dostoevskij: *The Double*
the party; the flight. (Chapters 4
and 5)

b) Chapter 2 (*Die Gesellschaft
im Keller*): encounter with
Schlemihl and Spikher

the encounter with the Double
(Chapter 5)

c) Chapter 3 (*Erscheinungen*)
d) Chapter 4 (the motif of the
lost mirror-image)

Mr. Goljadkin's dream (Chapter 10)
the repeated motif of the mirror-
reflections

THE SECOND COLLECTION OF TALES:
DIE NACHTSTÜCKE

1. *Der Sandmann* (Volume I)

"Pogorel'skij": *The Baleful Consequences of an Unbridled Imagination*

central episode of the mechanical
doll
Nathanael-Olimpia-Spalanzani-
Lothar

plagiary of the entire episode

Polevoj: *The Felicity of Madness*
Antiox-Adelheid-Schreckenfeld-
Leonid (in combination with
parallel figures from *Meister
Floh*)

opening letter: boy's childhood haunted by supernatural figure of evil	Odoevskij: *The Igoša* (*Variegated Tales*, No. 5) (?) the boy's life plagued by the imaginary monster, the Igoša
the mechanical doll that seemed to be a woman	Odoevskij: *The Tale of How Dangerous it is for Girls to Walk in Groups on the Nevskij Prospekt* (*Variegated Tales*, No. 7) the girl who was made into a doll
Spalanzani-Coppelius and Nathanael	Odoevskij: *The Improvisor* Segeliel' and Cipriano
Nathanael's opening letter; Coppelius	Dostoevskij: *The Landlady* Ordynov's view of Murin as a sinister, half-supernatural monster
general atmosphere of psychological terror	general atmosphere of psychological terror
2. *Die Jesuiterkirche in G.* (Volume I) painter-hero (Berthold) in Italy	Polevoj: *The Painter* painter-hero (Arkadij) in Italy
art-problem-tale with sombre outcome	art-problem-tale with sombre outcome
hero's blessedness in finally completing painting of the Virgin and St. Elizabeth	Arkadij's blessedness in finally completing painting of Christ among the children
Angiola, Berthold's spurned wife	Polevoj: *Emma* (?) Emma, the spurned angel of Paul (influence claimed by Rodzevič)
Berthold as "murderer" and artist	Dostoevskij: *Netočka Nezvanova* Chapters 1, 2, and 3 Efimov as pseudo-artist and murderer
3. *Das öde Haus* (Volume II) daemonic attraction to the mysterious house	Puškin: *The Queen of Spades* (?) Hermann's daemonic guidance to the house of the old Countess
	Lermontov: the "Štoss Fragment" Lugin's daemonic guidance to Štoss's house
the opening scene in the confectioner's shop: narrator-proprietor — the old man with the dog	Dostoevskij: *The Insulted and Injured* the opening chapter in the confectioner's shop: narrator (Vanja)-proprietor (Müller) — the old man (Smith) with the dog
4. *Das Majorat* (Volume II) the ghost; the snowy night	Gogol': *The Overcoat* (?) the ghost: the snowy night

THE THIRD COLLECTION OF TALES:
DIE SERAPIONSBRÜDER

1. the frame-tale device

"Pogorel'skij": *The Double*
the frame-tale device

(the frame-tale device of Odoevskij's *Russian Nights* was specifically denied by Odoevskij himself as being an imitation of *Die Serapionsbrüder*.)

2. *Rat Krespel* (Volume I)

(source of Odoevskij's epigraph for *Beethoven's Last Quartet*)

Krespel as violinist

Dostoevskij: *Netočka Nezvanova* (?)
Efimov as violinist (details only)

3. *Die Fermate*
narrator (Theodor) — Lauretta — Teresina
episode of the unruly horse

Dostoevskij: *A Little Hero*
narrator — "the teasing lady" — Madame M.
episode of the runaway horse

4. *Fragment aus dem Leben dreier Freunde* (Volume I)
evocation of Berlin streets
pursuit of the unknown beauty by three friends, with alternate outcomes: one sentimental-serious, the other two tragi-comic
the hypersensitive Severin
the pathetic lunatic Nettelmann who thinks he is King of Amboina and who is taken away to the madhouse
evocation of the city streets; the pursuit of the unknown beauty by a sensitive young man

Gogol': *The Nevskij Prospekt*

evocation of Petersburg streets
pursuit of different unknown beauties by two friends, with alternate outcomes: one tragic and the other satirically comic

the hypersensitive Piskarev
Gogol': *The Diary of a Madman*
Popriščin as a pathetic lunatic who thinks he is King of Spain and is taken away to the madhouse
Dostoevskij: *White Nights*
evocation of Petersburg streets; the pursuit of the unknown beauty by a sensitive young man
Dostoevskij: *The Insulted and Injured*
Part I, Chapter 8, as a variant version of the situation in *White Nights*
Dostoevskij: *Petersburg Visions in Verse and Prose* (the "Amalia" episode)
a further variation of the situation in *White Nights*

5. *Der Artushof* (Volume I)
the theme of Art versus Philistine life

Polevoj: *The Painter*
the theme of Art versus Philistine life

Traugott-Christine Roos	Arkadij-Veren'ka
Italy as the refuge of artists	Italy as the refuge of artists
Traugott-Berklinger-Felizitas- Christine Roos	Lermontov: the "Štoss Fragment" Lugin-Štoss-Štoss's daughter- Minskaja
	Dostoevskij: *The Landlady* Ordynov-Murin-Katerina-Tinxen Špis
the over all plan (up to the point where Traugott leaves for Italy)	the over all plan

6. *Nussknacker und Mausekönig*
(Volume I)
the battle with the mice

"Pogorel'skij": *The Black Chicken* (?)
details of the subterranean kingdom; the rat-hunt

Pate Drosselmeier and his
mechanical toys for children

Odoevskij: *The Cosmorama*
Dr. Bin and his gift of the magic
toy, the "cosmorama", to little
Volodja

Čajkovskij: *The Nutcracker* ballet

7. *Meister Martin der Küfner und
seine Gesellen* (Volume II)

(praised by Dostoevskij in "Three
Tales of Edgar Poe")

8. *Die Brautwahl* (Volume III)
incidental details; the multiple
doubles of Tusmann

Dostoevskij: *The Double*
incidental details: the multiple
doubles of Mr. Goljadkin

the inappropriate marriage of
the elderly Tusmann and
young Albertine

Dostoevskij: *A Christmas Tree and a
Wedding* (?)
Julian Mastakovič and his child
bride

Tusmann's adventures in the
streets of Berlin; "alcoholic"
phantasmagoria

Dostoevskij: *An Unpleasant Predicament*
Pralinskij's adventures in the streets
of Petersburg; alcoholic phantasmagoria

9. *Der unheimliche Gast*
(Volume III)
the Sicilian Count S---i, the
sinister hypnotist

"Pogorel'skij": *The Hypnotist*

the Neapolitan Marquis, the sinister
hypnotist

Dostoevskij: *The Landlady*
Murin as *apparent* sinister hypnotist

Margurite as the accomplice of
Count S---i

Katerina as Murin's *apparent*
accomplice

10. *Das Fräulein von Scudery*
(Volume III)
the police officials, La Régnie
and Desgrais

Dostoevskij: *Crime and Punishment*

Porfirij Petrovič and "the explosive
lieutenant" Zametov

11. *Spielerglück* (Volume III)

Odoevskij: *The Tale about how Collegiate Councillor Ivan Bogdanovič Otnošenie Was Unable to Offer Holiday Greetings to his Superiors on Easter Sunday* (?)
(*Variegated Tales*, No. 4)

the infernal spell of the playing cards

the infernal spell of the playing cards

the gambling mania, involving the sacrifice of a pure girl's love

Puškin: *The Queen of Spades*
Hermann's gambling mania and his sacrifice of Lizaveta Ivanovna's love

Lermontov: the "Štoss Fragment" (author's note)
the card-sharp's wagering and loss of his daughter

12. *Der Baron von B.* (Volume III)
the Baron as violinist who could not play the violin

Dostoevskij: *Netočka Nezvanova* (?)
Efimov as violinist who could not play the violin

13. *Signor Formica* (Volume IV)
(alias: *Salvator Rosa*)

(praised by Dostoevskij in "Three Tales of Edgar Poe")

14. *Der Zusammenhang der Dinge* (Volume IV)
the final scene
Euchar-Viktorine-Ludwig

Dostoevskij: *The Eternal Husband*

the basic situation; the final scene
Velčaninov-Natal'ja Vasil'evna-Trusotskij

THE POSTHUMOUS FOURTH COLLECTION OF TALES: DIE LETZTEN ERZÄHLUNGEN

1. *Haimatochare* (Volume I)
the over-all plan of a jesting mystification in epistolary form

Dostoevskij: *A Novel in Nine Letters*
the over-all plan of a jesting mystification in epistolary form

2. *Die Irrungen* (Volume I)
self-parodying "discontinuity" of episodes and deliberate non-resolution of mysteries

Gogol': *The Nose*
parody of Hoffmann's manner in "discontinuity" of episodes and deliberate non-resolution of mysteries

Dostoevskij: *The Double* (?)
technique similar to the above

pursuit of the mysterious beauty and her aged male companion

Dostoevskij: *The Landlady*
pursuit of the mysterious beauty and her aged male companion

Baron Theodor von S. — the beautiful Greek lady-Schnüspelpold; the lady as Schnüspelpold's ward

Ordynov-Katerina-Murin; Katerina as Murin's ward
(in conjunction with parallel figures in *Der Artushof*)

exoticism (Greece) in costume, Oriental splendor, etc.

Lermontov: the "Štoss Fragment" (?)
Lugin — the card-sharp's daughter — Štoss
the entrance of Štoss's daughter (?)

ironic humor applied to the mystifications

ironic humor applied to the mystifications (?)

the story as a whole

Turgenev: *Spring Freshets* (Chapter XII)
Gemma's erroneous recollections of the story as a whole
the author's use of the story as evocative of the mood in Russia in 1840

3. *Datura fastuosa* (Volume II)

"Pogorel'skij": *The Baleful Consequences of an Unbridled Imagination*

the Spanish villain Fermino Valies

the "Spanish" villain Venturino

the over-all plan

Puškin-Titov: *The Lonely Cottage on Vasil'evskij Island*
the over-all plan

Eugenius-Gretchen-widow Helms-Fermino Valies-Countess Gabriella

Paul-Vera-Vera's widowed mother-Varfolomej-the Countess I.

Fermino Valies and Gretchen in the garden

Dostoevskij: *A Christmas Tree and a Wedding*
Julian Mastakovič and the little girl in the arbor

4. *Die Genesung* (Volume II)
Theodor (narrator) as unintentional observer of the lovers' tryst in the beautiful rural spot

Dostoevskij: *A Little Hero*
the narrator as unintentional observer of the love tryst between Madame M. and "N." in the beautiful garden